STEERING SUSTAINABILITY IN
AN URBANIZING WORLD

Steering Sustainability in an Urbanizing World

Policy, Practice and Performance

Edited by
ANITRA NELSON
RMIT University, Australia

ASHGATE

Published by
Ashgate Publishing Limited
Gower House
Croft Road
Aldershot
Hampshire GU11 3HR
England

Ashgate Publishing Company
Suite 420
101 Cherry Street
Burlington, VT 05401-4405
USA

Ashgate website: http://www.ashgate.com

British Library Cataloguing in Publication Data
Steering sustainability in an urbanizing world : policy,
    practice and performance
    1. Urban ecology 2. Urban policy 3. Sustainable development
    4. Social change
    I. Nelson, Anitra
    307'.1'216

Library of Congress Cataloging-in-Publication Data
Steering sustainability in an urbanizing world : policy, practice and performance /
edited by Anitra Nelson.
        p. cm.
    Includes bibliographical references and index.
    ISBN 978-0-7546-7146-6
    1. Urban ecology. 2. Urban policy. 3. Sustainable development. 4. Social change.
I. Nelson, Anitra.

    HT241.S74 2007
    307.76--dc22   2007014528

ISBN 978 0 7546 7146 6

Printed and bound in Great Britain by TJ International Ltd, Padstow, Cornwall.

Contents

List of Figures and Tables

Notes on Contributors

Dr Sarah Bekessy, Senior Lecturer in environmental studies (RMIT University, Melbourne), specializes in sustainability science and university education for sustainability. Sarah researches biodiversity planning in urban fringe landscapes and tools to support transparent decision-making for environmental management.

Professor Mike Berry is a leading scholar of urban studies and public policy. His research at the RMIT–NATSEM Centre of the Australian Housing and Urban Research Institute (AHURI), Melbourne, focuses on urban development processes, alternative financing approaches for affordable housing, environmental economics and policy, urban social theory, economics and public policy, housing markets and digital centres.

Geoffrey Binder, who has a wealth of experience in education, organizational change and advocacy, is completing a research doctorate at RMIT University. Geoffrey is using the suburban Aurora development as a case study of the internal and external organizational relations and processes of VicUrban – the Victorian Government's flag bearer of environmental sustainability – as it plans for sustainable urban development.

Dr Dick Copeman practises and teaches permaculture at Northey Street City Farm (Brisbane), having been involved since it began (1994). He trained as a doctor, worked in Aboriginal health and general practice, was a Senior Lecturer at the University of Queensland and has campaigned in community health, consumer and environmental movements, especially on food policy, sustainable agriculture and urban transport.

Professor Tony Dalton researches with the RMIT–NATSEM Centre of AHURI. This research is closely connected to contemporary issues and policy development in the areas of housing market restructuring, the environmental performance of housing and policy making processes. Tony has contributed over many years to non-government sector policy work and advocacy.

Dr Richard Denniss was an economics lecturer (University of Newcastle, NSW), chief of staff for an Australian Democrats leader, Deputy Director of the Australia Institute (Canberra) and is currently adviser to the Australian Greens Party. He has researched policy impacts on economic efficiency and equity, the economics of environmental regulation and co-authored, with Clive Hamilton, *Affluenza* (Allen and Unwin, 2005).

Nutana Donaldson, a Senior Consultant with EnviroCom Australia® – an environmental consultancy providing education, training and research services to industry and government organizations across Australia's eastern seaboard – has spent the last decade supplying sustainability education services to local government and industry, especially in south-east Queensland.

Dr Paul Downton is an internationally renowned ecocity advocate and theorist and a prize-winning architect and designer. Paul has specialized in ecological architecture and ecocity development in Australia. In 1991, he was founding convener of Urban Ecology Australia and has been a key member in the establishment of the showcase residential ecologically sustainable development, Christie Walk, in the City of Adelaide.

Glenn Eales is Queensland Manager of the environmental consultancy EnviroCom Australia®, which provides education, training and research services to industry and government organizations across Australia's eastern seaboard. Glenn has focused on waste education, training and research, and is currently completing his doctorate of education at Griffith University (Queensland).

Dr Mark Gibson is Senior Lecturer in Media and Communications at Monash University, Victoria. He has recently moved from Murdoch University, Western Australia, where he was Director of the Centre for Everyday Life. He is Editor of *Continuum: Journal of Media and Cultural Studies* and has published widely on television, everyday life and cultural politics.

Dr Ascelin Gordon completed his doctorate in physics at the University of Melbourne, then became a postdoctoral researcher at RMIT University, focusing on making conservation strategies more effective within urban and peri-urban environments. He applies advances in ecological modelling and mathematical optimization to measure and model biodiversity and its relationship to urban development.

Peter Graham is Lecturer in Architecture in the Faculty of the Built Environment at the University of New South Wales (UNSW, Sydney). He is Stream Leader of Technologies in the architecture program and has developed undergraduate and postgraduate environmental studies courses for building professionals in Australia and Singapore. Blackwell published his book, *Building Ecology* (2003). University of Melbourne PhD candidate **Margaret Kam** co-authored his chapter with **Bill Randolph**.

Tim Grant is President of the Australian Life Cycle Assessment (LCA) Society, Assistant Director of the Centre for Design (RMIT University, Melbourne), Adjunct Research Fellow with CSIRO Atmospheric Research and has a LCA consultancy (Life Cycle Strategies Pty Ltd). His broad experience developing and applying LCA methods for companies and organizations includes running professional development courses.

Professor Wim Hafkamp is Scientific Director of the Netherlands Institute for City Innovation Studies, which creates partnerships between cities and university research groups to address complex urban issues by generating, applying, disseminating and sharing knowledge. An environmental economist with a research record in transport, infrastructure, environment and urban development, Wim is Professor of Environmental Sciences at Erasmus University (Rotterdam).

Mike Hill, co-proprietor of WestWyck, has 18 years of close involvement with local governments, including periods as mayor of Brunswick and Moreland city councils. Mike is Chair of both the Victorian Local Sustainability (Ministerial) Advisory Committee and the Moreland Energy Foundation (a local climate change project) and has been the chair of EcoRecycle Victoria and a board member of the inaugural Board of Sustainability Victoria.

Dr Ralph Horne is Director of the Centre for Design (RMIT University). After completing a doctorate in environmental assessment and climate change his research interests expanded into wider dimensions of sustainability, the role of design and planning processes. He was Senior Lecturer (Resources Research Unit, Sheffield Hallam University, UK) and an Associate of North Energy Associates (an energy services consultancy).

Joe Hurley was the project manager of the award winning Urban Water Conservation Demonstration and Research Facility at the Brunswick (Victoria) Centre for Education and Research in Environmental Strategies (CERES), an internationally renowned environment park, then joined the Centre for Design (RMIT University) to complete a doctorate on ecologically sustainable performance in urban fringe developments.

Richard Hyde is Reader and Associate Professor in the School of Geography, Planning and Architecture (University of Queensland). Teaching duties and research interests include developing indicators for sustainable housing and urban planning, technology, computer applications and building construction. His co-authors and their affiliations are: **Richard Moore**, Centre for Sustainable Design (University of Queensland); **Dr Lydia Kavanagh** (Senior Lecturer in Design and professional chemical/environmental engineer) and **Karen Schianetz,** both from the School of Engineering (University of Queensland); and **Melinda Watt,** General Manager of the Earthcheck Organization Australasia, Brisbane.

Margaret Lee coordinates a suite of interdisciplinary Re-imagining the Australian Suburb research projects in the RMIT Centre for Design. Her Masters of Social Science (International Urban and Environmental Management) involved discovering and developing alternative methods and models to facilitate sustainable development, especially through community development, facilitating change and building capacity.

Associate Professor Dave Mercer coordinates the International Urban and Environmental Management program at RMIT University. He researches local, national and international natural resource management and environmental policy and politics. Dave is an elected Fellow of the Environment Institute of Australia and New Zealand, and in 2002 was appointed to join the five-person Victorian Environmental Assessment Council advising the Minister for Environment on managing public lands and waters.

Dr John Merson is Executive Director of the Blue Mountains World Heritage Institute and coordinates the graduate research program in Environmental Policy and Management at the University of New South Wales. His current research focuses on environmental policy and management as well as sustainable development. His co-author (with Tavis Potts) is **Michael Kachka** a BMWHI consultant (Randwick, Sydney).

Dr Anitra Nelson is Senior Research Fellow, Sustainable Housing and Urban Planning, at the RMIT–NATSEM Centre of AHURI (Melbourne). Anitra's research, teaching and publications focus on community-based sustainability, urban land-use planning, ecological economics, sustainable regional development, community forestry and, most recently, the uses of digital technologies in homes, communities and offices.

Professor Peter Newman is Professor of City Policy and Director of the Institute for Sustainability and Technology Policy (ISTP), Murdoch University, Western Australia. Chair of the Western Australian Sustainability Roundtable, which advises the Premier on how to implement the State's sustainability strategy, Peter was also Sustainability Commissioner in NSW from 2004 to 2006 and a Fulbright Scholar in 2006–2007.

Adjunct Professor Alan Pears (RMIT University) pioneered visions of a sustainable Melbourne in a low fossil fuel intensity world, co-writing *Seeds for Change: Creatively Confronting the Energy Crisis* (Patchwork Press, 1978). Contributing to Victorian government building energy codes, environmental rating schemes, software tools and public information materials, Alan has been on the Australian Building Codes Board's energy efficiency steering committee and runs an environmental consultancy (Sustainable Solutions).

Lorna Pitt, a Melbourne City councillor for nearly a decade, has a history of involvement in campaigns to save and rebuild public infrastructure. Lorna campaigned for Melbourne's Queen Victoria Market, fought to save Melbourne's bluestone laneways, and became a key champion of Royal Park, the lungs of Melbourne.

Dr Tavis Potts lectures on coastal management (Scottish Association for Marine Science, Oban). Before this position, he was a Postdoctoral Fellow at the University of Western Sydney (UWS), Centre for Innovation and Industry Studies, where his research and outreach focused on developing strategies for sustainable innovation and 'green' business and systems for triple bottom line reporting and decision making.

Professor Bill Randolph is Director of the City Futures Research Centre (UNSW) and Deputy Director of the UNSW–UWS AHURI Research Centre. He previously spent six years as director of the UWS Urban Frontiers Program and was head of research at London's National Housing Federation after working at the Open University and UK Department of the Environment.

Dr Ingrid Richardson is Senior Lecturer in Multimedia and Cultural Studies at Murdoch University. Her research interests include philosophy of technology and science, phenomenology of new media and televisual interfaces, embodied interaction and corporeal feminism. She has published on the cultural and somatic effects of media screens, mobile devices, virtual environments, and biomedical imaging.

Dr Jan Scheurer trained in architecture and urban planning in Hamburg, and then completed his doctorate on mobility management in innovative housing developments at Murdoch University. An Associate Researcher in the RMIT–NATSEM Centre of AHURI (Melbourne), he has lectured at RMIT and Murdoch universities and is a consultant in urban design and sustainable transport.

Dr James Whelan is an activist, educator and researcher. He convened a postgraduate Environmental Advocacy course (Faculty of Environmental Science, Griffith University) and is Co-Director of thechangeagency.org. His research, training programs and publications focus on social movements, civil society, community action and engagement.

Acknowledgements

Without the encouragement and full support of Professor Gavin Wood, Director of the RMIT–NATSEM Centre of the Australian Housing and Urban Research Institute (Melbourne, Australia), this book would not have eventuated. Initiated as a responsibility of Anitra Nelson – Senior Research Fellow (Sustainable Housing and Urban Planning) – it relied on considerable efforts by other centre colleagues, especially Professor Mike Berry and Professor Tony Dalton, and research assistance from Rilke Muir and Yolande Strengers. RMIT Professor of Sustainability, John Fien, also contributed enthusiastically to publication plans. As outlined in Chapter 1 – with special thanks to Professor Lyndsay Neilson, Christine Kilmartin and Scott Rawlings – the Department of Sustainability and Environment (Victoria) provided valuable advice on chapter drafts and financial assistance for contributors to participate in face-to-face workshops. Finally, thanks to Frans Timmerman, who assisted with copy editing and proofreading.

Various contributors acknowledge support specific to their chapters: Professor Tony Dalton and Geoffrey Binder (Chapter 15) thank Barton Williams (VicUrban) for support, advice and recommendations; Richard Hyde et al. (Chapter 8) acknowledge the support of the Australian Cooperative Research Centre (CRC) for Sustainable Tourism; James Whelan (Chapter 11) sincerely thanks Jill Jordan, Lois Levy, Sheila Davis, Susie Duncan, Katrina Shields, Jon Woodlands, Peter Oliver and Neil Lazarow for their reflections and insights; and the research and preparation of Chapter 19 (Mike Berry et al.) was conducted within the Australasian CRC for Interaction Design, which was established and supported under the Australian Government's Cooperative Research Centre Program.

Permissions to reproduce material associated with the boxes, figures and tables listed below were gratefully received from the following publishers and copyright holders:

'Western Australian framework for sustainability' (Box 2.1) derived from WA Government (2003), *Hope for the Future: the Western Australian State Sustainability Strategy* (Perth: Department of the Premier and Cabinet).

'EcoIndicator 99 model' (Figure 5.1) originally published in Goedkoop, M. and Spriensma, R. (1999), *The EcoIndicator 99: A Damage Oriented Method for Life Cycle Impact Assessment* (Amersfoort: PRé Consultants bv).

'LCA performance of Aurora Homes' (Figure 5.3) originally produced by the Centre for Design, RMIT University and the Global Footprint Network (2006), *Ecological Footprint Analysis of Aurora Residential Development* as a report for the Victorian Environmental Protection Authority, VicUrban and Building Commission, Melbourne.

'Australian consumption of select materials' (Table 6.2) originally published in Newton, P. et al. (2001), *Human Settlements, Australia. State of the Environment Report 2001* [Theme Report] (Canberra: CSIRO Publishing for the Department of Environment and Heritage), available at <http://www.publish.csiro.au/pid/3002. htm> Commonwealth of Australia reproduced by permission.

'Average hours worked per employed person per annum (2000)' (Table 13.1) derived from Gittins and Tiffen (2004), *How Australia Compares* (Melbourne: Cambridge University Press).

'International comparison of paid annual leave and public holidays' (Table 13.2) originally published in Denniss, R. (2003), *Annual Leave in Australia: an Analysis of Entitlements, Usage and Preferences* [Discussion Paper 56] (Canberra: The Australia Institute).

'Sustainability Charter priorities, objectives and performance measures' (VicUrban) (Table 15.1) VicUrban (2006), *Sustainability Charter Making Our Communities Better (Draft)* [February] (Melbourne: VicUrban).

List of Abbreviations

ABARE	Australian Bureau of Agricultural and Resource Economics
ABS	Australian Bureau of Statistics
$A	Australian dollars
BASIX	Building Sustainability Index
BCA	Building Code of Australia
BEA	Building Environmental Assessment
BIEC	Beverage Industry Environment Council
BMCC	Blue Mountains City Council
BMWHI	Blue Mountains World Heritage Institute
BedZED	Beddington Zero Energy Development
CERES	Centre for Educational Research in Environmental Strategies
CSIRO	Commonwealth Scientific and Industrial Research Organization
DIY	Do-it-yourself
EPR	Extended producer responsibility
ESD	Ecologically sustainable development
GCCC	Gold Coast City Council
GDP	Gross domestic product
Gecko	Gold Coast and Hinterland Environment Council
HEP	Halifax EcoCity Project
HIA	Housing Industry Association
ICT	Information and communication technology
ILO	International Labour Office
ISO	International Organization for Standardization
LA21	Local Agenda 21 (aka Agenda 21)
LCA	Life cycle assessment
LED	Light-emitting diode
NABERS	National Australian Building Environmental Rating Scheme
NSW	New South Wales
OECD	Organization for Economic Cooperation and Development
PPP	Public–private partnership
REIN	Regional Environmental Innovation Network
SA	South Australia
SHED	Sustainable human ecological development
UK	United Kingdom
USA	United States of America
UEA	Urban Ecology Australia
UNEP	United Nations Environment Program
WA	Western Australia

Chapter 1

Steering Sustainability: What, When and Why

Mike Berry and Anitra Nelson

How does 'evidence' speak to 'power'? (Pawson 2006, 1)

Climate change presents a unique challenge for economics: it is the greatest and widest-ranging market failure ever seen. (Stern 2006, Executive summary, i)

Introduction

Although the contributors to this collection write from an Australian perspective, the context within which they discuss urban sustainability – the issues, approaches and challenges – is global. They address two main challenges: understanding the forces leading to unsustainable social and environmental outcomes in advanced capitalist, urbanized nations and encouraging creative ways of moving society onto more sustainable paths. In this latter task, governments have a critical role as major consumers of resources, providers of infrastructure, and through powers to tax and regulate. Hence, one theme running through the book focuses on how researchers and policy makers can 'speak' to each other and how timely credible research can inform and improve policy formulation, implementation and evaluation.

The theme of intertwining the dialogues and respective activities of researchers and policy makers guided the practical process of developing this book. Senior policy makers and advisers of the Department of Sustainability and Environment from the State Government of Victoria, Australia, kindly agreed to read and comment on early drafts of chapters and to reflect on how they saw sustainability policy developing and impacting on the environment, economy and society. At a workshop held in mid-2006, departmental officers and authors discussed the issues, methods and implications raised in the various contributions. The aim was to produce a thoroughly practical policy manuscript facilitated by a dialogue in which authors and policy makers challenged one another to articulate what a 'good' sustainability policy is and how it is delivered most effectively.

Inevitably, differences of view and values emerged, both between and among the participating researchers and policy makers, resulting in a robust and informative debate that proved to be invaluable. On the day following the workshop the authors met as a group and exhaustively reviewed the insights gleaned from their exchange with the policy makers and worked through the changes suggested. Both workshops were critical in setting the direction for the production of the final chapters that appear in this book. This approach has much to recommend it as a process for getting researchers and policy makers to speak and listen, and therefore understand each other.

Steer *What?*

The 'steering' reference in the title of this book reflects major changes in public policy development and analysis over the past twenty years in advanced capitalist nations. Neo-liberalism has emerged as the dominant policy paradigm, especially in the Anglo-democracies of Australia, Britain, the United States, Canada and New Zealand (Bell 2002). From this viewpoint, the role of government is to 'steer, not row', to set the legal and institutional framework within which 'the market' operates to allocate productive resources and to distribute the fruits of economic activity across the population and between countries and regions. What is clear, however, is that the challenge of steering economic and social development in productive, benign and above all *sustainable* ways is more complicated and difficult to achieve than the standard model of neoclassical economics proposes. Myriad 'market failures' intervene between rowers and navigators. The most obvious and – as the Stern quote above suggests – serious challenge is the complex, interacting set of effects resulting in long term, accumulating and irreversible climate change. Other failures are generated by negative externalities and distributional inequities associated with resource extraction, polluting activities, the abuse of political and market power and ecosystem breakdown.

Achieving sustainability requires a society to adequately deal with the full range of market failures facing that society, many of which will be cross-border and global in scope. In this context, Dovers (2006, 7) defines sustainability as 'the ability of human society to persist in the long term in a manner that satisfies human development demands but without threatening the integrity of the natural world'. He characterizes sustainable development as the capacity to deal with threats generated across four domains: diminution and degradation of resources; pollution and waste; ecosystem services; and 'society and the human condition' (Dovers 2006, 9). In each domain, deliberate government policy can help or hinder societies seeking sustainable development trajectories. However, due to the nature, scale, timing and scope of the threats posed, policy develops in a highly uncertain environment and, as such, is likely to be iterative, piecemeal and radically incomplete. Many of the processes driving economic, social and environmental change are complex in the technical sense and pertain to the operation of complex adaptive systems (Beinhocker 2006). Therefore it is impossible to accurately forecast their effects on the ground. This fact imparts an open-ended dynamic – a dose of 'fractal uncertainty' – to sustainability policy.

Why Steer, and *When?*

Many of the detrimental environmental impacts of human activities interact and form complex feedback mechanisms, with complex and synergistic long-term consequences that render attempts to steer outcomes even more difficult. Thus, sustainability policy must deal with drivers and effects that cut across conventional boundaries of academic disciplines and national boundaries, that have long-term gestation periods and impacts, and that entail chronic uncertainty. This imperative follows from the fact that effects and impacts – such as extreme climate events – display what founders of complexity science call 'wild randomness' (Mandelbrot and Hudson 2004). Instead of being normally distributed around a clear median with 'small tails' – infrequent extreme events, such effects tend to follow 'a power law' – there is a much larger frequency of both very small and very large impacts. Hence, policy makers should expect more 'one in a hundred year' events. Although path dependent to a degree, these events cannot be accurately forecasted in advance but contingency response plans will lessen the scale of their impacts when they do eventuate. The aftermath of Hurricane Katrina in the New Orleans region is a sad reminder of policy failure in this respect.

Policy makers need to recognize the constraints placed on their capacity to influence events by the long time horizons over which effects unfold, the paucity of workable models and relevant data, and the sensitivity of outcomes to the initial conditions prevailing in any specific context. Such constraints are magnified by weaknesses in institutional systems. Most policy systems with which we are familiar are poorly placed to deal with either the lack of knowledge of likely outcomes over the longer term and the 'back-end loading' of many of those events. To the extent that the negative consequences of unsustainable current practices are concentrated in the middle-to-distant future, current policies are likely to be inadequate. The way in which advanced industrial countries build their housing systems is a useful example.

Market forces tend to focus the minds of both housing providers and residents on the immediate costs of accessing the dwelling, not on the lifetime costs of living in it. Indeed, a house is a physical asset with a long life, typically servicing a few generations. If the extra cost of building-in energy or water-efficient features and fittings adds significantly to the up-front purchase price, the market will ruthlessly weed out these initiatives, even though they might have repaid the residents in dollars and amenity many times over during the life of the dwelling as well as reducing the overall 'environmental footprint'. In circumstances of clear market failure, appropriate and well-targeted government interventions can make a positive difference – in this case, by providing positive incentives to house builders and residents to include environmentally sensible features or regulating to achieve the same outcome.

Some environmental impacts are so large and pervasive that they defeat the reach of any one government to address them through targeted, piecemeal policies. Global warming falls into this category. In this case, the appropriate response must be collective, involving contributions from government, industry and community organizations at the local, regional, national and international levels. Because of the cumulative, irreversible nature of the problem and the huge potential costs of getting it wrong, collective action will need to be 'front-end loaded'. The Executive Summary of the Stern *Review* (2006, i) has underscored the crucial importance of action, given the inertial build-up of greenhouse gases:

The effects of actions now on future changes in the climate have long lead times. What we do now can have only a limited effect on the climate over the next 40 or 50 years. On the other hand, what we do in the next 10 to 20 years can have a profound impact on the climate in the second half of this century and the next.

Early collective action in such circumstances will not only reduce the eventual costs of greenhouse emissions over the long term but, according to the Stern *Review*, will also minimize the total costs of mitigation and adaptation entailed. However, the barriers to effective collective action at the various levels are immense. Barriers include the high transaction costs of reaching and implementing collective action, 'free riders' and the short policy horizons of governments locked into conventional electoral cycles.

Conversely, the scale and chronic uncertainty of some impacts can provide a strategic case for invoking 'precautionary principle' or 'wait-and-see' options. This requires policy makers to avoid or delay making decisions where the impacts are unclear until better intelligence is available to assess and manage the risks. Such an injunction runs counter to most approaches to public policy, which tends to implicitly attach a zero value/cost to potential effects that cannot be readily quantified and given a probability measure. Somewhat akin to the precautionary principle, the maxim of 'minimum regret' invites policy makers and others in the broader 'policy community' to place themselves at some distant time in the future and speculate on levels of regret if particular negative scenarios play out, and then to return to the present and choose a policy path that would give them the lowest cause to regret.

The issue of *when* governments should intervene in areas that have very long-term impacts is also intimately tied up with concerns over intergenerational equity – questions related to what we owe future generations. The original definition of sustainable development introduced by the Brundtland Report, *Our Common Future* (WCED 1987), explicitly raised this concern. Where the impacts are large, irreversible and long lasting, government policy interventions are required earlier rather than later to protect the rights of unborn generations. This essentially ethical prescription places a heavy burden on current governments, especially in view of the fact that unborn generations do not vote. The latter's interests are represented (tenuously) in democracies such as Australia only to the extent that today's voters and governments accept the responsibility for their future welfare and act accordingly.

New Policy Drivers

It is clear that climate change, and the issues surrounding it, will be a dominant factor in public policy in the coming decade. In addition to the specific problem of dealing with the effects of climate change, the following drivers, mostly mutually reinforcing, will concentrate the minds of policy communities around the world:

1. *Energy.* 'Peak oil', the point at which the known world supply of oil reserves has peaked and begins to decline, will pose increasing economic pressures on industrial and industrializing countries. The task of finding alternative energy sources and technologies will become more pressing. The nuclear energy

option has been raised as a means of combating greenhouse gas emissions, which raises massive problems for institutional systems, particularly national governments, concerning the storage of nuclear waste and threats of nuclear weapons proliferation and terrorism. The heavy dependence of many countries on relatively plentiful supplies of coal to generate the rapidly increasing global demand for electricity makes it difficult to bend policy in favour of more environmentally benign alternatives, especially in major coal-exporting countries, such as Australia. Debate over policy developments tends to oscillate between encouraging the exploitation of alternative energy sources and developing 'clean coal' technologies.

2. *Water.* In many countries the adequate and secure supply of water for agriculture, industry and dwellings is increasingly at risk. Water access, within and between countries, threatens to be a major cause of conflict. Water scarcity may force mass intra- and international migrations and require very large infrastructure investments for solutions such as long distance delivery and desalination. Policy systems will be massively challenged to respond in such conflicts. Overstressed river ecosystems are likely to collapse if adequate water flows are not maintained or regained, affecting other environmental and economic assets. Australia, as a dry, 'old' continent, is at the forefront of this particular challenge.

3. *Pollution.* Rapid industrialization continues to generate escalating volumes of pollution, given current technological trajectories traversed by the developed world and fast-growing econom, especially China and India. Instances include air pollution from motor vehicles, water pollution from industrial discharges and residential waste disposal.

4. *Population Growth and Ageing.* Population growth, particularly in the less developed countries, places increasing stress on fragile environmental and resource bases. The global population shows weak signs of stabilizing, a major hope being that increasing living standards in China and India will result in continuing falls in birth rates. Ageing populations in countries such as Australia place increasing and expensive demands on governments to meet the needs of older citizens – appropriate housing, mobility and leisure services but, above all, access to adequate health care.

5. *Health.* Besides aged care, governments will be faced with major challenges posed by current and possible future pandemics. AIDS and bird flu prefigure the potential scale and cost of such challenges and the difficulties of achieving effective international responses. Other diseases, such as malaria, tuberculosis and chronic eye diseases, are savage suppressors of economic and social development in underdeveloped regions.

6. *Poverty and Insecurity.* Widespread poverty in underdeveloped countries can deny such societies economic resources to engage in sustainable practices. Continued loss of forests, overexploitation of fishing stocks and pollution generated by overurbanization result partially from poverty. Successful efforts by countries like China to break out of poverty place different stressors on the environment, especially to the extent that they follow the natural resource-dependent technological path of advanced industrial nations. Increasing

insecurity in strategic areas threatens access to key resources, notably the Middle East and oil. It is difficult to see major advances in sustainability globally unless and until governments respond collectively to the problems of extreme poverty and insecurity.

7. *Financial Markets.* As the cost of unsustainable development rises exponentially, world financial markets are factoring in environmental risk when valuing the worth of businesses, reflected in cost and availability of insurance, the rapid growth of 'socially responsible investment', and shifts by investors towards companies that 'screen' positively on social and environmental grounds. As monitoring techniques, data bases and financial asset allocation become more sophisticated, companies that fail to move beyond 'greenwash' activities will bear higher costs of finance than more environmentally responsible competitors and bear increasing damage to their reputation (affecting sales).

The Urban Question

Many of the drivers and impacts noted above are associated with remorseless global processes of urban growth and concentration. For the first time in history, most people live in urban centres. There are more than twenty city-regions with more than twenty million inhabitants, most located in Asia. Current urbanization patterns impose unsustainable lifestyles on urban residents and unsustainable systems of resource use, transportation and waste disposal. 'Steering sustainability' really means dealing with the unwanted consequences of urban growth. This imperative calls for governments to improve the rate of urban metabolism, increasing 'good' life-sustaining outputs while reducing 'bad' outputs (such as pollution) and resource inputs. As in the Chinese example, this might entail government controls on immigration rates to the largest and most congested urban centres in favour of smaller centres.

Contributors to this book adopt a deliberate urban focus. More specifically, the focus is on the lived experiences of people in urban and suburban settings. They deal with a range of issues and approaches to improving sustainability 'on the ground' and argue for policy makers to steer people towards the mass adoption of more sustainable practices. Central themes running through the book include environmental democracy and the lifestyle (behavioural) changes necessary to achieve sustainable outcomes and holistic social learning. Each contributor identifies key sustainability principles and practices, frameworks, approaches and concepts for achieving sustainable housing and urban development outcomes. All the authors ask, in a constructive way: What policies and practices are most effective in enabling and forcing desirable social change, and what are the barriers that must be overcome to do so?

Transforming Cities

The book is divided into four sections. In Part 1 Transforming Cities, the contributors offer four overarching approaches to understanding the challenge of shifting urban growth trajectories to more sustainable paths. Each contributor operates from a distinct perspective, highlighting implications for policy makers.

Newman (Chapter 2) focuses on what constitutes a sustainable residential urban form in a growing metropolitan region. Newman speaks at the level of national policy making and metropolitan-scale planning, drawing on his personal experiences as a senior adviser on sustainability policy to the Western Australian Premier and a stint as the New South Wales Sustainability Commissioner (2004–2006). He begins with Western Australia's framework for sustainability definition of sustainability, elaborating on its implications for housing, in terms of the framework's principles, which attempt to ground and operationalize complex and contentious concepts such as 'intergenerational equity'. Newman identifies car dependence as a critical area for action – a topic considered by Scheurer in Chapter 7 too – and categorizes housing within three urban planning and development patterns: walking cities, transit cities and automobile cities. Analysing city sprawl in these terms, he presents economic as well as equity and environmental arguments in favour of transit-oriented centres and walking city centres.

Downton (Chapter 3) introduces the concept of 'the ecopolis', defined as minimizing ecological footprints (biophysical) and maximizing human potential (human ecology) in order to repair, replenish and support processes that maintain life. He has been a principal practitioner specializing in ecological architecture and is a resident founder of the Christie Walk project, a sustainable urban residential demonstration model or 'urban fractal' in Adelaide, the capital of South Australia. Downton sees the ecological city as 'the next evolutionary step for urbanism' and presents three model demonstration projects, 'urban fractals'. Downton speaks at the grainy level of community-inspired action and as an architect/designer. Nevertheless, his contribution and strategy is neither parochial nor small-minded. In fact it offers a philosophical, social and historical 'big picture' perspective of how to address sustainability challenges. Thus, he elaborates on ten ecopolis development principles, presents seven aspects of the sustainable human ecological development process (such as bioregional 'placing' and biozoning), introduces a novel 'frogstick' measure (urban ecology checklist) and proposes four conditions for ecocities (seeing the city within its hinterland, integrating knowledge, cultural change for ecological sustainability, and urban fractals).

Copeman (Chapter 4) switches the gaze to the micro level. He offers a simple, straightforward and eloquent introduction to permaculture and how its principles and perspective can be applied in urban planning and policy making as well as at the grassroots level (where it originated and has been most evident). He defines 'permaculture' as a sustainable approach to living with nature through applying three ethical principles – care for the earth, care for the people, share surplus resources – and twelve design principles (that structure the chapter). His points are illustrated by examples, such as Brisbane's Northey Street City Farm, where he has worked since 1994. He emphasizes third way organizations, neither public nor private enterprises, but cooperatives, collectives and networks that support growth of food in cities and so on. Alternative technologies, managed at the grassroots, mimic and control nature to modest human ends.

More broadly, Copeman sees permaculture as a way to heal the historical separation of rural and urban forms: 'by creating mosaics of housing, industry, shops, offices, farmland and bush right through and around cities, which would facilitate interesting and productive interactions at the boundaries of different areas, not only in the inner city but also in the suburbs and on the urban fringe.' In this view, social diversity complements ecological stability. Permaculture has often been practised and perceived as a rural development but Copeman uses the community garden as an exemplar of *urban* permaculture while standing his ground that decentralization is an ecological necessity. In this way his vision can be distinguished from Newman's and Downton's.

Grant (Chapter 5) adopts an explicitly technical cast. He presents life cycle assessment (LCA) as a critical lens through which to track and interrogate sustainability outcomes. He defines LCA, outlining its short history and applications with respect to sustainable housing and urban planning. Grant introduces the notion of 'environmental folklore' to refer to the shared knowledge of understanding and working towards sustainability. He positions LCA as a system to evaluate the comparative potential and limits of strategies, activities and products to progress sustainability. LCA is proposed as a humanistic *science*, which helps 'renew environmental folklore and provide more rational and responsive decision making in urban planning'.

Grant outlines a systematic approach to measuring the environmental impacts of manufacturing products and providing services and discusses its application in *Aurora*, a master-planned estate on the northern fringes of Melbourne, which aims to improve environmental standards and performance of suburban homes and households. Aurora is the focus or reference point for other contributors too – Dalton and Binder (Chapter 15) and Hurley and Mercer (Chapter 9). Compared with other chapters in the first part of this book, LCA appears very technical and limited in scope. However, Grant presents it as a set of overlapping techniques which, broadly applied, might offer a general and big-picture analysis of sustainability that can support effective government policy and improve environmental performance in both business and household sectors.

Collective Practices

The contributions to Part II Collective Practices focus on 'fields' of sustainability, such as water and waste. They provide overviews of contemporary challenges and discuss practical policies and strategies to address such challenges. A recurrent theme is the need for developing consistency and complementarities between individual and household-level sustainable practices and collective urban systems and infrastructure.

Pears (Chapter 6) examines non-transport (stationary) energy supplies and uses within an urban metabolism framework, which analyses inputs, outputs, dynamics and impacts. He highlights an integrated perspective arguing that, for instance, high-density settlements might economize on energy uses and costs but limit potential solar energy collection, storage and use and involve social disadvantages. Thus he discusses policy options within a real world of urban lifestyles, technological and economic developments, analysing 'diversified solutions' which take into account the various stakeholders and actors: industry, planners and regulators as well as consumers. Pears argues for policy making to be open, flexible, adaptive and innovative while challenging lifestyle choices that demand high energy-use, such as the trend towards larger houses despite a decline in household size.

Scheurer (Chapter 7) addresses challenges associated with moving from car dependence, which Newman (Chapter 2) identified as the key barrier to urban sustainability. Framing his discussion in a supply–demand model, Scheurer argues for integrated solutions: innovative energy-saving and resource-saving technologies; well-planned and organized urban transport systems; and changes in transport practices at the level of individuals. He offers European models and solutions to transport dilemmas as options for Australian policy makers. He discusses types of travellers, i.e. travel practices, as well as forms of travel (such as bicycle riding), arguing that urban structures need to be examined, understood and developed as systems of mobility choices and limits.

While sustainability indicators and audits proliferate, Hyde et al. (Chapter 8) argue that there have been insufficient assessments of how well these tools assist policy makers to implement, monitor and evaluate their sustainability strategies. To promote an emerging debate, they examine building environmental assessment tools, which aim to contribute to the successful implementation of sustainability policies and initiatives in housing, identifying their assumptions, weaknesses and practical benefits. Hyde et al. offer examples from Britain and Australia. They argue that, in as much as building environmental assessment tools are able to accurately predict, measure and monitor sustainable buildings, they have a role in evidence-based policy making and usefully contribute to correcting and otherwise reforming policy and practices.

Hurley and Mercer (Chapter 9) make a comment applicable to other areas considered in this book, that 'know-how and technology available to save water and improve water quality are far in advance of the majority of practices'. Living in a 'fool's paradise', urban Australians have expected free plentiful water supplies but today face radical limits on domestic water use. For instance, the Victorian Government has a target of reducing Melbourne's water consumption by 75 per cent by 2015. Watering gardens, showering, washing cars and filling outdoor swimming pools are regulated or under scrutiny. Technology, household practices, water agencies, supplies and services must change to achieve reductions in water use. Hurley and Mercer emphasize the importance of community education, referring to Aurora estate innovations to reduce demand and improve sustainable domestic water supplies, as well as a range of social, regulatory and economic initiatives that represent models for future practices.

Eales and Donaldson (Chapter 10) outline the evolution of integrated waste management as a response to outdated landfill methods for dealing with urban waste. They focus on the 'waste hierarchy' – avoid, reduce, reuse, recycle, recover energy and dispose – as the heart of managing waste for sustainability. Again attention is drawn to the significance of education and actions at a household level for waste-management systems to succeed.

Community and Civil Society

The successful implementation of sustainability policies in urban areas relies heavily on the practices of individuals and households in the contexts of community learning and neighbourhood action. In Part III Community and Civil Society, the contributors analyse the complexities of creating sustainable communities, citizens for sustainability.

Whelan (Chapter 11) argues that urban futures will be determined through vigilant and resourceful action by residents' groups and environmentalists. His analysis focuses on community action with respect to planning and developments in Maleny and along the Gold Coast (Queensland). His contribution is unique in arguing that women have fulfilled a 'pivotal role' and that alternative economic exchange systems are significant. Whelan addresses conflicts that commonly arise between grassroots groups and local councillors and bureaucracies, revealing that we have few effective political processes to engage with and harness community energies already supporting sustainable developments. He concludes that permanent engagement and reform based on shared understandings and decision making is crucial to achieve sustainability.

Mike Hill and Lorna Pitt (Chapter 12) have been prominent political figures, especially in local government and specifically concerned with sustainable urban planning and design. Instrumental in turning a former inner suburban primary school into a showpiece sustainable housing development, Hill and Pitt summarize their experiences and challenges in creating WestWyck as an urban ecovillage for educational purposes. They detail the practical challenges of integrating energy and water efficient techniques and technologies, using recycled materials and addressing transport needs. In this 'market oriented' development, the neighbourhood community is an active concept involving rights and responsibilities to ensure that the local ecology, local community and local economy coexist in sustainable ways.

Work–life balances are intricately associated with economic activities that impact on the environment. Denniss (Chapter 13) points out that most Australians are working longer, earning and spending more, yet still want to increase consumption. He argues that less working and spending is likely to have a positive impact on the environment. A political adviser for years, Denniss is currently attached to the Greens Party national leader Senator Bob Brown. His approach is practical. Referring to the 'slow food movement', the 'simple living network', the 'buy nothing day' and so on, he suggests actions for individuals and community-based groups to alter the situation. Finally, Denniss lists fourteen policy options that federal, State and local governments might consider to support less work, less consumption and a more sustainable environment.

Potts et al. (Chapter 14) discuss ways of operationalizing UN Local Agenda 21 – 'global talk to local action' – drawing on experiences of partnerships between business, government, university researchers and communities. They define partnerships as 'tools that promote dialogue, cooperation and education across different sectors and stakeholders' with a specific utility for achieving sustainability and refer to two case studies to argue that universities can facilitate community-based sustainability by acting as independent brokers – scoping ways forward and assisting in resolving conflicts between interested stakeholders. This role complements research advice, identifying, collecting and analysing appropriate information to enhance local understanding, knowledge building, and conducting trials of sustainability solutions.

Transforming Suburbs

Part IV Transforming Suburbs focuses specifically on issues related to sustainable housing: government as an agent for change, affordable sustainable housing, sustainable renovations ('retrofitting the suburbs'), policies and strategies to conserve nature in urban settings, and the sustainability aspects of high-technology 'smart' homes.

VicUrban is a State-owned land development agency involved with urban housing provision in Victoria. In the last decade housing sustainability performance and its measurement have become key concerns for such agencies. VicUrban has developed the Sustainability Charter, a performance-based planning initiative, which Dalton and Binder (Chapter 15) analyse in the context of a decline in housing affordability and difficulties with providing services for residents of low-density developments in sprawling suburban fringes. They identify three policy challenges: housing affordability, service delivery, and reducing the environmental impacts of low-density suburban developments. They identify a major weakness, public transport, over which VicUrban has little direct control, highlighting the agency's limitations and the need for holistic, whole-of-government approaches to sustainability.

Randolph et al. (Chapter 16) consider minimum environmental performance standards for new housing in the light of affordability to conclude that equity issues and affordability have lost out. This chapter is a plea to make housing affordability a central element of the housing sustainability debate and practice: 'Unless these two issues are tackled concurrently in policy development, we risk having to compromise both qualities – an outcome which undermines the triple-bottom-line equity aspirations of genuine sustainable housing.' The chief problem is that environmentally sustainable housing is costing more than traditional housing, which mainly excludes low-income households that will not benefit much from any 'trickle-down' effect.

Dalton et al. (Chapter 17) consider gaps in research and policies with respect to residential housing improvements conforming with and improving environmental housing performance standards. The authors review a series of 'important but uncoordinated initiatives' to identify questions inadequately addressed in the literature: Why do householders alter their homes? How concerned are they with improving the sustainability performance of their homes? How, and to what extent, are renovators informed about improvements for sustainability outcomes? Barriers to improving environmental features of alterations and additions to existing housing stock include limited information and hidden costs and benefits, complicating assessments of the economic benefits of environmental improvements and accentuating risk factors. The authors conclude that institutional change and focus is required to highlight the invisible potential of enhancing the sustainability of housing improvements.

Conservation is an urban issue in Australia, where settlement and subsequent urbanization has tended to develop along the coast, in areas of high ecological value, high biodiversity, dependable rain and fertile soil. Land incorporated into our sprawling cities has been virtually unmanaged for its ecological values. In line with international trends, and challenging the implied balance of outcomes in concepts such as environmentally sustainable development, Bekessy and Gordon (Chapter 18) argue that 'short-term economic gains consistently win over biodiversity concerns on a localized case-by-case basis'. Experts in preserving biodiversity have not contributed sufficiently to urban planning. Land requires integrated management across landscape and biological scales distinct from the socially created zones, powers and responsibilities of governments. To address the challenge of managing urban biodiversity – 'nurturing nature in the city' – the authors present a vision of 'Biodiversia', 'a suburb ... designed with the preservation of biodiversity as a top priority'.

There is a long history of political and economic leaders hailing or following technological 'advances' to address challenges facing humankind. Through the first half of the twentieth century home automation (the robot) was viewed as a way to save effort and time on household chores and maintenance. During the second half of the century, home automation has been applied to reduce risks and to improve security, safety, comfort and entertainment in homes. Most recently, housing-related technology (such as water and energy meters) has been applied for sustainability ends. Such features have been integrated into smart designs and developments, high-tech and 'more sustainable' dwellings. Chapter 19, by Berry et al., gives a critique of the concept of the smart home from four perspectives: historically, the point of view of policy making, in the context of innovation and, finally, through a review of 'non-determinist ways of interpreting human–technology relations'.

In the concluding Chapter 20 Nelson returns to an holistic perspective: what are the principles, processes and practices that will steer sustainable urban futures?

References

Bell, S. (ed.) (2002), *Economic Governance and Institutional Dynamics* (Melbourne: Oxford University Press).

Beinhocker, E. (2006), *The Origin of Wealth: Evolution, Complexity and the Radical Remaking of Economics* (Boston: Harvard Business School Press).

Dovers, S. (2006), *Environment and Sustainability Policy: Creation, Implementation, Evaluation* (Sydney: The Federation Press).

Mandelbrot, B. and Hudson, R. (2004), *The (Mis)Behaviour of Markets: A Fractal View of Risk, Ruin and Reward* (London: Profile Books).

Pawson, R. (2006), *Evidence-Based Policy: A Realist Perspective* (London: Sage Publications).

Stern, N. (2006) *The Economics of Climate Change – The Stern Review* [website] HM Treasury [website], <http://www.hm-treasury.gov.uk/independent_reviews/ stern_review_economics_climate_change/sternreview_index.cfm>(for Executive summary, see long version).

WCED (1987), *Our Common Future* [Brundtland Report, World Commission on Environment and Development] (Oxford: Oxford University Press).

Part I
Transforming Cities

Chapter 2

A Sustainable Cities Framework
for Housing

Peter Newman

Introduction

Sustainability has become a key concept for planning cities' futures. All Australian cities now have metropolitan planning strategies framed around sustainability. This chapter applies the framework developed by the Government of Western Australia (2003) for its State sustainability strategy to cities, with an emphasis on housing policy. The WA framework for sustainability included a definition and a set of principles (see Box 2.1) that can be applied to demonstrate how to think about sustainability in any area of human activity. This chapter uses these principles as the framework of an approach to housing for a sustainable city.

Box 2.1 Western Australian framework for sustainability

Definition of Sustainability

Sustainability is meeting the needs of current and future generations through an integration of environmental protection, social advancement and economic prosperity.

Sustainability Principles – Foundation Principles

1. *Long-term Economic Health*

Sustainability recognizes the needs of current and future generations for long-term economic health, innovation, diversity and productivity of the earth.

2. *Equity and Human Rights*

Sustainability recognizes that an environment needs to be created where all people can express their full potential and lead productive lives, and significant gaps in sufficiency, safety and opportunity endanger the earth.

3. *Biodiversity and Ecological Integrity*

Sustainability recognizes that all life has intrinsic value and is interconnected, and biodiversity and ecological integrity are part of the irreplaceable life support systems upon which the earth depends.

4. *Settlement Efficiency and Quality of Life*

Sustainability recognizes that settlements need to reduce their ecological footprint (i.e. less material and energy demands and reductions in waste), whilst they simultaneously improve their quality of life (health, housing, employment, community…).

5. *Community, Regions, 'Sense of Place' and Heritage*

Sustainability recognizes the reality and diversity of community and regions for the management of the earth, and the critical importance of 'sense of place' and heritage (buildings, townscapes, landscapes and culture) in any plans for the future.

6. *Net Benefit from Development*

Sustainability means that all development, and particularly development involving extraction of non-renewable resources, should provide a legacy of enduring value and thus should strive to provide net environmental, social and economic benefit for future generations.

7. *Common Good from Planning*

Sustainability recognizes that planning for the common good requires acceptance of limits to consumption of public resources (like air, water and open space) so that a shared resource is available to all.

Sustainability Principles – Process Principles

8. *Integration*

Sustainability requires that economic, social and environmental factors be integrated into planning, assessment and decision-making by applying all the principles of sustainability at once, and seeking mutually supportive benefits with minimal trade offs.

9. *Accountability, Transparency and Engagement*

Sustainability recognizes that:

a) people should have access to information on sustainability issues;

b) institutions should have triple bottom line accountability on an annual basis;

c) regular sustainability audits of programs and policies should be conducted;

d) public engagement lies at the heart of all sustainability principles.

10. *Precaution*

Sustainability requires caution, avoiding poorly understood risks of serious or irreversible damage to environmental, social and economic capital, designing for surprise and managing for adaptation.

11. *Hope, Vision, Symbolic and Iterative Change*

Sustainability recognizes that applying these sustainability principles as part of a broad strategic vision for the earth can generate hope in the future, and thus it will involve symbolic change that is part of many successive steps over generations.

Source: Adapted from Government of Western Australia (2003).

Long Term Economic Health

Humans can live in many different habitats but cities have become the preferred habitation for half the world. The thousands of years of experimentation in cities, since agricultural surpluses were found to be tradable for various urban services, has created *homo urbanus*. Globalization of the economy has accelerated the growth of cities as the places where opportunities exist to participate in global economic and cultural activity. By the mid-1990s, based on economic opportunities, cities were growing on average at 2.3 per cent per year but rural areas at only 0.5 per cent per year (UNEP/Habitat 1996).

Australian cities have firm strategies to accommodate growth, which seems inevitable. Decline or collapse is not on the agenda. However, long term views of history should include this possibility. Cities, and parts of cities, can collapse and die (Diamond 2005). If the economy is not firmly rooted in the reality of the city's bioregion, its use of resources and its ability to adapt to change, then a city is unsustainable. The dark clouds on the horizon of cities include climate change and its threat to water supplies as well as the peaking of world oil production, which has fed the past century of urban economic growth (Campbell 1991; Deffeyes 2005; Kunstler 2005). Such threats to future urban growth should be taken seriously.

Some commentators on apocalyptic possibilities suggest that cities are likely to be abandoned in favour of a new kind of ruralized urban area where everyone produces their own food and only local economies exist (Trainer 1995). Whilst recognizing the importance of local food and the bioregion, this option is unlikely. The history of cities shows that sharing services and the division of labour create far more opportunities. A return to Eden will not happen (Newman forthcoming). The forced ruralization programs of Pol Pot and Mao were economic and environmental disasters, apart from their social destruction, and their cities were soon rebuilt and refocused as the basis of their future.

Nevertheless, economies must adapt to the reality of new challenges to sustainability. We build housing that will last around fifty to a hundred years, but markets only see six months or so ahead. Long-term planning and housing strategies that go beyond the market's ability to respond and that can be built into a new sustainability agenda are needed.

Critical to the new sustainability agenda in cities is managing car dependence. Increasingly a feature of planning strategies, managing car dependence is seen as a major factor in the economics of managing a city. All Australian cities now have metropolitan strategies emphasizing alternative transport infrastructure and more densely built centres and corridors based around public transport. What is the basis for this?

Cities are shaped by transport priorities, increasingly understood in terms of the 'Marchetti constant' (Marchetti 1994). This travel time budget means that city residents travel, on average, no more than half an hour to work and half an hour home again. The Marchetti constant has universal application (Newman and Kenworthy 1999) and has been found in data on United Kingdom cities for six hundred years (SACTRA 1994). Historically this means:

- Walking cities were (and still are) dense, mixed-use areas, no more than 5 km across. This was the major urban form for 8000 years. The centres of Australian cities were formed and continue to function as walking cities.
- Transit cities, which developed 1850–1950, were based on trams and trains. This allowed them to spread 20–30 km with dense clusters of corridors following rail lines and stations. Most Australian cities, especially Melbourne and Sydney, grew rapidly in this era and retain their transit city corridors.
- Automobile cities, from the 1950s on, could spread 50 km in all directions and at low density. Since 1950, this form has dominated Australian urban development.

Australian housing can be classified in terms of these distinct urban forms, which shape how we use transport and create structures around which most urban issues are defined. For example, residents in the high density walking cities of Sydney and Melbourne use just 3–5 GJ of transport fuel per capita, the inner-area transit city residents use around 15–20 GJ per capita and the outer-area automobile city residents use 30–50 GJ per capita (Newman and Kenworthy 1999).

Different economies tend to be emerging around these distinct urban forms. The walking city and the transit city are increasingly centres of wealth in the new economy and feature most urban services, including diverse transport options. The automobile city is finally reaching its Marchetti limits based on car dependent sprawl as well as other ecological limits discussed in other chapters of this book. The dense walking city and the medium density transit city have higher concentrations of service jobs partly due to the economies of scale and density required to ensure services can be provided but also due to different urban lifestyle preferences. Those with smaller houses and apartments generally spend less on maintaining their house and block and spend more on local services. Automobile city areas are more oriented to consumption and less to personal services, such as restaurants, health clubs, bookshops and cinemas. The differences in urban service provision reflect the diversity of the city and inherent resilience due to multifunctionality. However, equity issues relate to public transport limits in outer suburbs.

Serious long-term economic problems are linked to car dependence. Not only will car-dependent cities be more vulnerable to peak oil, they already show vulnerability to global economic competition. Apparently, car dependence does not enhance the economy of cities. Car-dependent cities have the highest proportion of total transport costs as a proportion of city wealth. In a sample of 100 cities, rail-oriented cities were 43 per cent wealthier than car-oriented cities (Kenworthy and Laube 1999). This is understandable in terms of the sheer space taken up by cars (around twenty times more space compared to rail), the cost of road building, and the cost of driving.

The future economic health of cities demands a more sustainable balance between different forms of transport. The overemphasis on car-based development must be replaced by a greater emphasis on transit-oriented centres in suburbs, on walking centres in the city business district and sub-regional centres and on housing built into these centres. The provision of more walking city centres and transit corridors need not be at the expense of economic health. In the City of Vancouver, the emphasis on high density walking-city redevelopment has been an economic success: over 50,000 people have moved into the area; there have been significant reductions in car use (31,000 fewer trips per day); and increases in walking and biking to 107,000 more trips per day (City of Vancouver 2006.)

Equity and Human Rights

Equity considerations drive a lot of public policy, especially in housing (see Chapter 16). Affordable housing has been a major driver shaping Australian cities in the past fifty years. Subsidized suburban infrastructure and assisted mortgages have supported the sprawl and car dependence of Australian cities. Only recently has the assumption of car dependence in housing policy been challenged. Australian cities now face an equity problem in which the lower income proportion of our society is increasingly located in outer, fringe and coastal peri-urban areas, with very few options for travel other than car use to link them to jobs and urban services. The wealthy have taken over the inner suburbs with most transport and service options. Inner suburban residents spend a very low proportion of their incomes on transport (less than 5 per cent) while outer suburban households spend as much as 30–40 per cent.

Affordable housing strategies need to incorporate models that are not car dependent, such as the Vancouver policy for social housing in central and inner areas. Social housing is especially necessary in new middle and outer suburban centres. This might mean offering affordable houses in the form of more low-cost small units than in standard suburban developments (see Chapter 16). While such an approach is discounted by housing lobbyists who see cheap housing on cheap land at the urban fringe as the only affordable option, this traditional route to housing affordability is no longer sustainable (Newman 2002; 2004).

Achieving a balance between fringe-based and density-based affordability is the new challenge for housing policy. It is feasible to build attractive apartment housing for less than \$A100,000. Many of the oversized standard houses being built on Australia's urban fringe are two to three times this price. Using density to create affordability includes the critical transport dimension, assuming that denser housing is built in centres well served by public transport or where services are provided within walking distance. Such well-placed development needs to be managed to achieve affordable housing benefits as the strong market for well-located housing means that developers gain high profits. Institutional responses must ensure a certain proportion of well-located units for social housing.

Affordability in housing must include sustainability in water and power supplies. Building houses that leak energy or are poorly engineered for water harms the poorest and endangers the earth. The role of sustainability assessment in the development approvals system is critical to mandate ways of saving water and energy (see chapters 6 and 9).

Biodiversity and Ecological Integrity

The earth cannot be neglected in housing policy deliberations. The Melbourne Principles developed by the United Nations Environment Program to guide cities to become sustainable ecosystems (Newman and Jennings forthcoming) are being adopted by cities around the world to adapt developments to bioregions and especially to local biodiversity. The recent metropolitan strategies for Australian cities all stress this ecological factor in planning. Perth and Sydney, in particular, have acknowledged that their metropolitan areas are very high in biodiversity. Ecologist Steve Hopper has suggested Perth may have the highest biodiversity of any city in the world. The Sydney Basin was recently nominated the fifth most biologically diverse area out of 85 Australian bioregions. Nevertheless 267 species of plants and animals within the Sydney bioregion are listed as 'threatened', 35 per cent of all threatened species listed in NSW, despite the fact that Sydney covers only 5 per cent of the State (Department of Planning 2005).

Both Perth and Sydney have well-established programs to protect key environmental areas. Perth has a mechanism for purchasing open space, a special Metropolitan Improvement Fund that buys up land ahead of the urban front or areas later discovered to be rich in biodiversity. New Land Release areas follow Perth's approach to purchasing new biodiversity and open space areas through a land development levy managed by the NSW Growth Centres Commission. Almost half of Sydney is set aside as National Park, State Forest, regional and local open space, water catchments, wetlands and beaches.

However, threats to biodiversity and ecological integrity are overwhelming. The Millennium Ecosystem Assessment (2005) reports make grim reading: the loss of ecosystem function, which is the biggest threat to biodiversity, is clearly observable in 60 per cent of the 24 global ecosystems assessed. Ecosystem functioning and ecological integrity provide any city with: provisioning services (food, fresh water, fuel wood and genetic resources); regulating services (climate, disease and flood regulation); and cultural services (spiritual, recreational, aesthetic, inspirational and educational resources). The Millenium Ecosystem Assessment (2005) did not focus on cities where many of the key policy levers for changing sustainability problems exist. Ways of regenerating bush and renewing waterways degraded by previous development are being created, especially in Sydney (Dixon 2006).

Clearly there is a need to integrate housing responses to urban bioregions. Examples include Adelaide's Christie Walk (see Chapter 3) and the Somerville ecovillage at Chidlow, Perth (WA). Ecovillages (Gilman 1991) are laboratories of sustainability innovation, often arising from a base of ecological integrity and involving new small-scale technologies. Lessons from such experiments need to be mainstreamed into urban policy.

However, ecovillage experiments where people essentially become rural-based food producers whilst commuting to the city for work are not sustainable. They result in loss of good agricultural soils to fringe urban suburbs and hobby farms, which are generally unproductive. Australian residents in fringe urban areas, such as Sydney's Central Coast and Melbourne's Mornington Peninsular have three to four times the average fuel consumption, eight times that of an inner city resident. If we are serious about oil depletion and sustainability, we need to ensure that the countryside is more rural and the city more urban.

Bioregional food production needs to be facilitated through mechanisms such as local food policy councils and community-supported agriculture. Australian cities can achieve this by establishing horticultural precincts immediately adjacent to cities. Such areas of good soil need to be set aside and retained in perpetuity for horticulture rather than being wasted as 'market garden superannuation' for the next suburb. In such areas, we can get serious about recycling waste water, as water agencies cannot invest in pipes and technology unless certain about the area's future. This is a practical way for cities to protect the ecological integrity of their bioregions into the future whilst dealing with central resource issues.

Settlement Efficiency and Quality of Life

The best way to simply state the sustainability agenda for cities is summarized in efficient settlement and quality of life, a principle based on the Extended Metabolism Model (Newman and Kenworthy 1999), applied in the Australian State of the Environment report and in the metropolitan strategies of Sydney and Perth. This simple idea is a radical reform because cities have traditionally improved quality of life by increasing their ecological footprint. The only way to change this is at a fundamental structural level and through technological innovation.

The most likely fundamental change will be for cities to localize infrastructure solutions. The modernist solution to infrastructure has been to apply 'one best way' at the broadest scale. Thus energy, water, waste and transport systems are very large scale and often at odds with recently acknowledged ecological and renewable options. Smaller-scale water systems have emerged with the local reuse of grey water, recycling of sewage into horticultural precincts, and trapping stormwater for reuse. Similar local-scale systems are emerging for energy with mini-grids that use renewables and with co-generation, such as in Japan (NEDO 2005). What is likely to happen is that small-scale systems will be grafted onto larger regional-scale technologies and integrated through clever electronic control systems. Thus local-scale diversity will fit into regional-scale systems.

This is also a model for rebuilding public transport infrastructure – regional-scale 'backbones' of fast rail feeding out into a myriad of small-scale systems around local centres. The transport solution will combine transport infrastructure and land-use policy as well as household education programs, such as TravelSmart, which have already successfully reduced car use. Approaches that reduce ecological footprints whilst improving urban services is recognized in all the recent metropolitan strategies in Australian cities, which are committed to policies that reduce car dependence. The major problems are not in the dense and mixed land use inner suburbs, relatively well served by public transport infrastructure, and where fuel consumption per person is comparable to European cities. Unfortunately poverty is concentrating in the newer suburbs in the outer areas built in the last half century, which are heavily car dependent, with fuel consumption similar to US cities.

The looming problem of 'peak oil' makes efficient settlement an even higher priority. Global oil production is near to peaking, or has already peaked, resulting in the need to reduce oil consumption. The more sustainable city will be the more resilient city, not so vulnerable and dependent on oil, which will require fast transit and viable centres throughout the suburbs.

The *Sustainable Cities* report of the Australian House of Representatives (2005) recommends the provision of infrastructure funds for cities, especially for rail, and particularly in the middle and outer suburbs. Most other national governments, even in the USA, provide such funds. Such a critical shift needs to be made in federal policy in Australia. Money for such infrastructure exists from substantial capital funds associated with the state of the deficit. Also a mechanism could be developed to invest superannuation funds in our cities. If an urban infrastructure program were started, partnership funding of the required rail systems and integrated transport programs would follow. Perth's new rail system, which has cost $A2 billion and has given the city a 180 km modern electric rail system with 72 stations, was built without any federal funds. However, the freeway it passes down was funded almost entirely from federal coffers. This railway has been justified over many elections as a way of oil-proofing the city (Newman 2001). New developments are planned around these stations to take advantage of accessibility and amenity. Nevertheless, much of Perth, like all Australian cities, remains highly vulnerable to peak oil.

Community, Regions, 'Sense of Place' and Heritage

Sustainability in cities is finding new synergies with those who emphasize place and local identity. A sense of place can make a city more oriented to its basic ecology. However, as Seddon (1968, 2005) has shown, it is intensely human to belong, to relate to a local place through history and architecture, culture, food, music, and even football. The local food movement adds to this an ability to control the quality and environmental acceptability of food. But peak oil makes us see that we will need to be even more locally oriented in the future. In the 'Long Emergency', James Kunstler (2005) says that in response to peak oil, 'Our lives will become profoundly and intensely local.' Localism is the required *modus operandi* for the post-peak oil world, just as globalism was for the cheap oil era.

Globalization of economies began as the first cities traded beyond their immediate region – probably 4000 years ago – and will continue post-peak oil. But its character will alter as the extent of trade and mobility is unsustainable. Peak oil will ensure more clever movement of goods globally. As mentioned, there are social movements pushing us more towards localism: the need for local identity and sense of place; the slow food movement and its base in local foods; the ecocity movement with its desire to enable local community to be the basis for managing local resources and local infrastructure.

The value of the Internet and phone and computer video conference facilities will become even more obvious to maintain global interaction. In the same way that governments facilitated businesses to export globally and pushed international tourism, they need to facilitate localism now. Demonstration models need to be funded: where there is a need to create industrial ecology of businesses to share wastes as resources or work together to ensure local resources are used and reused; where local food linkages can be made between peri-urban growers and urban communities to directly supply fresh goods; where local enterprises can be facilitated and based on local resources and talents; and where local tourism can be marketed to local people. Such initiatives will help create a deeper sense of place whilst simultaneously reducing the ecological footprint.

Net Benefit from Development

Finding 'net benefit' from all development so that it can provide a legacy of 'enduring value' is the most practical way of demonstrating sustainability (Newman et al. 2005). Sustainability assessment is a way governments can address development approvals (Pope et al. 2004). This approach grew out of major resource projects in WA but sustainability assessment can be applied in other cities' strategic plans and through statutory development assessment processes (Newman 2005). Many local governments have sustainability scorecards. The NSW BASIX building sustainability system requires all new developments to design for 40 per cent less water and 25 per cent less greenhouse gas use than average homes and Victoria has similar requirements (Reardon 2005, Section 1.10). Recently, more complete sustainability assessments have been done on projects, such as Sydney's new land release areas (NSW Department of Planning 2007), introducing a 'policy gateway' style approach already implemented by some European governments (Sustainable European Regions 2007).

Common Good from Planning

Town planning attempted to achieve common good from development, a principle that needs reinterpreting for each new age. Today it means planning for sustainability (Newman 2003; 2005). The new metropolitan strategies will probably be seen as attempts at this. To achieve common-good outcomes, mechanisms to buy public space and build infrastructure are required.

The biggest threat to achieving common-good outcomes is the public–private partnership (PPPs) for infrastructure. PPP in the transport sector have been thrust into the public policy spotlight by the Cross City Tunnel controversy in Sydney, which has demonstrated how an infrastructure project funded entirely by the private sector can undermine local accessibility and public transport in order to ensure profits. Such PPPs totally undermine the basic approach of sustainability, which seeks to achieve common-good outcomes.

Australian cities have a critical need for infrastructure that can support more sustainable outcomes, in particular, in water and transport. Rail systems, with the exception of Perth, are not fit for the purpose, whilst traffic growth is out of hand and the problems of car dependence continue. Funding such infrastructure has reached a fork in the road – or the tracks. Australia can choose either a more traditional PPP where governments find most of the capital or a more experimental PPP where the private sector finds most of the capital. There are problems with either approach, but the reality is that cities cannot wait for a perfect model; they desperately need help right now.

I prefer a publicly funded infrastructure model based on evidence of State government planning and assessment processes to achieve common-good outcomes. The Perth rail system shows that a modern Australian city can build a competitive and efficient rail option using public funds. All Australian cities have plans to direct priorities towards new and revamped public transport systems with centres and corridors to reduce car dependence. However, this option needs federal government support. It cannot work because State governments favour health and education, unless designated capital funds are unlocked from Canberra. If not, then we must head down the path of the privately based PPP, with all its risks and questions about the common good.

Integration

Planners talk about 'balance' in making decisions, which is often code for 'trade-offs'. Sustainability wrestles with problems to make trade-offs unnecessary or minimal (Gibson et al. 2005). To avoid trade-offs, space must be made for 'policy learning' to occur in the system of decision making. Inherent conflicts that arise when traditional approaches and disciplines reach their limits must be resolved through new kinds of dialogues. My experiences wrestling with sustainability with governments across Australia reveal that opportunities for creating sustainable solutions are facilitated when a kind of 'magic' happens, with innovative solutions emerging from such dialogues (Newman forthcoming).

Accountability, Transparency and Engagement

Sustainability recognizes that:

- People should have access to information on sustainability issues.
- Institutions should have triple bottom line accountability on an annual basis.
- Regular sustainability audits of programs and policies should be conducted.
- Public engagement lies at the heart of all sustainability principles.

The magical solutions to sustainability problems that evolve from new kinds of dialogue only occur when part of the 'policy learning' process involves community engagement (see Chapter 11). Processes of deliberative democracy have become totally enmeshed in what sustainability means for cities and regions. The approach taken in Perth to develop a Dialogue for the City was the core thrust behind the Network City Plan (Hartz-Karp and Newman 2006). A similar process involving citizens randomly invited from the electoral role to be a 'citizen for the day' was attempted in Sydney at over twenty small public engagement sessions and led to Sydney's Metropolitan Strategy. All Australian cities have similar projects. Politics will always be part of planning in cities, but the processes of community engagement will enable much of the learning necessary for any public debate. Sustainability can only be a legitimate approach to the city if it encompasses the values of its citizens about their long-term visions for the city.

Precaution

The precautionary principle is sometimes identified as an unnecessary barrier to action. However, avoiding activities when we are unsure of the consequences can also force us to do more work. In planning it is obvious that we should not build on flood plains or coastal dunes, where water hazards might damage artificial constructions. However, it is not clear what risks are associated with climate change or peak oil. Adaptation strategies are only beginning to be discussed and research to ascertain the best strategies are not nearly as well funded as detailed scenarios of potential terrorist attacks. Strategic research on how our cities need to adapt to inevitable physical limits must become the highest priority. In a sustainability context, the precautionary principle should also mean that we do not risk social and economic capital in irreversible ways. Rebuilding our cities to reduce car dependence is an example of a policy that can enhance natural, social and financial capital.

Vision and Hope

Historically, demonstrations are at the core of advancing sustainability in cities. Every Australian city has icon commercial buildings, ecohouses for display, and a range of other sustainability demonstrations, such as the Perth hydrogen fuel-cell buses. The next stage is mainstreaming these demonstrations into policy packages. We have strong examples, so now we need strategic visions that feed these innovations into a series of successive steps over generations. This is how we can create hope in our cities based on sustainability.

References

Campbell, C. (1991), *The Golden Age of Oil 1950–2050: The Depletion of a Resource* (Dordrecht: Kluwer).

City of Vancouver (2006), *Transportation Plan* (Vancouver BC: City of Vancouver).

Department of Planning (2005), *City of Cities: A Plan for Sydney's Future* (Sydney: NSW Government).

Deffeyes, K. (2005*), Beyond Oil: The View from Hubbert's Peak* (New York: Hill and Wang).

Diamond, J. (2005), *Collapse: How Societies Choose to Fail or Succeed* (New York: Viking Books).

Dixon, P. (2006), 'Opportunities Within the Urban Footprint for Ecological Sustainability. What Landscape Architects Can Do to Work Towards This and the Problems Encountered with Current Design and Planning' [paper] Australian Institute of Landscape Seminar, Sydney, 2 May.

Gibson R., Hassan, S., Holtz, S., Tansey, J. and Whitelaw, G. (2005), *Sustainability Assessment Criteria, Processes and Applications* (London: Earthscan Publications).

Gilman, R. (1991), 'The Eco-Village Challenge', *In Context* 29.

Government of Western Australia (2003), *Hope for the Future: The Western Australian State Sustainability Strategy* (Perth: Department of the Premier and Cabinet).

Hartz-Karp, J. and Newman, P. (2006), 'The Participative Route to Sustainability', in Paulin (ed.).

House of Representatives (2005), *Sustainable Cities* (Canberra: Parliament House).

Jonker, J. and DeWitte, M. (eds) (2005), *Management Models for CSR: A Comprehensive Overview* (Heidelberg: Springer Verlag – Management Sciences).

Kenworthy, J. and Laube, F. (1999), 'The Significance of Rail in Building Competitive and Effective Urban Public Transport Systems: An International Perspective', *Global Mass Transit*, November, 69–74.

Kunstler, J. (2005), *The Long Emergency: Surviving the End of the Oil Age, Climate Change, and Other Converging Catastrophes of the Twenty-First Century* (New York: Atlantic Monthly Press).

Laird, P., Newman, P., Kenworthy, J. and Bachels, M. (2001), *Back on Track: Re-Thinking Australian and New Zealand Transport Policy* (Sydney: UNSW Press).

Low, N. and Gleeson, B. (eds) (2003), *Making Urban Transport Sustainable* (Basingstoke: Palgrave Macmillan).

Marchetti, C. (1994), 'Anthropological Invariants in Travel Behaviour', *Technical Forecasting and Social Change* 47:1, 75–78.

Millenium Ecosystem Assessment (2005), [website], <http://www.maweb.org>, accessed 5 December 2006.

NEDO (2005), *Safeguarding the Future of the Earth: Environment and Energy* (Tokyo: National Energy and Industrial Technology Development Organization).

NSW Department of Planning (2007), *Metro Strategy* [website], <http://www.metrostrategy.nsw.gov.au>, accessed 16 January 2007.

Newman, P. (2001), 'Railways and Reurbanisation in Perth', in Williams and Stimson (eds).

Newman, P. (2002), *Sustainability and Housing: More Than a Roof Overhead* [the 9th Annual F. Oswald Barnett Oration] (Hawthorn: Swinburne University of Technology).

Newman, P. (2003), 'Global Cities, Transport, Energy and the Future: Will Ecosocialisation Reverse the Historic Trends?', in Low and Gleeson (eds).

Newman, P. (2004), 'Sustainability and Global Cities', *Australian Planner* 41:4, 27–28.

Newman, P. (2005), 'Sustainability Assessment and Cities', *International Review of Environmental Strategies* 5:2, 383–98.

Newman, P. (2006), 'After Oil: Will Our Cities and Regions Collapse?' [submission to the Senate Inquiry into Australia's Future Oil Supply and Alternative Transport Fuels], Australian Parliament House [website], <http://www.aph.gov.au/senate/ Rural and Regional Affairs and Transport/>, accessed 2 January 2007.

Newman, P. (forthcoming), 'Can the Magic of Sustainability Survive Professionalism?', in Sheldon, C. (ed.) *Environmental Professionalism And Sustainability: Too Important to Get Wrong* (London: Greenleaf Books).

Newman, P. and Jennings, I. (forthcoming), *Cities as Sustainable Ecosystems* (Kobe: UNEP-ITEC).

Newman, P. and Kenworthy J. (1999), *Sustainability and Cities: Overcoming Automobile Dependence* (Washington DC: Island Press).

Newman, P., Stanton-Hicks, E., and Hammond, B. (2005), 'From CSR to Sustainability Through Enduring Value', in Jonker and DeWitte (eds).

Paulin, S. (ed.) (2006), *Communities Doing It for Themselves: Creating Space for Sustainability* (Perth: University of Western Australia Press).

Pope, J., Annandale, D. and Morrison-Saunders, A. (2004), 'Conceptualising Sustainability Assessment', *Environmental Impact Assessment Review* 24, 595–616.

Reardon, C. (ed.) (2005), *Your Home Technical Manual*, 3rd Edition. (Canberra: Commonwealth of Australia, Department of the Environment and Heritage, Australian Greenhouse Office).

SACTRA (1994), *Trunk Roads and the Generation of Traffic* (London: Department of Transport).

Seddon, G. (1968), *Sense of Place: A Response to an Environment, the Swan Coastal Plain, Western Australia* (Perth: UWA Press).

Seddon, G. (2005), *The Old Country: Australian Landscapes, Plants and People* (Melbourne: Cambridge University Press).

Sustainable European Regions (2007), SER [website], <http://www.sustainable-euroregions.net>, accessed 17 January 2007.

Trainer, T. (1995), *The Conserver Society: Alternatives for Sustainability* (London: Zed Books).

UNEP/Habitat (1996), *An Urbanizing World: Global Report on Human Settlements* (Oxford: Oxford University Press).

Williams, J. and Stimson, R. (eds) (2001), *Case Studies in Planning Success* (New York: Elsevier).

Chapter 3

Ecopolis: Concepts, Initiatives and the Purpose of Cities

Paul F. Downton

Introduction

The ecological polis, 'ecopolis', defines the purpose of a city: minimizing ecological footprints (biophysical) and maximizing human potential (human ecology) in order to repair, replenish and support processes that maintain life. As the basis for strategic planning for translation into effective policy, this chapter presents four key propositions, ten core principles, and seven steps towards ecological city making. Using the concept of urban fractals, demonstration projects, it explores challenges to achieving sustainable practices, such as institutional inertia, in a world threatened by climate change.

Ecopolis

Making and maintaining cities creates the greatest human impact on the biosphere so it is vital to understand their processes and purpose. A city is more than the sum of its buildings. Cities include services and infrastructure that consume energy and land. First and foremost, a city is a place of culture (Register 1987). For our species to survive, we need a culture that creates urban ecosystems that contribute to the ecological health of the biosphere.

The ecopolis is the next, perhaps most important, evolutionary step in urbanism: built to fit its place, co-operating with nature, a place of human culture that consciously sustains the cycles of atmosphere, water, nutrients and biology in healthy balance whilst empowering the powerless, feeding the hungry, and sheltering the homeless.

Although the ecopolis is about creating human environments specific to their time and place, the concept is timeless and universal. To create appropriate places for everyone, in every land, for all time, cities need to be different, reflecting the unique characteristics of peoples, places and times. This 'universal regionalism' can only come about through the persistent application of principles embedded in an explicit culture of city making. The challenge is to embed processes that are as natural to life in cities as bones are in bodies.

Three Urban Fractals

> Models and strategies are required for eco-neighbourhoods in urban areas in order to
> practically demonstrate innovative and appropriate solutions which could be readily
> applied by other neighbourhoods. (Rudlin and Dodd 1998, 2.)

Since 1991, attempts to apply and test the developing theory of 'ecopolis' have been
undertaken by the author and colleagues in South Australia in three projects initiated
through the non-profit group, Urban Ecology Australia Inc. (UEA), and sustained by
substantial community effort.

The projects tested propositions (outlined later in this chapter): that a city is part
of its region (Proposition 1); that there was enough extant knowledge and adequate
techniques and technologies to begin making ecological cities (Proposition 2); and
that the driving force for change depended on 'communities' and 'active citizenship'
(Proposition 3). Each project was conceived as an ecopolis in microcosm, 'urban
fractals' able to be repeated and scaled up or down whilst retaining the essential
aspects of the original (Proposition 4).

Christie Walk

In the heart of Adelaide, the capital of South Australia, lies a small urban village,
a living community that demonstrates every aspect of urban sustainability on
just 2000 m² (half an acre). Named 'Christie Walk', in memory of environmental
and social activist Scott Christie, this small urban fractal was recognized with an
international Asia Pacific Forum for Environment and Development (2006) award
for outstanding achievement in the promotion of socially equitable and sustainable
development in the region. Constructed in a six-year period, knitted into the fabric
of its neighbourhood, it is a fraction of an ecocity and has been used to test many of
the precepts and principles of the ecopolis.

A key aspect of Christie Walk is its location in the most mixed-use, least wealthy
and most culturally diverse part of Adelaide, which required the designers to address
complex inner-urban contexts (Reardon 2005, Section 7.3). However, the context
supplied solutions as well as challenges: transport energy use is minimized by the
proximity to public transport and walkable distances to major urban facilities. Twenty-
seven dwellings, including an apartment building with community facilities on one
street frontage, have been built on a total site area equivalent to two quarter-acre blocks.
Residents have planned, organized and managed community gardens, including South
Australia's first 'intensive' roof garden. Several housing types are represented, some
linked physically and all connected through landscaping that has been designed to be
an integral part of the passive climate response of the dwellings.

This project expresses important aspects of ecopolis practice, including:

- Community processes and structures based on mutual aid and direct
  democracy.
- Consideration of social impacts related to financial decision making (involving
  Community Aid Abroad Ethical Investment Trust and Bendigo Community
  Bank).

- Indicating how design can integrate sustainability technologies – healthy construction, water capture and reuse, solar power, and innovative on-site sewage treatment linked to irrigation of a nearby public park.
- Showing how urban form reduces transport demands and high densities facilitate community and conviviality.
- Demonstrating how appropriate technology and funding reinforce local community processes to achieve sustainable human ecological development.

Observe (Table 3.1) the advantages of Christie Walk compared with a conventional development, according to significant measures of sustainability. Developed without any support from governments, the Christie Walk fractal would be much easier to replicate within a policy environment that assisted communities to engage with the complicated spheres of construction, finance and development.

Table 3.1   Christie Walk compared with a conventional development

Features	Conventional Development	Christie Walk
Site area	2000 m²	2000 m²
Number of dwellings	24	27
Productive landscape	200 m²	700 m²
Productive roof area	NONE	170 m²
Resource conservation, including material recycling/reuse	NO	YES
Energy efficiency	NO	YES
Non-toxic construction	NO	YES
Community space	NO	YES
Stormwater capture	NO	YES
Effluent treatment	NO	YES
Renewable energy	NO	YES
Community engagement	NO	YES
Educational programs	NO	YES
Diversity of dwelling types	NO	YES

Whyalla EcoCity Development

Following several moderately successful public workshops, a 15 ha site in the heart of Whyalla, South Australia, was zoned an 'ecocity' with subsequent developments and modifications on site. The Whyalla EcoCity Development attracted a critical mass of support in a city of just 27,000 people. Whyalla had a significant group of citizens who understood and were committed to the ecocity vision, many closely associated with local religious and cultural organisations. Pressure from economic reductionists seeking to replace community areas with commercial concerns tested their knowledge and advocacy skills. They would have benefited enormously from a council that practised policy consistency with the original project goals. Most significantly, the partial physical realization of the Whyalla EcoCity Development has had less impact than the continued international influence of the theoretical Halifax EcoCity Project (Downton 1994; 1996; 1998).

Halifax EcoCity Project

During the late 1980s and early 1990s, the Halifax EcoCity Project (HEP) coevolved with the UEA, which had convened the 1992 Second International EcoCity Conference. The HEP proposal for an ecocity microcosm for 800 people – community facilities, cafés, shops, offices, an ecology centre, marketplace, and so on – was conceived as a means of catalysing redevelopment in the City of Adelaide and as a device for promulgating development that integrated social justice and community control with strong ecological goals.

The car-free, mixed-use proposal of three to five storeys followed a similar density to traditional European cities. Environmental targets included: reducing the ecological footprint of the neighbourhood to an ecologically sustainable level, analysing life cycle costs and impacts, applying ecological design principles and environmental purchasing criteria, eliminating fossil fuels for power and heat, creating a closed water system, exploring food production possibilities, reducing car use and developing community planning.

An important goal of the HEP was to influence the wider community and raise consciousness of the potential of urban development action and community-based politics. The project's success can be seen in the number of academic citations and courses that have incorporated the project as a case study, publications that refer to the project, media reports, exhibitions, and awards received for, or because of, the project. For instance, Rudlin and Dodd (1998, 1–3) identified the HEP as an ecological development case study exemplifying a genuine sustainable urban neighbourhood. The HEP catalysed the creation of Christie Walk and, in the *Ecopolis Now* video documentary (Stegman 2000), it was referred to as the 'Holy Grail' of urban environmentalism, indicating that virtual cultural fractals can be effective too.

Similar to the Whyalla project, the HEP might have been realized had city council policy makers not compromised on their initial publicly expressed support. Though the HEP never eventuated as a physical edifice, it remains a cultural construct and historical experiment in participatory, community development (Orszanski 1993).

Theory and Definition

> A 'sustainable city' enables all its citizens to meet their own needs and to enhance their
> well-being without damaging the natural world or endangering the living conditions of
> other people, now or in the future. (Girardet 2000.)

This is just one of numerous definitions of sustainable, green and ecological cities alongside claims to be ecological cities, notably Curitiba, Brazil, for its early hubris and influence. There has been no widely accepted, functional definition of an ecological city except as a place that Douglas Adams (1979) might have termed 'mostly harmless'.

Just as a biologist opens a biology textbook and fails to find a definition of 'life', so those of us concerned with the fate of cities and the sustenance of our environment imagine that we know what a city is, yet lack a clear, shared definition of its fundamental purposes. To open the debate and establish some ground rules, I address the question of why we make cities and provide a testable definition of an ecological city.

Cities have to be more than 'mostly harmless'. Today, they must support massive human populations, and repair and redress the enormous natural damage that humans have already done. I propose that an ecological city is exemplified by the concept of the ecopolis, where citizens consciously intervene and manage the sustainability of the biophysical environmental processes of a region. In other words, citizens of the urban ecosystem fit human activity within the constraints of the biosphere whilst creating housing and urban environments that sustain human culture. In its full realization, the ecopolis is a manifestation of a developed ecological culture, standing in contrast to the expressions of exploitative culture in our present-day cities.

I say 'ecopolis', rather than 'ecocity', to reinforce the definitional links between social and environmental purposes. 'Eco' refers to ecological purpose and 'polis' to the ideas and ideals of governance that encompass community and self-determination. I adopted the term in 1989, constructing the word from first principles, partly in response to the term 'multifunction polis' then prevalent in Australia. The ecopolis has been independently discovered or constructed internationally (Koskiaho 1994), adopted by others (Girardet 2004) and used to name international conferences (UEA 2006).

The ecopolis is about the way we organize knowledge, how we see ourselves and define the purpose of cities. I suggest that architecture and planning be redefined as the art and science, theory and practice, of creating sustainable human settlement – subsets of urban ecology (Brueste et al. 1998). In the early days of the ecocity movement it was not unusual to hear the comment that an 'ecological city' was an oxymoron. The 'mostly harmless' definition of sustainable cities reflects a failure of the imagination, a fear about making more mistakes, about trying to do as little bad as possible. What if we set out to be genuinely 'good' instead? (McDonough and Braungart 2002, 67).

Ecopolis Development Principles

Drafted in association with Chérie Hoyle and Emilis Prelgauskas, the initial twelve Ecopolis Development Principles were intended as a set of precepts for developing human settlement that restored, rather than destroyed, ecological health, minimizing biophysical ecological footprints (Rees and Wackernagel 1996). The revised version (Downton 2006) has ten principles divided into biophysical and biosocial, informed by the work of Norbert Schulz from Germany, an intern at UEA, in 1995:

Biophysical Principles (minimize ecological footprints)

1. **Restore Degraded Land:** use urban development to restore health and vitality

of land.
2. **Fit the Bioregion:** create human settlements that work with region's natural cycles.
3. **Balance Development:** balance development with the 'carrying capacity' of the land.
4. **Create Compact Cities:** reverse sprawl and stop ad hoc developments in landscapes.
5. **Optimize Energy Performance:** generate and use energy efficiently.

Human Ecology Principles (maximize human potential)

6. **Contribute to the Economy:** create work opportunities and promote economic activity.
7. **Provide Health and Security:** create healthy and safe environments for all people.
8. **Encourage Community:** cities are for everyone.
9. **Promote Social Justice and Equity:** equal rights/access to services, facilities and information.
10. **Enrich History and Culture:** respect the past. Look to the future. Celebrate diversity.

Overtaken by Glaciers

Making cities requires consideration of timescales that exceed the attention span of conventional commerce and politics. This is a problem. If cities are to be kept on the path of ecological fitness over time there must be concomitant socio-cultural structures and institutions to manage their passage. Brand (1999) draws attention to the lack of institutions or decision-making systems that deal with very long-term planning in contrast with traditional cultures that commonly looked back and forth across several generations.

Technology can hinder or facilitate cultural attitudes. The hegemony of unhealthy, energy-hungry, central air-conditioning systems has been partly due to the idea that any building could be made comfortable by plugging in a machine and flicking a switch. According to the canons of the architectural priesthood, this allowed 'design freedom' by separating the function of the building envelope from the need to moderate the climate. Conversely, ecocity design is understood and practised as a rich process of engagement by living creatures with their environment and with each other. It eschews the linear, compartmentalized process favoured by industrial society; it needs to be developmental, and it requires careful, continuous maintenance. It requires use of technology and management of a different kind than that bequeathed by militarism and production-line manufacturing processes.

It is ironic that, just as the realization is dawning that human systems and institutions need to accommodate and adapt to the long, slow rates of change of natural systems, the climate is moving. Glaciers are overtaking us, changing the world faster than our institutions. Climate change requires a heightened alertness to the bio-geophysical environment and constant activity to keep pace with the changes in natural systems precipitated by human affairs. However, there is a danger that institutional responses will continue to change too slowly and that policy-making will remain based on 'more of the same' thinking.

Seven Steps and Four Propositions

Although modern planning systems, including the New Urbanism, acknowledge the importance of land use they rarely apply available knowledge with the kind of practical ecological sensitivity demonstrated by McHarg (1971). The seven steps identified in the sustainable human ecological development (SHED) process (Table 3.2) are designed to reinforce the need to integrate land use planning with every aspect of making ecocities. For instance, Richard Register (1987) points out the positive potential of tall buildings, provided that there is a diversity of activities in such developments. Tall buildings save land for agriculture; promote energy saving by reducing travelling distances; make commerce, culture and social diversity more easily available; and, with imagination, can include multilevel greenhouses and roof gardens (such as the one at Christie Walk). Register reminds us that cities are three-dimensional entities, not flat maps, and asserts that a vital social life is essential for any community claiming to be ecological.

The seven steps can be interpreted as a basis for framing policy and constructing planning and development programs. SHED connects human and non-human life through the flow of water within ecosystems. A topographic built-form relationship between region and habitation is identifiable through their respective capacities and functions as shedders of water. Biological processes dominate the first four steps and provide the context for all the others, which highlight community processes. Although numbered sequentially, any practical step in the SHED process may come first.

Table 3.2   Processes within Sustainable Human Ecological Development (SHED) Steps

	**SHED 1.** *Shedding* – identifies the biophysical context and its inherent developmental constraints for city-making: watersheds; bioregions; design with nature (McHarg 1971); carrying capacity; ecological footprints; environmental space.
	SHED 2. *Placing* – explores cultural and spiritual aspects of a bioregional analysis (Sale 1991), placing people, seeking non-physical structures as a basis for maintaining deep continuities: genius loci; spiriting (discovering spirit of place); geomancy; feng shui; re-inhabitation (Berg 1981).

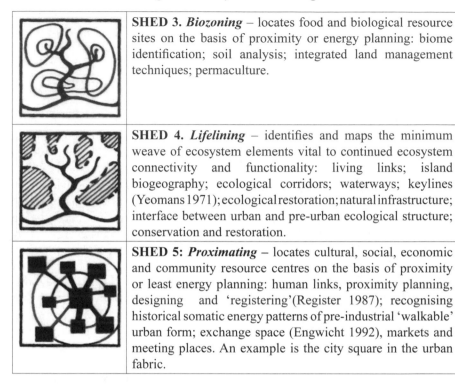

	SHED 3. *Biozoning* – locates food and biological resource sites on the basis of proximity or energy planning: biome identification; soil analysis; integrated land management techniques; permaculture.
	SHED 4. *Lifelining* – identifies and maps the minimum weave of ecosystem elements vital to continued ecosystem connectivity and functionality: living links; island biogeography; ecological corridors; waterways; keylines (Yeomans 1971); ecological restoration; natural infrastructure; interface between urban and pre-urban ecological structure; conservation and restoration.
	SHED 5: *Proximating* – locates cultural, social, economic and community resource centres on the basis of proximity or least energy planning: human links, proximity planning, designing and 'registering'(Register 1987); recognising historical somatic energy patterns of pre-industrial 'walkable' urban form; exchange space (Engwicht 1992), markets and meeting places. An example is the city square in the urban fabric.

The seven steps are about setting architecture and planning within the real biophysical and biosocial realities of place – part of the conscious making of ecological civilization, instead of attempting to incorporate sustainable processes within architecture and planning. Barton (2000, 28) said: 'The real challenge facing us is not one of building eco-villages, but of making the modern city, and the way of life lived in it, environmentally sustainable.' The intertwined relationships between cities, place and culture, and human and biophysical ecology may be understood through four propositions about the necessary conditions for making ecocities (Downton 2002):

- City-region: a city is part of its place.
- Integrated knowledge: all knowledge must be integrated (harnessed/holistic).
- Cultural change: eco-cities need to establish strong cultural structures that recognize social and ecological interdependency.
- Cultural (urban) fractals: Small demonstration projects are vital as catalysts for cultural change.

The Frogstick – An Urban Ecology Checklist

Environmental indicators are essential for measuring ecological performance in urban design and planning. Many such indicators have been created during the last decade.

Table 3.3   Example of a Frogstick Score Sheet for the City of Adelaide

	Away from Sustainability	-10	-7.5	-5	-2.5	+2.5	+5	+7.5	+10	Towards Sustainability
1. Air	Pollutes			X						Purifies
2. Water	Pollutes/wastes	X								Purifies/recycles
3. Earth (soil)	Destroys			X						Renews
4. Fire (energy)	Non-renewable		X							Renewable
5. Biomass	Decreases	X								Increases/stable
6. Food	Consumes		X							Creates
7. Bio-diversity	Decreases	X								Increases
8. Habitat	Destroys		X							Creates
9. Ecolinks	Reduces	X								Increases
10. Resources	Wastes	X								Recycles/reuses
Total Performance		**-50**	**-22.5**	**-10**						**- 82.5%**

The 'frogstick' (Downton 1991, 54) was inspired by Wells (1981, 33–40) – 'frog' because this species is so sensitive to its environment that its presence or absence in a preferred habitat provides an indication of the habitat's relative health. Designed for novices to understand, elements of the frogstick measure can be adapted and augmented to in-depth scientific enquiry (see example in Table 3.3). This checklist addresses minimizing the ecological footprint in the physical environment (a similar one is required to maximize human potential in the social environment).

Conclusion

In reviewing the case studies, it can be seen that HEP and Christie Walk were self-directed social experiments undertaken by people who freely chose to be part of an innovative, non-government initiative. The HEP managed to achieve semi-legendary status as an example of something genuinely achievable, whilst Christie Walk reinforced its credibility by being a partial 'microcosmic' realization of the HEP. They express the four propositions detailed in this chapter:

- The three projects were all designed in a consciously determined relationship to their broader regional contexts.
- The concepts, principles and techniques required to create human settlements that fit within the ecological systems of the biosphere whilst sustaining their biogeochemical functionality do exist.
- The creation of ecocities will depend on cultural change to transform the deep cultural inertia in local government.
- Each project depended on a created community with shared ideas and preparedness to translate those ideas into activity. Whether the broader community can be more completely involved with a relatively high level of consciousness of its evolutionary role can only be tested in time.

The role of the community as a system of mutual aid based on direct democracy is central to the ecopolis idea. Catalysing urban cultural fractals can only occur with a high level of participation in their design, development and maintenance by the wider community. Whilst government policy makers can assist or hinder community-based processes, they are unlikely to successfully initiate ecopolis projects. Direct democracy and active citizenship (as opposed to passive consumerism) require approaches to architecture, planning and urban design that are as responsive to the body politic and social demands as they are to the sun, the weather, and the living processes of the biosphere. Community-based 'bottom up' planning strategies, rather than 'top down' planning strategies, are fundamental to the foundation and sustenance of any ecologically viable human settlement in the long term. The role of policy makers is to actively assist urban communities by providing a coherent framework for retrofitting or new building projects, in existing urban environments or in new towns and cities.

It is time to define the purpose of cities and bring our understanding of that purpose into line with urgent concerns for sustainability and the health of humans and the biosphere. Now the purpose of the city must be to create an environment that generates health and enhances ecological sustainability. This is a major historical shift with substantial implications for policy makers.

Making cities is really about the creation and management of complex living systems, and cities are the primary habitats for human survival now. The developing theory of the ecopolis is predicated on an approach to the making of architecture and cities that defines them as potential living systems, as extensions of the human organism. Just as the constructions of living creatures can be seen as extensions of their physiology (Turner 2000, 27), buildings and cities can be conceived as components of living systems. This line of thinking promises a rich field of enquiry. If the making and maintenance of cities were analysed in terms of their being extended phenotypes of the human gene, it might be possible to look forward to achieving a kind of unified theory of urban ecology. Architecture and associated creative activity could then be seen as integral to life processes, as ways of making our habitat function better and increasing our chance of survival as a species through a purposeful, goal-directed approach to city making.

References

Adams, D. (1979), *The Hitchhiker's Guide to the Galaxy* (London: Pan Books).

Alexander, C., Ishikawa, S., Silverstein, M., Jacobson, M., Fiksdahl-King, I. and Angel, S. (1977), *A Pattern Language* (New York: Oxford University Press).

Asia Pacific Forum for Environment and Development (2006), APFED Awards [website], Winners 2006 [webpage], <http://www.iges.or.jp/en/apfed/award/winners/index.html>, accessed 1 January 2007.

Ball, P. (1999), *The Self-Made Tapestry: Pattern Formation in Nature* (New York: Oxford University Press).

Barton, H. (ed.) (2000), *Sustainable Communities: The Potential for Eco-Neighbourhoods* (London: Earthscan).

Berg, P. (1981), 'Devolving Beyond Global Monoculture', *CoEvolution Quarterly* 32:Winter, 24–30.

Bookchin, M. (1991), 'Libertarian Municipalism – An Overview', *Green Perspectives* 24.

Bookchin, M. (1986), *The Limits of the City* (Montréal-Buffalo: Black Rose Books).

Bookchin, M. (1992), *Urbanization Without Cities – The Rise and Decline of Citizenship* (Montréal: Black Rose Books, Institute of Policy Alternatives).

Brand, S. (1997), *How Buildings Learn: What Happens After They're Built,* Revised Edition. (London: Phoenix Illustrated/Orion).

Brand, S. (1999), *The Clock of the Long Now: Time and Responsibility* (London: Phoenix).

Breuste, J., Feldmann, H. and Uhlmann, O. (eds) (1998), *Urban Ecology* (Berlin: Springer-Verlag).

Downton, P. (1991), 'Solar Cities for a Sustainable World – Making Places Fit for Frogs', *Proceedings Solar 91 – Energy for a Sustainable World Volume 1* (Adelaide: Australian and New Zealand Solar Energy Society and Flinders University of South Australia).

Downton, P. (1994), *The Halifax EcoCity Project – A Community Driven Development* (Adelaide: Centre for Urban Ecology).

Downton, P. (ed.) (1996), *EcoCity Whyalla* [Booklets 1–7] (Adelaide: Centre for Urban Ecology).

Downton, P. (1998), 'Adelaide and Whyalla: The Practice of Urban Ecology in Two Australian Eco-City Projects', in J. Breuste et al. (eds).

Downton, P. (2002), 'Ecopolis: Towards an Integrated Theory for the Design, Development and Maintenance of Ecological Cities' [Unpublished thesis] Submitted to Mawson Graduate Centre for Environmental Studies, University of Adelaide.

Downton, P. (2006), Ecopolis [website], <http://www.ecopolis.com.au> and <http://www.ecopolisnow.com>, accessed 16 January 2007.

Engwicht, D. (1992), *Towards an Eco-City – Calming the Traffic* (Sydney: Envirobook).

Girardet, H. (2000), 'Cities, People, Planet', *Schumacher Lectures,* April, Liverpool.

Girardet, H. (2004), *Cities People Planet: Liveable Cities For a Sustainable World* (Chichester: Wiley Academy).

Koskiaho B. (1994), *Ecopolis – Conceptual, Methodological and Practical Implementations of Urban Ecology* (Finland: Ministry of the Environment).

McDonough, W. and Braungart, M. (2002), *Cradle to Cradle: Remaking the Way We Make Things* (New York: North Pint Press).

McHarg, I. (1971), *Design with Nature* (New York: Doubleday/Natural History Press).

Orszanski, R. (1993), 'The Design and Production of EcoCities: A Case Study of the Halifax Project' [Unpublished Masters dissertation] Submitted to Mawson Graduate Centre for Environmental Studies, University of Adelaide.

Reardon, C. (ed.) (2005), *Your Home Technical Manual*, 3rd Edition (Canberra: Commonwealth of Australia, Department of the Environment and Heritage, Australian Greenhouse Office).

Rees, W. and Wackernagel, M. (1996), *Our Ecological Footprint – Reducing Human Impact on the Earth* (Gabriola Island/Philadelphia: New Society Publishers).

Register, R. (1987), *Ecocity Berkeley: Building Cities for a Healthy Future* (Berkeley: North Atlantic Books).

Rudlin, D. and Dodd, N. (1998), 'Eco-Neighbourhoods: A Brief for a Sustainable Urban Neighbourhood', *Sun Dial: The Journal of the Sustainable Urban Neighbourhood Initiative* 6: Spring, 1–3.

Sale, K. (1991), *Dwellers in the Land: The Bioregional Vision* (Philadelphia: New Society Publishers).

Stegman, S. (2000), *Ecopolis Now* [video documentary].

Turner, J. (2000), *The Extended Organism: The Physiology of Animal-built Structures* (Cambridge/London: Harvard University Press).

UEA (2006), Urban Ecology Australia [website], <http://www.urbanecology.org.au/>, accessed 6 January 2007.

Wells, M. (1981), *Gentle Architecture* (New York: McGraw-Hill).

Yeomans, P. (1971), *The City Forest – The Keyline Plan for the Human Environment* (Sydney: Keyline Publishing).

Chapter 4

Permaculture: Design Principles for Urban Sustainability

Dick Copeman

Introduction

Australian cities are unsustainable. Water use exceeds available supplies, food systems are unsustainable, energy use contributes to global warming, climates are warming and drying, and traffic jams are worsening, as are economic inequality, family breakdown and social disruption. Rather than piecemeal solutions to these problems, what we urgently need is a design approach that offers a holistic program for sustainable living in cities. Permaculture offers such an approach.

Permaculture is a design system that can help Australian cities become environmentally sustainable and socially equitable. A movement of people who, in backyards, community gardens and elsewhere, is slowly but surely changing the face of our cities, the voice of permaculture needs to be heard in discussions about densification and decentralization, social equity and inclusion, and how to involve citizens and communities in planning for sustainability in our cities.

While the philosophy and methods of permaculture have been mainly applied at the grassroots, permaculture ethics and principles can guide the work of planners, regulators and developers to produce sustainable solutions to current problems with water, waste, transport, energy and food supply. This chapter outlines a permaculture approach to sustainable housing and urban design in Australia.

What is Permaculture?

Permaculture arose out of a growing awareness in the 1960s and 1970s that the environment was in crisis. At that time, ecology was coming of age as a separate discipline. Bill Mollison and David Holmgren devised 'permaculture', a system of applied ecology that drew upon 'observation of natural systems, the wisdom contained in traditional farming systems and modern scientific and technological knowledge' to achieve 'a design system for creating sustainable human environments' (Mollison with Slay 1991, 1). David Holmgren (2002, xix) has defined permaculture in more detail as a system for creating: 'consciously designed landscapes which mimic the patterns and relationships found in nature, while yielding an abundance of food, fibre and energy for provision of local needs. It is a vision of permanent (sustainable) human culture based on permanent (sustainable) agriculture'.

Permaculture includes three ethics and twelve design principles that encapsulate the ways in which people can manage land and plan and construct houses, gardens, farms and communities sustainably and equitably. The ethics of permaculture are *care of the earth, care of people* and *share surplus resources.* Equal emphasis is given to human wellbeing and to environmental protection, which differentiates permaculture from both the ecocentric, deep ecology perspective and also from the anthropocentric, social ecology perspective. It is true that, as Brendan Gleeson (2006, 160) says, 'Only just human institutions and tolerant caring societies can produce lasting solutions to the ecological crises that threaten Australia's cities.' However, the converse is equally true, namely that only cities that look after their environment can be truly just and fair to their citizens.

The principles of permaculture, as formulated by Mollison (Mollison with Slay 1991, 532), stressed design elements and their complementary interaction within landscapes, reducing energy use and utilizing biological resources. More recently, Holmgren (2002) has revisited the concepts, theories and practices of permaculture and reformulated the principles as:

- Observe and interact.
- Catch and store energy.
- Obtain a yield.
- Apply self-regulation and accept feedback.
- Use and value renewable resources and services.
- Produce no waste.
- Design from patterns to details.
- Integrate, do not segregate.
- Use small and slow solutions.
- Use and value diversity.
- Use edges and value the marginal.
- Creatively use and respond to change.

Holmgren (2002, 47–8) argues that permaculture offers the best hope of successful adjustment to the low-energy future that will follow the imminent peaking of global oil supplies, and that permaculture principles can guide us as we negotiate the 'culture of energy descent' that will be humanity's main preoccupation over the next century.

Cities as Solutions

Moving cities towards sustainability will require substantial changes to many facets of society and decision making. Permaculture offers an integrated approach to how we make these changes and how we involve all levels of society in the process. The key players who decide and influence the directions in which our cities develop and change are local and State government planning and regulatory authorities, the development industry, and the planning and design professionals who work for these groups. The remainder of this chapter outlines policy applications of permaculture principles that these players could implement to make cities more environmentally sustainable and more socially equitable. These policies complement the widespread changes already occurring at a neighbourhood and community level and support individual actions towards sustainable cities.

Observe and Interact

Creating an optimal design or plan requires a degree of familiarity with the place that is being planned or designed. Each place has its own unique climate, landform, vegetation and history. Observation of these specific local features, and interaction with local people by planners and designers before they start to create a design, is important.

Permaculture design works with nature and uses natural processes as much as possible. The ability to 'read the landscape' is a key skill for permaculture designers. Developing this skill requires that designers spend time out of doors, observing and interacting with nature. There is no better way to understand the requirements for handling water run-off, for example, than to stand on a site in the middle of a rainstorm. And there is no better way to find out whether the finished construction is successful in handling water run-off than to revisit it during another rainstorm.

Local communities often have detailed knowledge of the history and geography of a site that can be invaluable for planners of buildings, developments and infrastructure projects. Too frequently, however, that knowledge is not sought by the planners, or is sought by social scientists, not planners, or is sought only at a late stage in the planning when the main reactions that people have are negative. Early, informal interaction with local people by planners would identify potential problems and help achieve mutually acceptable and sustainable solutions.

Catch and Store Energy

Catching winter sun for natural warming and cool summer breezes for natural cooling, while blocking out hot summer sun and cold winter wind, are the common sense features of so-called passive solar design. Unfortunately, in contemporary Australian housing developments, these are honoured in the breach more often than not.

Solar hot water heating, the most efficient of all energy-saving technologies, is installed in only a small minority of Australian buildings. Also, almost all the rainwater that falls onto city roofs runs off into stormwater drains. The time has come to require passive solar design, solar hot water heating and rainwater collection, storage and use in all new houses and all houses undergoing major renovation (see Chapter 17).

Planning authorities can also work with design professionals, the construction industry, 'green' plumbers networks, the hardware industry, environment centres and community gardens to facilitate the dissemination of these sustainable design methods and technologies as well as the advice and 'know-how' required to support their adoption and installation.

Trees are very efficient at catching and storing solar energy in the form of both food and wood. Local authorities should broaden the focus of the tree planting that they have been doing in recent years with bush regeneration groups and individual landholders to include trees that can be harvested for fuel and food, as well for wildlife habitat and environmental improvement.

Obtain a Yield

The potential yield of food, fibre, fuel and fodder from Australian cities is enormous. They are mostly in the better-watered areas of the country and their low density means that there is plenty of open space.

Backyard production of vegetables, fruit, nuts, eggs and honey has a long tradition in Australia and is currently going through a minor resurgence. Production of food on public land, through community gardens and street plantings of food trees, is a newer development gaining momentum. Future needs may also include urban production of timber for construction and firewood and even fodder for animals.

Australian permaculturalist Rosemary Morrow, who has worked extensively in Vietnam, has compared the typical quarter acre block in the suburbs of Sydney with the typical Vietnamese small holding, also a quarter acre. The Vietnamese block contains fruit trees, vegetables, medicinal herbs, firewood, a pig and some chickens, a fishpond and a rainwater tank. This supplies most of their food needs and even produces a surplus to trade in the local market. Sydney suburbs could quite easily follow the Vietnamese example, Morrow (2005, 14–15) argues.

Urban agriculture has a long tradition in many of the world's large cities, from 'allotments' beside railway lines in Britain and Germany to the Chinese market gardens on creek flats in Australian cities before World War II. Shanghai grew most of the food for its many millions of inhabitants within the city boundaries until its recent rapid growth. Havana, the capital of Cuba, responded to the food crisis brought about by the cessation of Soviet support in 1989, and continuing US sanctions, by rapidly developing the capacity to produce much of its food within the city. Ten years after the crisis, average food consumption was almost back to what it was before the crisis (Cruz and Medina 2001, 4). Australian permaculturalists played a significant role in helping facilitate this transition.

Current planning policies aim to increase urban density in order to support greater efficiency of services, such as public transport, but these policies can lead to reductions of open space in cities. The challenge for planning policy is to increase urban density in a moderate and environmentally and socially sustainable way that ensures the continued availability of both public and private open space for urban production and yield, without creating alienating, high-rise ghettos or increasing road space for private transport. Increased density should never be a planning goal in its own right. Increased public transport use, for example, may be achievable just as readily by improvements in efficiency and coordination as by increasing residential density (Self 2000).

Community groups are developing new ways of obtaining a 'yield' or income through 'social' enterprises such as food cooperatives, farmers' markets, plant nurseries, gardening services, cafés and coffee shops. These 'third way' – neither 'public' nor 'private' – enterprises often employ disadvantaged people and involve others on the margins of mainstream society in a socially inclusive approach. These small enterprises can meet local needs and employ local people in a way that larger public and private employers often cannot. Policy makers and planners could assist these social enterprises by developing new forms of land tenure and other forms of support for them.

Apply Self-Regulation and Accept Feedback

As water and energy shortages become a fact of everyday life, planners, policy makers and authorities are setting targets and imposing restrictions on consumption. If these are imposed in a top-down, heavy-handed way, they risk alienating the people whose cooperation is required to achieve the targets.

Permaculturalists and other environmentalists have been working with and teaching communities and individuals for many years how to monitor their own consumption and how to use resources less and more efficiently. The notion of 'limits to growth' is central to permaculture policy and is now entering mainstream debate and policy. Planners and policy makers could work with permaculturalists and environmentalists to provide feedback to the public and to involve them in deciding how to limit growth and reduce consumption.

Feedback can come in many and varied ways. At CERES (2007) environment centre in Melbourne, sacred kingfishers were noticed to be arriving in spring a few years ago, after an absence of many years, providing feedback that efforts to revegetate the creek and bring back wildlife were working. This resulted in the 'Return of the Sacred Kingfisher' annual spring festival celebration.

Use and Value Renewable Resources and Services

We are still discovering, or rediscovering, sustainable ways of utilizing natural systems, such as plants and soil, to provide useful materials and to help us reuse our 'wastes'.

Earth and straw bales are renewable building materials that many permaculturalists have used to build their houses. However, the sustainable housing codes that have been developed to promote construction of houses with minimal environmental impact have, in the past, discriminated against the use of these renewable materials. This anomaly was rectified after some vigorous lobbying but it appears that the same thing is happening now in the area of grey-water reuse.

Permaculturalists pioneered effective natural systems of grey-water purification and reuse, using reed beds, banana circles and mulch trenches. However, officially sanctioned grey-water reuse systems for sewered areas in Queensland now require surge tanks, valves for purging to the sewer, soil tests, reticulation 100 mm beneath the surface and payment of an annual licence fee (Queensland Government 2006). The regulations do not make any allowance for the role that plants can play in taking up the grey-water nor do they acknowledge the importance of rotating grey-water distribution so that soil organisms can rejuvenate and any accumulated salts be flushed out. Permaculturalists risk acting outside the law if they continue with their proven systems.

The lessons from these episodes is that engineers and planners need to become more biologically literate, 'health' regulations need to reflect environmental health as well as human health and planning codes, and regulations that aim to regulate renewable systems should be formulated in consultation with the people who developed them in the first place.

Produce No Waste

It is a scandal that, in a country whose soils are infertile partly because they are very low in organic matter, a huge source of organic matter, in the form of urban green 'waste', is dumped in landfill (see Chapter 10). The green waste from urban kitchens and gardens should be composted and applied to our gardens and farmlands to improve fertility.

Adding compost to our soils could have another benefit. Tim Flannery (2005, 32) has suggested that increasing the level of carbon in soil by incorporating organic matter from compost and green manure into our farmers' fields would be one of the best, and quickest, ways to tackle the increase in greenhouse gases that is causing climate change.

Some local councils are experimenting with kerb-side pick-up of green waste and large-scale composting of it, while others are encouraging residents to compost at home. Some community gardens compost green waste from local restaurants and lawn-mowing contractors. These scattered and patchy efforts need to be coordinated, expanded and replicated nationwide. Local governments, through their State and national associations, are well placed to facilitate such efforts, which could become at least partly self-supporting through sales to farmers.

Reuse of building materials and retrofitting of older houses, office buildings and warehouses has become quite fashionable in certain quarters but, as with 'green' power, it often costs more to use the recycled product than it does to use the new, non-recycled alternative. Governments could help redress this imbalance by ensuring that the full costs are charged for new building materials, including environmental externalities and hidden subsidies such as the diesel excise rebate.

Design from Patterns to Details

The patterns of geography and climate in areas occupied by Australian cities are quite different but there is a boring sameness about the outer suburbs of all cities. The design details have not reflected the particular patterns of their local climate, landscape and vegetation.

Early versions of sustainable housing codes, which focused mainly on winter warming, not summer cooling, had the inadvertent effect of making houses hotter in summer. To make matters worse, climate patterns are changing, with summer heat waves becoming hotter and more prolonged. So sales of air conditioners are soaring as residents seek relief from the sweltering conditions in their suburban hot boxes.

Permaculture teaches the importance of assessing the flows of energy, including sun, wind, water, fire, frost, people and animals, across a site before designing structures or gardens and placing them on the site. Permaculture designs aim to harvest and use beneficial energy flows, such as cool summer breezes and winter sun, while blocking or deflecting harmful flows, such as cold winds or fire.

Sustainable housing codes must require subdivision and housing designs to take account of local patterns of climate, including the projected changes in the climate, as well as patterns of landscape and vegetation. Creeks, wetlands, ridgelines and significant vegetation all need to be taken into account in land use planning. Areas of productive soil will be particularly important in ensuring food security for cities in an oil-depleted future and should be protected from housing development. There can be no 'one size fits all' approach to housing development and design in countries as geographically diverse as Australia.

Integrate, Do Not Segregate

In Australian cities, work is segregated from home life, people are segregated from each other inside their individual houses or apartments, the poor are segregated from the rich, the disabled from the able bodied, and the elderly from their younger family members.

Mixed-use redevelopments incorporating residential, retail and commercial uses are beginning to break down this segregation but permaculture would integrate much further. Urban ecovillages, co-housing, housing cooperatives, social enterprises, community workshops and community gardens are just some of the initiatives being developed to integrate people, including the disabled, the disadvantaged and the elderly, into the larger society. Landuse zoning will need to change to allow for multiple uses for land and to reflect the smaller footprint of private land and the larger footprint of common or public land that such initiatives require.

This principle also incorporates the maxim of Mollison (Mollison with Slay 1991, 8) that, in a sustainable, integrated system, 'Each important function is supported by many elements'. For instance, to ensure secure water supply for cities, it would be best to use multiple water sources, including domestic rainwater tanks, stormwater retention basins and grey-water reuse, as well as implementing efficiency measures, such as flow reduction devices, dual-flush toilets and drip irrigation for gardens. For example, Bondi Junction, Sydney has a productive community garden in the midst of a sea of unit blocks and shops. Despite water restrictions, it is a green oasis thanks to two large tanks of rainwater harvested from the roof of the childcare centre next door.

Likewise, with energy, ensuring a secure supply would require use of a variety of sources, including solar hot water systems, photovoltaic cells and wind turbines as well as energy-efficient design and appliances. To ensure food security, food would be grown on balconies, in backyards, in community gardens and city farms and in public parks and along streets, as well as in market gardens on urban creek flats and on the urban fringe.

Use Small and Slow Solutions

Large houses on small lots is the pattern of most new developments in our cities, with unsustainable consequences, such as increased stormwater run-off and little room for rainwater tanks, grey-water reuse, vegetable gardens or children's play areas. The challenge for developers and architects wishing to create sustainable housing and limit urban sprawl is to design smaller houses that still provide the sense of space, comfort and privacy that buyers seek in larger houses.

Today's 'fast' society not only leaves many people behind but also deprives citizens of the richness and depth of experience of local culture, food and people. Contrast the social interaction and taste experience of buying food at a large supermarket with shopping at a local organic farmers' market or the sense of belonging to a neighbourhood gained from walking rather than driving through it. Visionary design for our cities needs to plan for a future in which walking, bicycles, bus and rail will be the predominant modes of transport and where people will be able to live their lives more fully in their local neighbourhood, rather than needing to travel all over the city to go to work, school or shops.

Diversity of Uses and Values

The biodiversity of the remaining natural areas in and around our cities has been depleted by development, while at the same time the diversity of human cultures is being reduced by modernization and globalization. In an effort to re-create pristine biodiversity, many local governments and community groups are involved in efforts to regenerate bushland in cities by planting species that are native to the local area and by waging a 'war on weeds'. They have been successful in bringing back plants, birds and animals that had vanished years before but, in many cases, have created new weedscapes.

Permaculturalists, and many conservationists, are now recognizing that biodiversity is not a static reality that can be re-created but rather is a dynamic and evolving feature of sustainable natural systems (see Chapter 18). Total eradication of weed species is impossible and many indigenous species no longer thrive where soils and water flows have been irrevocably changed. Fruit trees, bush foods and timber trees can be planted instead, to use productively the increased nutrients and water flows created by soil disturbance and run-off.

In regard to human diversity, the policy of multiculturalism has been successful in fostering acceptance and celebration of the diverse cultures within Australian society. But as David Holmgren (2002, 219) puts it:

> Multiculturalism itself contains the same paradox as the permacultural use of biological diversity, where the process of valuing and making use of nature's diversity contributes to changing it. Acknowledgement of the value of differing traditions goes hand in hand with a promiscuous hybridisation to create new local cultures of place.

Planners and local authorities thus need not only to be mindful of the different cultural groups within a local community but also responsive to ways that the community as a whole is evolving and creating its own local 'culture of place'.

Use Edges and Value the Marginal

In biological systems, edges, or boundaries between two different landforms or plant communities, are often regions of greater diversity and productivity. Similarly, in cities, the boundaries between different neighbourhoods or between residential and commercial areas are often lively and creative places.

The post-war separation of residential from commercial and industrial zones in Australian cities, plus the almost total exclusion of agricultural land, has created sterile, monocultural cityscapes. Permaculture planning would reverse this separation by creating mosaics of housing, industry, shops, offices, farmland and bush right through and around cities, which would facilitate interesting and productive interactions at the boundaries of different areas, not only in the inner city but also in the suburbs and on the urban fringe.

The growing inequality in Australia has left many people, not least the Indigenous inhabitants, marginal to mainstream economic and social systems. Non-Indigenous Australians can learn much from Aboriginal traditions about how to live in sustainable ways on this dry continent. Fire prevention and management is one area where Aboriginal knowledge has already been found to be useful. We would do well to learn also from them about the importance of a spiritual relationship to land, the social value of supportive, extended families and how to use and harvest the bushland areas, rivers and seas in sustainable ways.

Urban planners and local authorities could work with Indigenous people to establish Indigenous cultural centres in our cities and to facilitate planting and harvesting of bush foods as well as the sustainable harvesting of the urban wildlife, such as possums and scrub turkeys, whose numbers have increased dramatically in some Australian cities in recent years.

Creatively Use and Response to Change

Rapid and continuous change is a feature of modern life, which is often seen as negative. However, change can be harnessed for positive ends, as summarized in the permaculture aphorism, 'the problem is the solution'.

Demographic changes create opportunities for planners and authorities to support more sustainable housing, land use and lifestyles. The 'gentrification' of older suburbs is an opportunity to encourage the retrofitting of existing houses for sustainability, while the 'empty nest' change currently affecting many of the 'baby boomer' generation living in large family homes opens up possibilities for their homes to be modified to allow them to take in boarders.

Similarly, the advent of higher petrol prices creates an opportunity to develop alternatives to private, car-based transport, notably improved public transport, and to reduce the space allocated for roads and parking. The water crisis affecting many of our larger cities is an opportunity for Australians to revalue this most precious of resources and to change forever their assumption of unlimited supplies of potable water. The looming decline in the availability of oil that will follow 'peak oil' will also create a myriad of opportunities to redevelop strong and sustaining local communities and local economies.

Therefore, permaculture principles can provide inspiration for planners, designers and regulators to rethink the way we develop and organize our cities. These principles have also been a stimulus to people at the grassroots in our communities to take actions towards sustainability.

Community Action for Urban Sustainability

Until recently, the impact of permaculture has been greatest in rural areas. It has not been so visible in major cities. However, the rapid blossoming of community gardens is changing this. There are over two hundred community gardens in Australia in 2006, with more starting each year. They grow food and demonstrate sustainable ways to design gardens, use water and energy, keep animals and regenerate bush land. They also provide training, build community networks and support disadvantaged people.

Some community gardens operate enterprises such as nurseries, gardening services, market gardens, organic food markets, cafés, training courses in permaculture and organic horticulture and bicycle repair that allow people to make a modest income while meeting local needs. For instance, take a common scenario at Brisbane's Northey Street City Farm. It's a Saturday morning. Hundreds of people are milling through the organic farmers' market buying local organic produce from the farmers who grow it. Under the mango trees, people are drinking coffee and chai, chatting and singing. Others are wandering through the nursery, seeking advice about what to plant in their home gardens. In another corner, fifteen people are listening eagerly to a demonstration of how they can reuse grey water on their gardens. Across the road, three volunteers are putting finishing touches to a large mosaic mandala.

The gardens can help make the transition to sustainability interesting and fun, not difficult or threatening. By involving people socially, in gardening together, attending a workshop, building a cob oven, shopping at a farmers' market or planning a community event, community gardens help bring people together to work cooperatively on the sustainability project. Such a project exists in Melbourne's inner northern suburbs, where CERES city farmers weed and till the broad beans and garlic that grows on a fertile flat alongside Merri Creek. This creek flat has been cultivated continuously for over a century, first by Chinese market gardeners, then by a post-war immigrant family from Italy, and now by the CERES farmers.

Permaculture: Motivating for Change

Permaculture has motivated people to change behaviour because they have felt committed to a cause and have been involved personally and collectively in working towards achieving a worthwhile goal. They have felt connected to something that is bigger than themselves as individuals – a movement with a clear vision and practical strategies.

Permaculture has also motivated governments to change. By getting out and doing it, implementing sustainable housing and land management solutions on the ground, permaculture has had, and continues to have, an influence on policy makers and regulators.

Grey-water reuse, for example, has been practised by permaculturalists in urban as well as rural areas for many years, but only now, faced with water shortages, are urban authorities beginning to offer their imprimatur to this sensible strategy. Other examples of urban permaculture strategies being taken up by local authorities include composting toilets, swales or contour ditches for stormwater retention, farmers' markets and street plantings of fruit and nut trees. For example, visitors who use toilets at community gardens located at Murdoch University (Perth, Western Australia), CERES (Melbourne, Victoria) and Morningside (Brisbane, Queensland) help to take the load off city sewers and contribute to the fertility of the gardens. These gardens have all been at the forefront of trials of biological or composting toilets with on-site reuse of treated effluent in urban situations.

Permaculture is just one of many similar movements that work together to develop and promote sustainable living systems. Organic farming, community supported agriculture, slow food, ecovillages, co-housing, housing cooperatives, alternative finance, ethical investment, community recycling, community arts and sustainable transport are some of the other movements. Together they form a powerful network of 'people power' that is slowly but surely beginning to transform the way we live.

Decentralization

Lack of water is likely to limit the size and density of Australian cities. Arguably, many of Australia's major cities are approaching, or possibly are already beyond, a size and density that can be sustained by the available water. Permaculture strategies for more decentralized human settlements, which harvest their own water and grow much of their own food, will be vital for ensuring the sustainability of Australian settlements in a future that is likely to be drier than now.

Energy use could increase during the transition to a decentralized pattern of settlements, as 'sea changers', 'tree changers' and rural 'new settlers' use their private, often four wheel drive, vehicles to commute to and from cities and regional centres for work, family visits, shopping, education, health care and cultural experiences. However, permaculture inspired ecovillages, such as Crystal Waters near Maleny in Queensland, have sought to minimize the need for residents to travel by creating a critical mass sufficient to support basic service provision on site. Other permaculture inspired rural subdivisions in New South Wales, such as Jarlanbah in Nimbin and The Bend in Bega, have been sited on the edges of existing country towns so that residents can use the existing services and community activities provided in those towns.

Australian cities and coastal regions grappling with issues of sustainable population numbers need decentralization policies. They should aim to limit the sprawl of small rural acreage holdings around our major cities and along coastal strips and to promote instead the rejuvenation of existing country towns and villages.

Conclusion

As an amalgam of science, philosophy, traditional agricultural and land management systems, along with practical design techniques, permaculture provides a holistic approach to reordering our living systems. Permaculture has much to offer Australian cities confronted by and grappling with dramatic environmental and social changes.

References

CERES (2007), Centre for Education and Research in Environmental Strategies [website], <http://www.ceres.org.au>, accessed 5 January 2007.

Cruz, M. and Medina, R. (2001), *Agriculture in the City: A Key to Sustainability in Havana, Cuba* (Kingston: Ian Randle Publishers).

Flannery T. (2005), *The Weather Makers* (Melbourne: Text Publishing).

Gleeson, B. (2006), *Australian Heartlands: Making Space for Hope in the Suburbs* (Sydney: Allen and Unwin).

Holmgren, D. (2002), *Permaculture: Principles and Pathways Beyond Sustainability* (Hepburn Springs: Holmgren Design Services).

Mollison, B. with Slay, R. (1991), *Introduction to Permaculture* (Tasmania: Tagari).

Morrow, R. (2005), 'The Blossoming of Surburbia', *The Planet – The Journal of Permaculture International Limited* 13, 14–15.

Queensland Government (2006), *Guidelines for Councils of Greywater for Residential Properties in Queensland Sewered Areas* Queensland Department of Local Government, Planning, Sport and Recreation [website], <http://www.lgp.qld.gov.au/docs/building_codes/sustainableliving/GreywaterGuidelines.pdf>, accessed 15 September 2006.

Self, P. (2000), 'Is Effective Democratic Planning Possible?' in Troy (ed).

Troy, P. (ed.) (2000), *Equity, Environment Efficiency – Ethics and Economics in Urban Australia* (Melbourne: Melbourne University Press).

Chapter 5

Policy Approaches Incorporating Life Cycle Assessment

Tim Grant

Introduction

In the development of 'green' or 'sustainable' design practice, a range of guides, checklists, advice and green mores develop as sustainable design folklore. 'Folklore', as used here, is not derogatory, simply describing how a knowledge base develops over time and passes between people in both formal and informal channels, in guides and policies and also in conversations and marketing. Such folklore is based on experience and analysis, what is known at any given time or for a significant period before any given time. What is important from a policy perspective is that this folklore is renewed as situations change and new knowledge and innovations occur. A culture of challenging and testing sustainable design folklore has developed so that responses to sustainability are fresh, unique and tailored to specific situations, rather than rigidly implementing a set of rules.

Onc important tool in the evaluation of new approaches and the development of new folklore is life cycle assessment (LCA), a method of evaluating the environmental impacts of products and services across their whole life cycle. LCA focuses on how human activities in the economy affect the environment. It reaches beyond attributes of products and services, such as 'natural' or 'renewable', to specify and evaluate the net environmental damage or improvement to the environment of those products and services.

This chapter outlines why LCA is important for developing sustainable housing and urban planning culture and practice. A brief history and an examination of current LCA applications in this area are provided. Trends in analytical techniques of LCA and results emerging from LCA in relation to sustainable housing and urban planning are discussed and recommendations made for embedding these approaches into the thinking of planners, designers and policy makers.

What is Sustainable?

In a book on steering sustainability, it is important to deliberate over the central question: What is sustainable? The first aspect of this question is philosophical, being how to balance social and equity goals with economic and environmental goals. However, at a more mundane level, having reached agreement on the broad principles of sustainability, there remain complex questions about which courses of action lead to sustainability, how far they go, and whether they are enough.

Currently, most opinions about what is good for the environment are based on historical experiences of environmental issues and reactions to environmental pressures, collectively condensed into environmental folklore encapsulated in very general terms, such as 'natural', 'degradable' or 'renewable', or in acts such as the move to avoid the use of polyvinylchloride, the shift to smaller vehicles, and so on.

The limitation of environmental folklore is that it generally develops in an ad hoc way. More importantly, it is often outdated, representing responses to historical concerns and pressures, even a generation out of date. Such folklore may not be based on a quantitative assessment of effectiveness and rarely takes into account wider environmental concerns. For example, the initial response to the problem of increasing plastic waste in the 1960s was to look for biodegradable plastics in an attempt to reduce litter and disposal problems (Bonifaz et al. 1996). Through one of the first LCAs undertaken in Europe, it became clear quickly that biodegradables were not a solution, due to the resources required to produce them and because biodegradable material increases gas emissions and leachate in landfills. Despite this, a folklore pertaining to plastics, the (non) issue of not degrading in landfill or in the environment persists, and biodegradables are still regularly sought as a solution.

Another problem is that the complexity of the modern economy and its interaction with the environment, a more complex system than the economy, makes intuitive responses vastly inadequate. As a response to the failure of current systems of city design and agriculture, Chapter 3 (on the ecopolis) and Chapter 4 (on permaculture) describe efforts to make human activity and the economy emulate natural systems. Each approach addresses the limitations of the current systems. However, to determine the respective values of theses approaches both as alternatives to the current system and in terms of their superiority to other alternatives, it is necessary to dispassionately evaluate whether they deliver the net environmental benefits sought and, if so, at what cost to other environmental and sustainability priorities. Ultimately, we would also like to know how far these achievements take us towards sustainability. However, to suppose that we can quantify sustainability endpoints is overly ambitious given the complexities and dynamic natures of the economy and the environment.

Applying Life Cycle Assessment

LCA is a method for determining the efficacy of strategies, policies, actions and products to advance sustainability when compared with current practice or with alternative future options. LCA provides a framework for a systemic assessment of environmental impacts. LCA aims to calculate the extent to which human activities, such as product manufacture and use, involve exchanges with the environment, such as the use of resources or the release of pollutants (air emissions, radiation and so on). LCA relates these exchanges to environmental indicators, analysing scientific causes and effects. The types of impacts examined depend on the study and the practitioner, but should cover all the important impacts, and should be scientifically valid: there should be a clear cause-and-effect relationship between emissions and endpoint damage.

This approach recognizes that any set of environmental indicators or concerns is socially constructed and is not a set of absolute or intrinsic environmental 'rights' of the biosphere. Examples are provided by different approaches to environmental protection. For instance, some seek to protect aspects of nature dating from specific time periods (in Australia, usually pre-settlement) while the permaculture movement (advocating a form of sustainable agriculture) considers the biosphere in terms of sustainable productivity. Urban environmental issues are often framed around short-term and medium-term health concerns about air and water pollution.

This chapter will show how, in order to renew environmental folklore and provide more rational and responsive decision-making in urban planning in future, LCA impact assessment, coupled with quantification of the scale and causes of such damage, is essential.

How Life Cycle Assessment Works

LCA seeks to measure the environmental impacts of human activities by breaking down those activities into constituent parts and measuring how each part contributes to environmental impacts. The scope of the environmental impacts taken into account is limited by the available science for characterizing the links between activities and environmental impacts and by the scope set by the LCA analyst and client, who may define environmental criteria of interest. Taking a broad definition of environment as 'everything that surrounds an organisation' (Standards Australia 2004), derived from the international standards on environmental management, the impact need not be limited to biophysical impacts but could include social, cultural and economic impacts. However, traditionally, LCAs have been limited to biophysical impacts.

The approach to constructing a cohesive set of environmental impacts begins with identifying key areas of protection for humans. In other words, what do we as humans see as the most important things to maintain or enhance in the face of the pressure from modern industrial societies? The main failing in this approach is the lack of consistent positive frameworks for what humans wish to achieve. Areas of protection acknowledged internationally are: human health, ecosystem health, resources stocks and climate systems. Environmental effects that cause damage to such areas of protection are identified, and cause-and-effect chains between releases and materials used by productive systems and damage are established. An example of an LCA impact method is EcoIndicator 99 (Goedkoop and Spriensma 1999, 10), shown in Figure 5.1. It shows how the area of protection that we call 'human health' is affected partly by respiratory disease, which is in turn linked to changes in hydrocarbon concentrations from volatile organic carbon emissions. Other pathways include land use and its effect on habitat size, and consequent effects on vascular plants, which, in turn, affect biodiversity. In routine LCA practice, the impact methods are taken from existing models rather than being developed from first principles.

Figure 5.1   EcoIndicator 99 model

Figure 5.2 shows how extractions from the environment and releases to the environment are accounted for at each stage of the life cycle: from raw material production, to material manufacture, to product manufacture, to packaging and use, on to disposal of the product (Standards Australia 1998). In LCA, something is deemed released to the environment when it leaves human control or management, such as before human transformation. Releases to the environment are not treated as problems until an impact on one of the areas of protection is identified. Although, in physical terms, all of these interactions occur within the environment, the movement of polluting substances within the economy is not counted as a problem. For example, while lead is a major pollutant in air and water, the use of lead in car batteries is not a problem to human health as long as the lead can be maintained and managed within that product. While the cause and effect between emissions or resource use and the areas of protection is difficult to quantify, a clear link is required before they are assessed within the LCA framework.

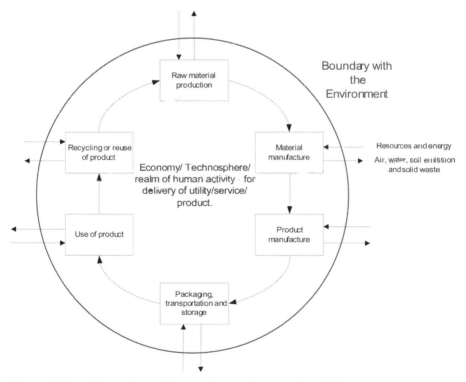

Figure 5.2   Interactions between the environment and the economy

While the framework for LCA is built from the top down – that is, identifying the areas of protection, looking for damaging effects to those areas, then looking at emissions which lead to those effects – in practice LCA works from the bottom up. Data on emission flows and resource use are collected from production systems investigated through the LCA. This is usually based on specific products or services which are assessed to determine the least damaging, or most beneficial, manner in which a service or product can be supplied. In this way, LCA is always assessed per unit or function (referred to as the 'functional unit').

Standards Australia (1998) describes LCA as a four-stage process. This process begins by defining the goal and scope of the LCA, including an accurate definition of the service under study (the functional unit), the indicators to be used, and the specific aspects of the production system to be examined. The second stage involves measuring emissions and resources used in production systems to produce the functional unit, although this is usually collected from pre-existing environmental databases rather than gathered first-hand. The culmination of this second stage is the addition of all emissions and resource flows across the entire production system. The third stage of the LCA takes the inventory, which may consist of hundreds of individual emissions, and assigns to them indicators selected for use in the study. The fourth stage of the LCA is the interpretation phase, which examines significant issues highlighted by the LCA and tests the assumptions and data sources with checks such as sensitivity and uncertainty analysis.

Systematic and Explicit

In LCA, quantification and methodological developments in search of causes and effects do not build towards a single unified model of either the environment or sustainability. The choices made in the development of LCA indicator sets are just that: choices supported with information about current states of knowledge of how human activity affects human health and the environment. This is a vastly different approach from other environmental perspectives, such as government policy, which is often based largely on piecemeal responses to a series of single-issue crises that have occurred over the last fifty years or so. Issues such as waste avoidance and recycling are a response to landfill shortages, poor amenity around landfills, and pollution arising from landfill leachate. Energy resource policies have been a response to energy shortages since the 1970s. Climate change is simply the latest pressure, which draws our attention to responses, most embedded in the economy. Most responses to climate change affect a range of other environmental issues in both positive and negative ways.

The purpose of the LCA framework is to look past the historical baggage and labels attributed to different products, services and approaches, and to evaluate, in a transparent and objective way, the positive and negative outcomes of alternative approaches to decision making about issues associated with production and consumption. Within this framework, attributes such as 'natural', 'degradable', 'renewable', 'recyclable', 'reusable', 'phosphate free', 'chlorine free' and so on are evaluated on their merits rather than simply placed in perspectives which rely on their historical significance. Both the utility provided by products and the damage to areas of protection for human beings are succinctly identified to allow maximum opportunity for alternative interpretations and approaches to emerge. For example, in the area of utility, the functionality of cars focuses on mobility, to allow consideration of alternative modes of transport, and then on accessibility and community services provided by mobility. Through such reasoning, the necessity for mobility might be reduced by bringing destinations closer together.

Just as functionality can be deconstructed to reveal the underlying benefits derived from products and services, environmental impacts can be deconstructed to reveal underlying issues of concern. As part of a plastic bag study produced for the Australian government (ExcelPlas Australia et al. 2004), the impacts of litter from shopping bags were separated into aesthetic (visual impacts of litter, both natural and constructed) and marine animal impacts. Within this framework, slowly degrading materials were interpreted as hardly affecting the aesthetic impacts, as most litter in many locations was collected before it degraded. In the case of marine mammals, the density, not the degradability, of the material was shown to be the most important feature. Removing from the water stream material with a density of 1 or lower, which tends to remain suspended in waterways and oceans for weeks or months, was most significant because heavier materials sank within days of entering waterways.

Integrating LCA into Decision Making and Planning

There are numerous problems associated with LCA, not least of which are the time and expense that it takes to undertake LCA research and studies. It is neither practical nor desirable to use LCA, as currently designed, for all significant decision making in any sector from packaging through to housing and urban planning. The cases where LCA is justifiable within a single decision context are few and, despite the investment of significant resources, LCA may not always provide clear answers to specific questions.

The value of LCA lies in the learning and understanding it provides and the new insights into how and why different materials, production and approaches affect environmental concerns. Using a consistent and considered analytical framework, LCA is creating new environmental folklore beyond single-issue concerns that essentially respond to the latest crisis.

What is required to drive the development of this new environmental folklore is a solid research foundation of LCA and life cycle inventory with respect to existing and proposed approaches to housing and urban development. For instance, recent work on the ecological footprint of the Aurora green development in northern Melbourne (see Chapter 15) has highlighted significant potential benefits from installing solar hot water systems, improving the thermal performance of houses and, most importantly, reducing the average house size across a diverse mix of housing options (CfD at RMIT and Global Footprint Network (2006).

The theoretical performance of an average Aurora dwelling compared with conventional dwellings is shown in Figure 5.3. The environmental indicator used in this study was a measure related to the ecological footprint that principally considers land use and greenhouse gas emissions (converted to a land use equivalent). The value of this approach was as a tool of communication. The ecological footprint is understandable and simple for housing designers and land developers to use. Many other initiatives either made little difference to the environmental loads of the house construction or were not well enough characterized to determine resulting benefits.

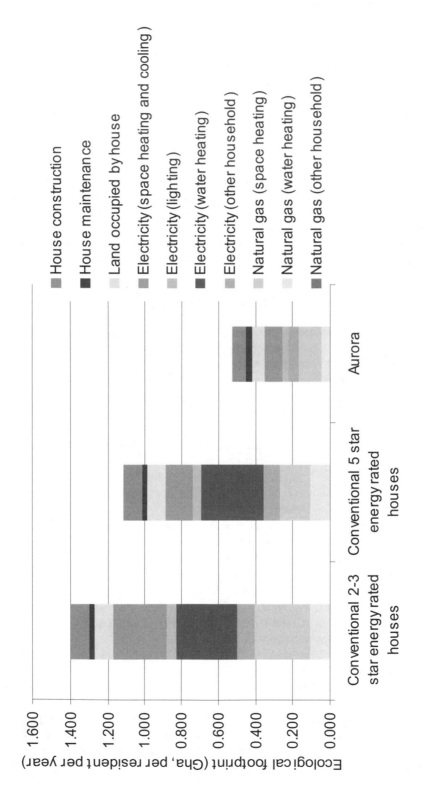

Figure 5.3   LCA performance of Aurora homes

The number of organized material ratings and assessments being undertaken in Australia now means that the evolution of environmental folklore should be faster than before. Figure 5.4 proposes how LCA can function, through guides and case studies, to regenerate environmental folklore.

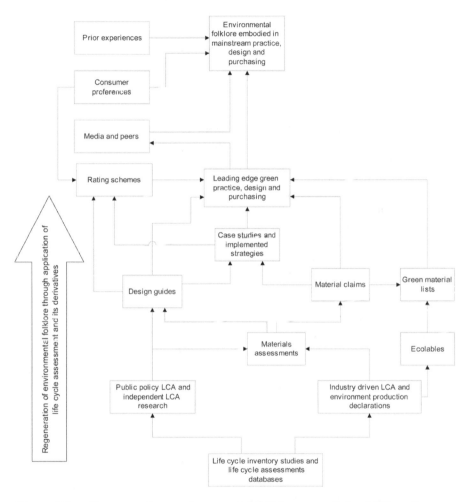

Figure 5.4   Regenerating environmental folklore – applying LCA and its derivatives

The data and lessons arising from LCA differ from what we have known previously. LCA data and interpretations are neither as stable nor as simplistic as a lot of previous environmental folklore. Subtlety is important in both interpretations and applications of environmental principles. This insight is not new, as existing environmental folklore also required subtle interpretation. However, subtlety is not possible without deeply understanding the rationale behind certain aspects of environmental folklore.

Folklore without a clear understanding of the rationale and appropriate application of a principle or insight tends towards environmental dogma. A good example is provided through a discussion of the development of biofuels, which promised positive benefits for the environment. Biofuels, made from renewable feed stock, are almost entirely non-toxic and can be considered 'natural', depending on whether agriculture is defined as natural or not. Early LCA studies showed mixed results for different biofuels, with land use impacts such as fertilizer application and water use being significant for some crops. Also, processing impacts, particularly for ethanol fuels, is considerable, depending on the source of energy (Beer and Grant 2003). However, as the biofuels industry has developed and responded to these studies, and associated science and information has improved, results for biofuels have been shifting positively. Details of the system matter, and subtlety is important.

The appropriate approach in this new era of multiple and complex environmental, social and economic objectives involves scepticism and dynamism with respect to information use, and continuous inquiry into what works for sustainable practices over time. Scepticism need not lead to indecision. It is important to act on the best available knowledge. However, policy makers as well as other decision makers need to be careful not to get locked into set positions and solutions so that flexibility is possible when refinement or changes in strategy are required at a later point.

We need to be responsive and reflexive in the application of our environmental knowledge, as changing technology, social preferences and pressures will make tomorrow's solution different from today's and outdated by the day after tomorrow. Not only market-based players, such as manufacturers, product developers and consumers, but also advocates and policy makers need to be willing to challenge their assumptions and beliefs without relenting on a commitment to a more sustainable outcome. What LCA approaches provide are ways of considering both the breadth of environmental impacts, rather than just an immediate issue, and all the stages of the production use and disposal chain. LCA highlights systematic approaches and learning, not just a reductionist calculated 'answer'. LCA suggests that solutions only have value when elucidated in terms of causes and potential solutions.

Another significant aspect of applying LCA is the need to incorporate dynamic models which look ahead, not only at existing impacts and environmental performance but also at the potential performances of alternatives and the likelihood of sustainable practices continuing. The most striking example of this is in the petroleum sector where synthetic products generally perform well (high) in most environmental indicators, but are based on diminishing reserves of oil or 'natural capital' (Hawken et al. 1999). Much of the system's efficiency results from the scale of production and the quality of the original feed stocks. Obviously competing processes based on lower quality, recycled or natural feed stocks generally have higher manufacturing impacts. Nevertheless, the potential for ongoing sustainable production of natural products over synthetic products is of great interest to making decisions relating to sustainability.

Conclusion

LCA is a central element for steering sustainability. It provides a compass in what is a multidimensional space for solutions, assessing product performance against a range of environmental impacts in different parts of the supply chain. It provides well-developed and tested methods to introduce sustainable practices into our urban environments. LCA advisers and researchers can assist policy makers through a suite of strategies, such as applying LCA methods to practical challenges, training and advising policy bureaucrats and technocrats, monitoring and evaluating the results of government LCA applications, and through independent research, including research on policy recommendations.

References

Beer, T. and Grant, T. (2003), *Life-Cycle Assessment of Emissions From Fuel Ethanol in Vehicles. National Clean Air Conference: Linking Air Pollution Science* Policy and Management. (Newcastle, Australia: Clean Air Society).

Bonifaz, O., Nikodem, H. and Klopper, W. (1996), 'LCA – How It Came About – An Early Systems Analysis of Packaging for Liquids', *International Journal of Life Cycle Assessment* 1:2, 62–5.

CfD at RMIT and Global Footprint Network (2006), 'Ecological Footprint Analysis of Aurora Residential Development' [Unpublished report prepared by the RMIT Centre for Design and Global Footprint Network for the Victorian Environmental Protection Authority, VicUrban and Building Commission, Melbourne].

ExcelPlas Australia, CfD at RMIT, and Nolan-ITU (2004), *The Impacts of Degradable Plastic Bags in Australia: Final Report to Department of the Environment and Heritage* (Melbourne: Centre for Design at RMIT).

Goedkoop, M. and Spriensma, R. (1999), *The EcoIndicator 99: A Damage Oriented Method for Life Cycle Impact Assessment* (Amersfoort: PRé Consultants bv).

Hawken, P., Lovins A. and Lovins, H. (1999), *Natural Capitalism: Creating the Next Industrial Revolution* (Boston: Little, Brown and Co.).

Standards Australia (1998), *AS/NZS ISO 14040: 1998 Environmental Management – Life Cycle Assessment – Principles and Framework* (Sydney: SAI Global Ltd).

Standards Australia (2004), *AS/NZS 14004: 2004 Environmental Management Systems – General Guidelines on Principles, Systems and Support Techniques* (Sydney: SAI Global Ltd).

Part II
Collective Practices

Chapter 6

Stationary Energy: A Critical Element of a Sustainable Urban Metabolism

Alan Pears

Introduction

This chapter focuses on the role of stationary (non-transport) energy supply and use in the urban context, and proposes some policy options to help shift it towards a less unsustainable path. Stationary energy is an important direct input, and an input to other inputs, to urban development and activity. Supply and use of stationary energy drives aspects of the dynamics of the urban system and contributes to positive and negative sustainability outcomes. Table 6.1, which is loosely based on the urban metabolism model (Yencken and Williamson 2000, 121), lists major roles energy plays in an urban context, providing a framework for this discussion.

Table 6.1   Roles played by stationary energy in urban systems

Inputs	Dynamics	Outcomes/ Impacts
Direct energy inputs *Energy as an indirect input for*: food (agriculture and processing); materials (mining and processing); and water (pumping, treatment and embodied energy in infrastructure).	*Operating energy* for buildings and urban infrastructure. *Operating energy* for business, industrial and household activities (including recreation).	*Gain or loss* of amenity. *Impacts* of gaseous, liquid and solid wastes. *Need for treatment or recycling* of pollutants and wastes.

Energy use in urban areas can create tensions and dilemmas. For example, development at higher density potentially reduces energy use and energy costs of urban infrastructure, but may limit access to solar radiation, change the level of building embodied energy, and may create significant social and amenity issues. Also, distributed electricity generation, such as cogeneration (the production of heat and electricity on site, usually using natural gas), or solar cells may cut greenhouse gas emissions but impact negatively on local air quality and amenity in comparison to remote centralized power stations. Some methods of treating waste water for reuse, and even supplying drinking water, such as desalination, can have significant energy implications as well.

To develop urban policies that promote a transition towards a sustainable energy future, we need to look at the direct and indirect ways that energy is used, the forms of energy used and how they are supplied, and find ways of responding to the tensions and dilemmas that emerge.

Inputs, Dynamics, Outcomes and Impacts

The following discussion of energy issues within the urban metabolism conceptual framework of inputs, dynamics and outcomes or impacts highlights the critical necessity for an integrated, societal approach to energy policies related to energy production, supply and use.

Inputs

Energy is a critical input to urban systems. In Australia, energy is mostly produced from fossil fuels mined or extracted and converted into useful forms, such as electricity and processed natural gas, at locations distant from cities. Electricity and natural gas dominate Australia's urban stationary energy supply, although wood, liquid petroleum gas, various forms of petroleum, and even some coal, are also used. The provision of this energy has enormous environmental and locally significant social implications, such as pollution and land-use conflicts in Victoria's Latrobe Valley. Non-transport energy use, mainly used in urban systems, was responsible for 49 per cent of Australia's total 2003 greenhouse gas emissions (AGO 2005a), and grew by 37 per cent between 1990 and 2003 (AGO 2005b).

Various options for sustainable energy supply have been proposed, including shifting to renewable energy, geosequestration (capturing and storing greenhouse gases from fossil fuel use), and even nuclear power. Energy efficiency improvement is a key aspect of any sustainable energy strategy because, whatever energy source is used, efficient usage reduces the capacity required and, hence, social and environmental costs.

Each energy option creates challenges, for example:

- Ongoing use of fossil fuels contributes to climate change, while geosequestration, storing carbon dioxide from combustion underground, is in its early stages of development and is likely to require replacement of all existing power stations, at substantial cost.
- Development of wind farms in some parts of Victoria has provoked strong opposition from some sections of the community.
- Many Australians have long-standing concerns about the risks of nuclear power and uranium mining.
- Energy efficiency policies are often opposed by entrenched interest groups, such as some building industry organizations, and elements of the timber industry have strongly opposed introduction of more stringent building energy regulations (Pears 2006, 50–51).

In principle, energy supply should not be considered in isolation from social and environmental issues. When it has, this has often led to inappropriate policies. For example, energy market reform in Australia has focused on supply-side strategies and narrow financial criteria, which has driven an increase in consumption and a larger share of coal-fired electricity. This has contributed to the rapid growth in stationary energy greenhouse gas emissions. Instead, the development of a comprehensive sustainable energy strategy needs to start at the point of consumption, examine the systems and services for which energy is an input, then analyse the range of energy resources available, to match needs and sources. When this approach is taken, consideration of energy efficiency and appropriate energy forms, such as heat or electricity, may lead to the selection of very different mixes of energy sources than has traditionally occurred (Saddler et al. 2004). Such issues are discussed further below.

Food supply to urban areas involves significant stationary energy inputs, both directly and indirectly, for agricultural activity, to produce fertilizers and chemicals and for processing into final products. Agriculture, forestry and fishing consumed 94.5 PJ in 2003–04, 4 per cent of Australia's total final stationary energy (ABARE 2006). Greenhouse gas emissions from livestock and soils further increase environmental impacts. The food processing industry uses even more energy than agriculture, 164 PJ in 2003–04, 7 per cent of Australia's total final stationary energy (ABARE 2006).

Energy use for mining and processing materials for urban buildings, infrastructure and business activity is another major sustainability issue. Table 6.2 shows annual consumption of select materials per Australian. This table highlights the significance of construction activity in terms of quantities of material used. The high-energy intensity of metals makes them worthy of close consideration. Australia's metals industry uses over a quarter of all stationary energy. Although a significant proportion of local production is exported, we import large quantities of metals as finished products (70 per cent of new cars purchased in 2005 were imported). High energy use in metal production cannot be ignored simply because most is exported.

Table 6.2   Australian consumption of select materials

Material	kg/person/year
Aluminium	34
Steel	478
Wood, woodchips	233
Paper	168
Coal (mostly as electricity)	2900
Plastics	72
Construction materials	5226
Crops	467
Meat	82
Dairy	242
Total	9902

Source: Newton et al. (2001, 40).

Several analysts have highlighted the magnitude of energy used to mine, process and transport materials for buildings and urban infrastructure. Such energy costs are referred to as 'embodied energy'. Crawford and Treloar (2005) have estimated that the energy embodied in an office building is 8 to 25.8 GJ/m², depending on the boundaries of the calculation. The lower value reflects only energy directly involved in producing materials while the higher value includes upstream energy inputs via an input–output model. The higher value is equivalent to estimated greenhouse gas emissions from energy consumption related to operating an average office building for up to twelve years, in which case operating energy dominates the life cycle impact. As buildings become more efficient, embodied energy will become a more significant proportion of life cycle building energy use, unless the energy involved in production of materials is also reduced.

Water supply involves energy use for pumping and treatment. ABARE (2006) estimates that Australia's total energy use associated with water, sewage and drainage is 8.9 PJ per year, of which 84 per cent is electricity. This is equivalent to 104 kWh of electricity per person per year, almost 4 per cent of average household electricity usage per person, and 70 MJ of other fuels (equivalent to about two litres of petrol) per person per year. In hilly urban areas, energy used in pumping water can exceed 2 kWh/kL. As we move towards strategies such as water recycling, desalination (which consumes 3 to 5 kWh/kL of water), or sourcing from distant locations, the energy cost of water is likely to become more significant. However, there is potential to offset some energy use by generating electricity from water as it flows downhill from high altitude storages to users. Indeed, some water suppliers are already installing mini and micro hydroelectric systems at dam outlets and in pipelines instead of pressure reduction valves.

Dynamics

Over 85 per cent of Australians live in cities, where most economic activity occurs. A high proportion of building and infrastructure energy use, building and infrastructure embodied energy, and household, business and industrial activity occurs in urban areas. The mainly urban commercial sector – office, retail, hotel, education and other services – uses 10 per cent of stationary energy and 22 per cent of all electricity while households, mainly in urban areas, use 18 per cent of all stationary energy and 28 per cent of all electricity (ABARE 2006). Most remaining stationary energy is used by industry, which provides inputs to urban areas as well as exports. While recreation may occur outside urban areas, most participants are from urban areas.

There is ongoing energy use associated with infrastructure, such as street and public lighting, energy losses from electricity and gas supply networks, local distribution of water and pumping of sewage. Around 0.5 per cent of all Australian electricity is used for public lighting (ESAA 2005).

Despite the major environmental impacts of urban energy use, energy is often a small component of total costs. In a typical household, non-transport energy accounts for around 2–3 per cent of expenditure on goods and services (ABS 2005). For the non-transport services sector, it is less than 1 per cent and for most industry less than 3 per cent (ABS 2002). Even if the full environmental and social costs were incorporated into energy prices, energy would still be relatively cheap. RCG/ Hagler Bailly and SRC Australia (1993) have shown that the greenhouse impact was the major environmental cost of Victorian electricity and that the inclusion of all environmental costs would increase the average retail electricity price by only around a third.

The total cost of delivery of energy services includes costs of appliances, equipment or buildings that convert energy into useful services. Australian households spend more on buying energy-consuming appliances than on direct energy inputs (ABS 2000). Expenditure on buying and renovating houses dwarfs expenditure on energy. Most purchases of appliances and houses are made with little regard for energy efficiency. Indeed, measures such as appliance energy labelling, minimum energy performance standards and building energy codes are usually justified by the argument that, without them, buyers would fail to capture cost-effective energy savings due to market failures and imperfections.

This means policies relying on market mechanisms that focus only on energy pricing do not necessarily deliver optimal policy outcomes. Incorporating environmental, social and economic costs into the price of energy would not make it sufficiently expensive to significantly change behaviour. Many decisions by manufacturers, retailers, installers and purchasers that drive energy consumption, involving purchase of appliances and design of buildings, are not made with a view to future energy consequences. In any case, most governments are reluctant to implement policies that increase energy prices, because of concerns about impacts on business and rural households. So policies to shift energy use towards sustainability must target a range of players – appliance and building designers, manufacturers, developers, builders, retailers, trades, purchasers and energy users – in ways that are likely to influence their behaviour in relation to energy. They need to involve measures such as incentives for sale and purchase of energy efficient appliances, equipment and buildings, as well as regulation.

People congregate in urban areas to conduct business, industrial and household activities, thereby shaping urban economic and social outcomes. Policy makers often believe, erroneously, that ongoing economic and social development depends on increased use of energy and available supplies of cheap energy. Energy is just one of a number of critical inputs. The types of activities conducted and the efficiency of practices influence the level of energy use for a given level of outcomes. For example, an efficient services-oriented economy is likely to use much less energy than a comparable level of economic activity based on the processing of resources and manufacture of commodities. Smil (2003) points to a wide variation in levels of economic activity of countries with similar energy intensities.

In 2003, Victorian household, small business and large business electricity prices were higher than in New South Wales by 37 per cent, 37 per cent and 5 per cent respectively (ESAA 2004). However, the Victorian economy performed well. Such data challenge the undue significance placed on low energy prices for business success. At the same time, it can be argued that total energy cost, not energy price, is likely to influence behaviour. Improving energy efficiency can reduce total energy cost or offset the impact of using more expensive energy sources.

Recreation is an important aspect of amenity in urban areas. The level of energy use required for different options varies widely. Sitting in a park reading a book, or sailing in a nearby lake use much less energy than flying interstate for a skiing trip, driving a speedboat or driving to a rarely occupied holiday home. While much of this energy is for transport, holiday homes and tourism facilities use substantial amounts of energy and often contribute disproportionately to expensive seasonal peaks in energy demand. For instance, many unoccupied holiday homes leave fridges, hot water services and equipment on standby.

Outcomes

Pollution and wastes from burning fuels and other activities that use energy have become major urban issues. Emissions from transport fuel combustion and stationary energy fuels produce the bulk of urban air pollution. In Melbourne, in the mid-1990s, non-transport fuel was responsible for almost 40 per cent of sulphur dioxide and volatile organic compounds (EPA 1998). Urban electricity use contributed to pollution in the Latrobe Valley, where the bulk of Victoria's electricity is generated from coal.

There is potential for higher urban energy use from processing water and materials for reuse and for increased generation of energy from what have traditionally been seen as wastes. At the same time, the emerging role of energy derived from wastes in the waste management hierarchy (see Chapter 10) will be increasingly debated. For instance, are there circumstances under which it is preferable to produce energy from waste paper instead of recycling it or using it for mulch? Will construction of a waste-to-energy plant encourage more wasteful behaviour and undermine recycling programs? Such questions highlight the holistic context within which urban energy supply and use must be considered and cluster around the key question of what paths are appropriate for achieving sustainable futures.

Policy Options to Support Sustainability

There is no single path towards sustainability. Technological and social developments mean that new options constantly arise. Therefore policies must be flexible and facilitate innovation if they are to assist in progress towards sustainability. Where private agents are expected to act, their ability to capture benefits that they value, and to manage risk (especially in the period before the benefits outweigh the costs), will strongly influence their inclination to act.

Given that energy use is the outcome of lifestyle and economic development choices, our energy future is sensitive to many factors. For example, the increase in average floor area of new homes in the 1990s drove a significant increase in home heating and cooling energy use, as well as higher material consumption. The shift towards large-screen plasma television sets and low-voltage halogen lights has also increased energy consumption. However, dramatic changes are improving domestic energy efficiency and use of renewable energy. Today's refrigerators use a third as much electricity as those of the mid-1980s. Features such as insulation make it possible to build homes that need little heating or cooling, in most Australian climates. Foreseeable technologies, such as light-emitting diode (LED) lighting, solar glazing that generates electricity and organic LED television sets, offer potential for very large reductions in energy demand, even while the quality and scale of services is enhanced.

On the energy supply side, technology is shifting rapidly towards greater diversity and distribution of energy conversion technologies. Cogeneration systems, renewable energy sources and fuel cells are increasingly feasible substitutes for traditional centralized electricity generation. More businesses and houses can access natural gas from extensions of gas pipelines. Energy storage technologies are improving, thus enhancing flexibility of energy systems.

There are some fundamental trends shaping future paths and creating policy issues to be addressed, including increasingly diverse mixes of supply and demand side technologies as energy, water, communications and other aspects of our lives are affected by miniaturization, modular construction, dematerialization, connectivity, multidimensional communication, utilization of diffuse energy sources, improving efficiency of use and recovery/reuse/recycling. For example, households and businesses increasingly will: collect and store solar energy and rainwater; use high efficiency technologies for more services from less energy, water and materials; and process water and materials for reuse. The next section explores some emerging policy issues associated with these new trends in supply-and-demand factors.

Support for Diversified Solutions

As we develop a more diverse range of technological and social energy service options that may be applied anywhere between the point of delivery of a service and the traditional centralized sources of supply, we must ensure fair and reasonable treatment for end users and their representatives as they interact with established infrastructure and service providers. For example, surveys have shown that many households installing grid-connected solar cells have had great difficulty gaining what they consider to be fair treatment from their electricity suppliers (Thornton and Washusen 2005). More widespread problems for cogeneration and demand-side measures have also been identified (CoAG 2002). Similar issues exist in telecommunications. Market regulation will need to be modified to send signals to support positive behaviour and control unfair actions.

National energy-market reform objectives specifically commit to 'stimulate sustained energy efficiency improvements' and 'encourage the development of less carbon-intensive sources and technologies' (CoAG 2002, 64). National policy also aims to address any structural, legislative or regulatory barriers to cogeneration, renewable energy and energy efficiency consistent with efficient operation of the market (Commonwealth of Australia 1998). Regulators have failed to ensure this. Indeed, Victoria's Essential Services Commission (ESC 2006) has a key objective of maintaining the viability of the industries it regulates, which seems incompatible with the fair treatment of emerging industries that compete with established electricity and gas industries.

There are examples of attempts to use market structures to promote sustainable energy, based on recognition of the social benefits of such a shift. The UK Office of Gas and Electricity Markets is required by legislation to account for the environmental impacts of its decisions and to consider 'how best it can contribute to sustainable development' (Ofgem 2005). The New South Wales Independent Pricing and Regulatory Tribunal has mechanisms to allow energy distributors to 'pass through' recovery of lost revenue from energy efficiency and distributed generation.

The energy market policy initiatives required include clear targets and key performance indicators for achieving fair treatment of sustainable energy options in energy markets, with clear penalties and contingency responses if they are not met. In the short term, compensating incentives for options adversely affected by market distortions must be introduced, along with formal demand-side incentive mechanisms, such as the New South Wales Greenhouse Gas Abatement requirement for electricity retailers (Greenhouse Gas Reduction Scheme 2007).

Technical protocols are needed for interaction of multiply dispersed systems and mechanisms for taking advantage of the benefits such systems offer. Distributed water collection or electricity generation and storage systems might interact with centralized supply systems to provide mutual benefits by cutting pressure on infrastructure at critical times, while storing energy or water at other times. The Australian Greenhouse Office protocol for the control of appliances demonstrates how government can play an integrating role. 'As of right' grid connections and guaranteed fair pricing agreements are critical, along with stable incentive frameworks that do not stop and start. German households that install photovoltaic electricity systems are guaranteed a minimum price for power they sell to the grid (Hunnekes 2004). Each year this guaranteed minimum is reduced by 5 per cent for new installations, which guarantees returns without entrenching the subsidy permanently and pressures the photovoltaic industry to reduce costs in a sustained manner.

The potential for large numbers of small energy generators and water treatment systems to operate might require management of risks, such as electrocution, falling off roofs and disease from poor quality water. The development of low-cost monitoring, feedback and safety systems, along with reasonable health and safety standards will be critical to substitute for simple conservative standards and bans.

Capturing and Sharing Benefits Equitably

Businesses and individuals can sometimes capture unfair benefits from their activities or shift costs and responsibilities unreasonably onto others as the balance of responsibilities shifts with changes in technology or market frameworks. The Productivity Commission (2004) has noted that some builders and developers have used performance-based building code provisions to shift costs from the building phase to the operating phase, potentially disadvantaging buyers and occupants. Likewise, it is widely accepted that energy prices will be distorted against sustainable options until a price based on the cost of limiting climate change within safe boundaries is placed on carbon emissions. Policy measures, such as demanding disclosure of performance at time of sale or lease, requirements to demonstrate performance claims, such as the Australian Building Greenhouse Rating scheme commitment agreement for new buildings (ABGR 2007), and monitoring and research to evaluate ongoing performance, can assist.

At the same time, we must create mechanisms so that those who generate benefits for others can capture a share of such benefits. Estimation of life cycle impacts and benefits for the whole of society can provide a basis for determining reasonable incentives for individuals to adopt measures with societal benefits. For example, a developer could be required to pay a charge equivalent to twenty-five years of greenhouse gas emissions from a new building. This requirement would create an incentive to reduce life cycle emissions because absorbing the charge into the price of the developer's building would make it less competitive than low-emission buildings designed using cost-effective strategies. Similar up-front charges could be linked to appliances, equipment and vehicles. Positive incentives could be based on the same approach, paid up-front and linked to life cycle greenhouse benefits. Incentives or fees could apply to water use and material content of products to encourage dematerialization, reuse and recycling. 'Intelligent' baselines can be designed to shift with sales-weighted average performance so that 'free riding' is minimized yet incentives for excellence are maintained.

Managing Trade-offs

Environmental and social impacts and trade-offs associated with distributed energy, water and materials management systems must aim to be effective, technically and socially. Air and noise pollution from distributed energy generation systems are obvious challenges. However, the logistics of managing materials responsibly on small building sites and heritage issues associated with urban consolidation and installation of features such as solar hot water services are also challenges. If utilization of urban biomass for energy increases, effective low-pollution technologies will be increasingly critical.

The late-1980s Brunswick–Richmond Powerline Review, which responded to community concerns by examining the proposing agency as well as the proposed options to establish high voltage powerlines through Melbourne's inner suburbs, and the community consciousness raising movement, Watermark Australia, provide models of community engagement and empowerment to develop improved solutions with multiple benefits and broad consensus. The energy sector has been seriously deficient in such processes. It is also important to develop improved decision-making tools to facilitate more sophisticated choices. For example, the FirstRate house energy rating software allows the designer to select a preferred mix of energy efficiency measures to achieve a required five-star outcome, so that individual circumstances, such as desire for a view or problems with lack of solar access, can be addressed (Reardon 2005, Section 1.10). We need similar tools to guide compliance with density guidelines, protect neighbours' solar access and guide other complex decision making processes.

Establishing More Sustainable Values and Practices

We must challenge our assumptions in practices that have implications for energy consumption. Do we really need open refrigerated display cabinets in supermarkets and extremely bright artificial lighting in retail stores? Is it appropriate to waste energy heating outdoor dining facilities on footpaths? How bright does street lighting really need to be, given that trees often block out much of the light anyway? How much lighting is needed in the middle of the night? Open community processes, education and formal research are needed to confront these issues, accept or change community attitudes and drive change where appropriate.

Fostering Innovation

Achieving practical transitions to sustainability will require us to foster innovation and explore the diversity of possible paths forward while capturing economies of scale and managing the risks of 'stranded assets' (loss of an investment's value). A theoretical example of a stranded asset is an expensive coal-fired power station that cannot be used because it exceeds greenhouse emission targets. We should be wary of investing in large, long-lived, specialized solutions at a time of rapid change and uncertainty.

While economic efficiencies are important, we should remember that short-term economic benefits can mean long-term disadvantages. Often sustainable energy solutions are criticized for being expensive and uneconomic. However, the extra cost of constructing a sustainable home is comparable with installing a quality kitchen and less than one year's depreciation on some car models often seen parked in house driveways. The economic risks associated with making mistakes in the sustainable energy field are small compared, say, with the depreciation cost of cars, expenditure on alcohol and gambling, as long as mistakes do not lead to energy shortages or blackouts. Minimizing the risks of change involves identifying niche opportunities where emerging technologies and services can develop profitably or at least at cost. For example, public advertisers could be required to use solar cells at a cost that is trivial compared with advertising revenue, providing a niche market for developing our solar-cell industry.

Future-Proofing Infrastructure and Equipment

Urban infrastructure and equipment is durable, and inflexibility associated with design may prevent or delay the adoption of sustainable technologies. For example, the cost of installing 'third pipe' (treated effluent) water networks in new subdivisions is low with common trenching. But retrofitting this option is extremely expensive. Similarly, installing wall insulation during the construction of new buildings is much cheaper and more practical than retrofitting it. It could be argued that installing hydrogen-compatible gas pipes in new developments in anticipation of a shift towards hydrogen might be a useful future-proofing strategy. However, inclusion of such features might involve costs that a private or corporate infrastructure provider would refuse to carry or cannot pass on, thus prompting regulation or incentives.

In the future we will need to redesign energy supply systems to more appropriately suit demand for specific services. As an example, maintaining reasonable comfort in hot weather is important to many people and potentially a matter of life or death for certain young, old or ill people. Yet those using air-conditioning are often portrayed as wimps and blamed for blackouts and the higher costs required for occasionally used energy supply infrastructure. We can provide comfort without such costs. A very well-insulated and shaded bedroom can be cooled by a highly efficient air-conditioner using no more energy than a ceiling fan. On-site photovoltaic panels could use the bountiful solar energy available at times when most cooling is required without overloading transmission and distribution networks. It is not an intrinsic problem; perceiving cooling as a 'problem' reflects current service provision through centralized electricity supply systems dominated by capital-intensive inflexible coal-fired power stations.

Limits of 'Renewable' Energy

We need to consider resource limits and other constraints and opportunities associated with renewable energy sources. Because renewable energy sources are dispersed, variable and diffuse, the quantities available for some purposes may be limited. It is critical that aggressive energy efficiency is pursued in parallel with renewables. Cutting the quantity of energy required for services will reduce the cost of sustainable provision to below the total costs of today's energy systems. We need to establish infrastructure to capture renewable energy sources that are wasted currently. For example, urban biomass (grass clippings, tree prunings and waste food) already provides a substantial potential energy resource which active management could substantially increase.

Conclusion

Change happens in ways that are often unexpected, particularly by existing industries and policy makers, who generally apply 'incremental' approaches.

Gas street lighting provides an interesting historical example of the tensions that exist as new energy technologies emerge. In Melbourne, in the late 1890s, gas street lighting was losing its market share to electric lighting. While the innovation of gas mantle lamps meant more light from less gas, so that gas might again compete with electricity, the gas industry was unenthusiastic about a new technology that would reduce gas sales in the short term, even though it meant the industry might have a more viable future. Therefore it was not the gas industry but retailers, McEwans and the Australian Incandescent Light Company, that initially imported the mantles (Proudley 1987, 103).

We face similar problems today as the gas and electricity industries struggle to respond to opportunities of energy efficiency and renewable energy. For example, the regulated financial return to gas network owners in Victoria is linked to the gas sales per kilometre of pipeline. Therefore the five-star energy regulations now mandated in most climatic zones in Australia for new single dwellings will adversely affect revenue by cutting demand for gas heating (MMA 2004), so it was not surprising that the gas industry actively opposed introducing the five-star regulations. Of course, revision of the regulatory framework could resolve this conflict, but this has not occurred.

A key factor underpinning the current policy challenge is the need to manage a period of transition and uncertainty as new solutions emerge and are often less than perfect, or impact on groups previously unaffected, while challenging existing solutions. Throughout this chapter many policy options and issues have been highlighted. The key to success will be use of a wide variety of policy tools that encourage creative responses and protect emerging solutions from the market power of entrenched interests.

References

ABGR (2007), Australian Building Greenhouse Rating [website], <http://www.abgr. com.au>, accessed 15 January 2007.

ABARE (2006), *Australian Energy Consumption and Production 1974–75 to 2004–05* Australian Bureau of Agricultural and Resource Economics [website], Table F1: Australian Energy Consumption, By Industry and Fuel Type – Energy Units [webpage], <http://www.abareconomics.com/interactive/energy/index.html>, accessed 15 June 2006.

ABS (2000), *Household Expenditure Survey 1998–99: Detailed Expenditure Items* [Cat. No. 6535.0] (Canberra: Australian Bureau of Statistics).

ABS (2002), *Business Operations and Industry Performance Australia 2000–01* [Cat. No. 8140.0] (Canberra: Australian Bureau of Statistics).

ABS (2005), *Household Expenditure Survey 2003–04 Summary of Results Australia* [Cat. No. 6530.0] (Canberra: Australian Bureau of Statistics).

AGO (2005a), *Tracking to the Kyoto Target 2005* (Canberra: Australian Greenhouse Office).

AGO (2005b), *Australia's Fourth National Communication on Climate Change* (Canberra: Australian Greenhouse Office).

Commonwealth of Australia (1998), *National Greenhouse Strategy* (Canberra: Australian Greenhouse Office).

CoAG (2002), *Towards a Truly National and Efficient Energy Market Energy Market Review Final Report* (Canberra: Council of Australian Governments/ Commonwealth of Australia).

Crawford, R. and Treloar, G. (2005), 'An Assessment of the Energy and Water Embodied in Commercial Building Construction', [paper] Fourth Australian LCA Conference, February, Sydney [website], <http://lca-conf.alcas.asn.au/2005/ Papers/Crawford_and_Treloar.pdf>, accessed 9 January 2007.

EPA (1998), *Air Emissions Inventory Port Phillip Region* (Melbourne: Environment Protection Authority).

ESAA (2004), *Summary of Statistics 2002–03* Energy Supply Association of Australia [website], <http://www.esaa.com.au>, accessed 3 July 2004.

ESAA (2005), *Electricity Gas Australia 2005* (Sydney: Energy Supply Association of Australia).

ESC (2006), *Energy: Our Role* Essential Services Commission [website], <www.esc.vic.gov.au/public/Energy/Our+Role.htm>, accessed 6 December 2006.

Greenhouse Gas Reduction Scheme (2007), [website], <http://www.greenhousegas.nsw.gov.au/ >, accessed 10 January 2007.

Hunnekes, C. (2004), 'Germany: photovoltaic technology status and prospects', International Energy Agency [website], <http://www.iea-pvps.org/ar03/deu.htm>, accessed 20 December 2006.

MMA (2004), *Economic Analysis of Impact of BCA and Plumbing Regulations on Gas Supply to New Estates* [Report to Department of Infrastructure and the Sustainable Energy Authority] (South Melbourne: McLennan Magasanik Associates).

Newton, P., Baum, S., Bhatia, K., Brown, S., Cameron, A., Foran, B., Grant, T., Mak, S., Memmott, P., Mitchell, V., Neate, K., Pears, A., Smith, N., Stimson, R., Tucker, S. and Yencken, D. (2001), *Human Settlements, Australia. State of the Environment Report 2001* [Theme Report] (Canberra: CSIRO Publishing for Department of the Environment and Heritage), available at the CSIRO Publishing [website], <http://www.publish.csiro.au/pid/3002.htm>.

Ofgem (2005), 'Environmental Action Plan Annual Review 2004/5'. Archived Publications [webpage], Ofgem [website], <http://www.ofgem.gov.uk>, accessed 30 January 2006.

Pears, A. (2006), 'The National Picture', *ReNew: Technology for a Sustainable Future* 95, 50–51.

Productivity Commission (2004), *Reform of Building Regulation Research Report* (Melbourne: Productivity Commission).

Proudley, R. (1987), *Circle of Influence: A History of the Gas Industry in Victoria* (North Melbourne: Hargreen Publishing).

Reardon, C. (ed.) (2005), *Your Home Technical Manual,* 3rd Edition. (Canberra: Commonwealth of Australia, Department of the Environment and Heritage, Australian Greenhouse Office).

RCG/Hagler Bailly and SRC Australia (1993), *Externalities Policy Development Project: Energy Sector – Selected Externality Values* (East Melbourne: Department of Energy and Minerals).

Saddler, H., Diesendorf, M. and Denniss, R. (2004), *A Clean Energy Future for Australia* (Sydney: Clean Energy Future Group and World Wildlife Fund).

Smil, V. (2003), *Energy at the Crossroads* (Massachusetts: MIT Press).

Thornton, K. and Washusen, J. (2005), *Impediments to Grid Connection of Solar Photovoltaic: the Consumer Experience,* Alternative Technology Association [website], <http://www.ata.org.au/wp-content/policy/impediments_to_grid_connection.pdf>, accessed 9 January 2007.

Yencken, D. and Williamson, D. (2000), *Resetting the Compass: Australia's Journey Towards Sustainability* (Collingwood: CSIRO Publishing).

Chapter 7

Sustainable Transport in Urban Neighbourhoods: Policy Approaches, User Responses

Jan Scheurer

Introduction

When viewed from a user perspective, reducing car travel in contemporary cities poses a specific challenge of coordination between demand and supply-based approaches in housing policy and urban planning. Experience suggests that buildings designed with resource saving technologies deliver comparative benefits regardless of their inhabitants' lifestyle choices (Gestring et al. 1997; Jensen 1994). Similarly, programs to build grassroots awareness and behavioural change often achieve improvements in sustainability performance independent of building or neighbourhood design and infrastructure. However, coordinating these approaches is highly desirable due to the synergies it can engender. With regard to sustainable transport behaviour, it can be described as imperative (Scheurer 2001).

Attempting to reduce car dependence, car use or car ownership immediately demonstrates the collective nature of transport networks. There is a frustrating paradox here: infrastructure for non-motorized modes and public transport services cannot improve sustainability performance unless significant numbers of transport users choose them. Conversely, an individual's best intentions of reducing their car use remains thwarted where infrastructure, services and urban form fail to offer acceptable alternatives.

This chapter argues that a key driver for progress in urban transport sustainability is innovative and experimental stakeholder relationships at various institutional and informal levels. The determinants of transport behaviour are examined from a user perspective, before highlighting the physical and social incentives required to promote non-car modes in local areas. In conclusion, some practical approaches to implement these insights on the ground are discussed.

Transport energy consumption and environmental impacts can be influenced by many factors beyond those raised in this chapter. Alternative transport fuels can increase or decrease environmental impacts, depending on their sources. Improving vehicle fuel efficiency is a critical means of reducing impacts per vehicle kilometre, while ongoing improvements in engine technology, linked to tighter fuel quality standards, are cutting some forms of pollution. However, such measures do not necessarily contribute to reductions in the overall amount of travel. In some cases they may even encourage more travel as the cost of transport decreases. Increasing capabilities of telecommunications and computers mean that many tasks that traditionally required travel can be conducted without travelling or by using less transport, though it is debateable whether these opportunities practically translate into lifestyles and logistic chains of reduced travel.

Neighbourhoods and Travel Patterns

Until the 1990s, transport and mobility were rarely included in toolboxes for instigating sustainable urban development in neighbourhoods, even though the extent and character of travel behaviour are quite clearly connected to the internal layout, functional diversity and interactivity of a locale. Rudlin and Falk (1999) note that it is possible to design an ecological neighbourhood featuring a host of resource-saving technologies and behavioural incentives in locales largely disconnected from the existing settlement context. This neighbourhood will be totally car-dependent whenever its members need to travel outside of it, offsetting many of the resource savings achieved within the community. Conversely, a highly accessible inner urban neighbourhood with inherently low car use may show better overall energy performance, even if the buildings are not designed to high standards of resource efficiency and residents are not resource conscious.

Therefore, there is an emerging trend to pay greater attention to the links between different aspects of transport infrastructure and mobility behaviour, in a quest to further the potential of reform towards more sustainable cities and neighbourhoods. Simultaneously, there is a more differentiated understanding of the concept of mobility and its relation to the various dimensions of urban space and the activities of transport users now. Jahn and Wehling (1999, 130) distinguish between:

- the physical-geographical space *(räumliche Mobilität)*, where mobility is determined by the availability and quality of technology and infrastructure, and therefore the ability to traverse physical distance efficiently and rapidly;
- the socio-physical space *(sozial-räumliche Mobilität)*, where mobility is determined by the cohesion and multiplicity of urban and local communities, economies and environments, and thus the ability to satisfy everyday needs and attend social activities outside the home conveniently and through minimum investment of time and money; and
- the socio-cultural space *(sozio-kulturelle Mobilität)*, where mobility is determined by aspirations and lifestyle preferences, and thus by the ability to participate in activities and expressions that are indicative of such choices and their associated social milieu.

A relatively widely discussed approach to explain the complex effects of lifestyles on mobility patterns concerns the conundrum between residential location, travel intensity and preferred travel modes. Different precincts of the city have specific characteristics that make them more or less attractive to groups aspiring to different lifestyles. Often these characteristics are connected to parameters of functionality, proximity and density.

Chandra (2005) and Newman and Kenworthy (1999) compiled a range of findings consistently showing that total distance travelled and the modal share of trips in cars increase with distance between place of residence and city centres. The most plausible explanation is that inner urban areas generally offer more opportunities within walking and cycling range and better public transport services, but pose constraints to unhindered car use (such as road congestion and limited, costly parking), while this situation is the opposite in outer suburbs. However, in reality numerous other variables exist.

Two Norwegian studies (Hjorthol 1998; Næss et al. 1995) confirm the tendency for car use to grow with distance of residence from a city centre, while revealing that public transit use and non-motorized travel do not simply reverse this pattern. The most prolific public transport users were residents of middle suburban areas with adequate public transport service and infrastructure (usually post-war settlers, not functionally integrated). In densely built-up inner areas and small towns on the urban fringe, non-motorized travel was more prevalent, and public transport use showed less correlation with the quality of service. As an explanation, it is suggested that inner urban residents enjoy better conditions for non-motorized mobility and thus have a choice of transport modes for many trips, while suburban residents effectively depend on motorized modes for most travel needs. Thus, the characteristics of the residential neighbourhood as such – accessibility of services, internal density, interactivity and integration of public transport – play a significant role.

However, Røe (1999) found that there was a much higher potential for non-motorized modes and public transit to substitute for each other where conditions were conducive than for either separately to reduce typical car use for the location. Moreover, an even jobs–housing balance in the spirit of urban decentralization appears offset by cross-commuting between suburbs and districts in environments of high access and low cost of motorized mobility. 'People do not choose where to live mainly because of the distance to work' (Næss et al. 1995, 350; see Sager 2005 too).

Gwiasda (1999), in a study on travel patterns in several precincts of Cologne, Germany, concluded that potential travel demand savings vary considerably between purposes of trips. The location of retail facilities near dwellings appears to encourage short shopping trips across all income groups. Residents in every study area allocated similar travel time budgets to shopping trips. Residents with shops nearby were far more likely to walk or cycle to them, and to visit more places. In the field of leisure, correlations between facilities within a precinct and their use by local residents are less pronounced, probably reflecting a widespread propensity to maintain social networks and organize associated activities over larger geographical areas. Repeated changes of residence and/or workplace usually have little effect on preferences for leisure activities.

Røe (1999) and Hjorthol (1998) agree that the activities of inner urban Norwegian households tend to be largely self-contained within a broader central area, particularly for entertainment and recreation, where choice of destination is more discretionary than for most other trip purposes. This is not surprising, since most cultural and entertainment facilities are centralized in Oslo, the capital. Inner urban residents use them more frequently than suburban residents. In contrast, shopping patterns appear

Table 7.1 Mobility styles in Freiburg

Mobility Style Group	Characteristics	Suggested Marketing Strategies	Modal Split by Trips	
Domestic Traditionalists (24%)	Conservative or unpronounced views. Value family and material security. Inconspicuous mode choices. Below-average number of trips and travel distance. Large share of seniors.	Promotion of public transport in conventional media, focusing on value-for-money aspect. Special fares for seniors. Improvements to pedestrian environment in neighbourhoods.	Car	36%
			Public Transport	15%
			Non-Motorized	49%
Risk-Oriented Car Enthusiasts (20%)	Cars – and, to some extent, bicycles – are regarded as symbols of independence and objects of technological fascination. Risky, aggressive drivers. Almost exclusively males.	Expansion of bicycle infrastructure to cater for faster movement and greater challenges. Campaigns on road safety (emotive message) and fuel-efficient driving (technical message).	Car	62%
			Public Transport	5%
			Non-Motorised	33%

Group	Characteristics	Policy recommendations	Mode	
Status-Oriented Motorists (15%)	Cars are regarded as symbols of status and participation. Car use perceived to be essential for leisure purposes. Safety concerns about walking and cycling. Aversion to public transport. Predominantly females.	Supply of status vehicles with car-sharing organizations. Image campaign for public transport, first class compartments and security staff. Prestigious bicycle training courses.	Car	54%
			Public Transport	12%
			Non-Motorized	34%
Nature-Oriented Traditionalists (24%)	Affinity to nature and to slow movement. Positive attitude to walking, cycling and public transport. Negative attitude to cars, though safety concerns sometimes lead to a preference for car use. Predominantly females.	Awareness campaigns on safety in public spaces and on public transport. Expansion of bicycle infrastructure to cater for slow movement. Separation of walking and cycling paths.	Car	25%
			Public Transport	18%
			Non-Motorized	57%
Decided Environmentalists (17%)	High affinity to cycling. Support public transport. Reject car for sustainability concerns. Predominantly younger people.	Material and symbolic incentives to discontinue car ownership (wrecking bounties, guaranteed ride home schemes). Better coordination of modes (such as rail-bicycle) with web-based, interactive information.	Car	15%
			Public Transport	25%
			Non-Motorized	60%

Source: Data derived from Götz (1999, 314–22) and Götz, K. et al. (1997)

to coevolve with local conditions. Inner urban households perform more frequent, impulsive, shorter, mostly non-motorized trips to shops. Suburban residents tend to plan less frequent shopping trips but are more likely to use cars and choose shopping facilities outside their neighbourhood. Snellen et al. (1999) report a comparable pattern from a survey in Dutch cities, where 70 per cent of weekday grocery shopping is non-motorized, while on weekends 48 per cent of shopping trips are made by car over longer distances.

Demographic differences, such as a higher number of young adult households and fewer households with children in inner urban neighbourhoods, can partly explain these observations. In addition, Hjorthol (1998) emphasizes that levels of education, gender and family size do influence mode choice – females, respondents with higher degrees and people with fewer children were found to use non-car modes more for most purposes. But Hjorthol (1998, 213) lends equal importance to the impression that inner urban residents are attracted to their environment precisely because its diversity and fine-grained structure reflect their aspiration to experience the city's 'character and soul'. At the periphery, residential aspirations revolve more around qualities such as easy access to nature and integration into a village community, ideals reported in the German case studies in Gestring et al. (1997).

Characterizing Styles of Mobility

In applying a combination of qualitative and quantitative instruments, the studies discussed indicate that any valid exploration of the lifestyle dimensions of measurable travel behaviour necessarily requires more than numerical analysis of transport statistics. Thus the difficult task of bringing together disciplines that have long led separated lives – social science, traditionally lacking spatial references, and transport research, traditionally blind to behavioural motives other than personal economic rationalism (Hesse and Trostorff 2000; Røe 1999). An outstanding example is Götz's (1999) approach to improving public transit, walking and cycling by investigating the underlying motivations and symbolic content of mode choice, and applying a classification of mobility styles for target-group specific marketing. Götz argues that mobility cannot be understood without integrating physical (movement), social (accessibility) and reflected (social positioning) aspects. The database acquired through surveying in Freiburg, Germany, helped identify clusters of lifestyle parameters and mobility styles with suggestions for marketing of sustainable transport modes. These strategies integrate elements of soft and hard policy for simultaneous application to unfold their synergistic potential. The five mobility styles drawn from the Freiburg sample and described in detail in Götz et al. (1997) and Götz (1999, 314–22) are summarized in Table 7.1.

The travel choices of the five groups that appear in Figure 7.1 originate from different dimensions of mobility, and of self (Jensen 1999). In the two groups labelled 'traditionalists', cultural/authentic aspects stand out as the dominant motivations for travel behaviour. Choices of transport modes and activity patterns evolve from a person's values and beliefs. The marketing strategies suggested were devised to reaffirm these beliefs but influence/change behaviour. Clearly, support from these two groups is crucial to build a popular majority for sustainable transport and to reduce car travel in mainstream society. However, neither group is expected to be susceptible to behavioural change perceived as radical, extravagant, or an agenda of political elites (Götz et al. 1997). In contrast, the mobility behaviour of 'status-oriented motorists' is largely determined by status awareness (Jensen 1999) so the suggested marketing approaches attempt to promote the status content of more sustainable behavioural choices, to induce individuals to reflect on their behaviour and reposition themselves in their societal roles.

The 'risk-oriented motorists' and 'decided environmentalists' act primarily from motives to transparently position themselves socially through choices of mobility behaviour (Jensen 1999). The affinity to respective preferred modes of transport derives from symbolic values and capacities to express a set of subjective persuasions, aspirations and affections. Thus suggested marketing strategies have a substantial content of emotional appeal aiming to affirm and intensify pre-existing behavioural impulses that appear desirable from a perspective of sustainable mobility. Under prevailing mobility conditions these groups offer less scope for practical behaviour change than the previous three (Götz et al. 1997).

Jahn and Wehling (1999, 134–8) describe how, in a programmatic framework of mobility management, such marketing approaches could translate into actor and target-group specific packages of instruments to foster a process of 'uncoupling mobility from automobility'. On a local level, it appears sensible to initiate such programs with groups or firms amenable to acting as *pioneers*, because they will generate noticeable impulses on changing mobility patterns and reliable markets for new mobility services. Of course Jahn and Wehling (1999) emphasize that the paradigm shift must eventuate in the three complementary realms identified earlier: spatial (physical) mobility, socio-spatial mobility (accessibility) and socio-cultural mobility.

In this context, Holzapfel (1997, 78–89) speaks of a dichotomy of lifestyle regimes, which he terms 'distance-intensive' *(entfernungsintensiv)* and 'experience-intensive' *(erfahrungsintensiv)*. In lieu of pursuing a moralistic approach towards ecological goals which, he argues, tends to consolidate the status quo rather than foster change, he emphasizes the need to promote an experience-intensive lifestyle incorporating proximity interactions, slowness and diversity as richer and more fulfilling than the predominant distance-intensive model. The attraction of experience-intensive lifestyles is not least seen in the reinstatement of personal autonomy over time, which has been largely lost in a quest to maximize autonomy over space through unhindered motorized mobility. Thus, it is recognized that top-down intervention is unsuitable for this task, and the question of how individuals really respond to the challenge of adjusting their mobility patterns to sustainability principles, regardless of where such a challenge may come from, remains open.

Use of Urban Space

By providing parameters for density, concentration and mix of land uses, planners determine conditions of movement within neighbourhoods (Barton 2000; Carmona et al. 2003; Newman and Kenworthy 1999). Total distances travelled and proportionate car use are usually lowest where neighbourhoods are closely integrated with the surrounding urban fabric, functionally and spatially connected to central facilities, which facilitates non-motorized travel, and where attractive public transport links exist to all relevant adjacent centres (Næss 1995; Taylor 2003).

Certain minimum densities of activities, population and jobs per hectare are necessary to generate sufficient levels of social and commercial interaction within easy walking distance from homes, so that numbers of journeys remain within the neighbourhood. The ideal settlement density required to bring about such benefits is contested (Mees 2000). However, New Urbanism-inspired planning and design guidelines in Australia, emerging since the late 1990s (for example, Department of Infrastructure 2002; WAPC 2000) seem to point to a critical subcentre size of 10,000 residents and jobs, and an optimal ratio of 1.5 jobs per residential household or around one job per two residents (Morris and Kaufman 1996; Newman 2003). Taking a walkable 800-metre radius around a 200 ha subcentre suggests a minimum density of fifty residents and jobs per hectare if the entire catchment area is developed, and a proportionally greater density in areas of geographical constraints or if existing land uses are resilient to redevelopment.

When density and multifunctionality focus on the neighbourhood centre, ideally clustered around the principal public transit station and decreasing towards the perimeter (Duany 2003; Taylor 2003), this tends to improve residents' access to public transport and important service facilities (Murray and Wu 2003) and contributes to lower energy use in transport (Næss et al. 1995).

To make walking within neighbourhoods attractive, it is critical to prioritize or at least provide equal rights to pedestrians over motorized traffic along internal road and path networks and to draw clear boundaries between public and private or semi-private spaces (Apel et al. 1997; Rudlin and Falk 1999). Employing traffic calming techniques, such as designing all vehicular roads for low speeds (30 km/h or less) and a legible, comfortable and direct network of pedestrian routes (Hathway 2000) best achieve this outcome. The elimination of physical barriers, particularly for wheelchair users, serves a similar purpose. Besides promoting non-motorized modes, such measures ensure that streets, squares and open spaces meet circulation needs and encourage civic interaction, thus restoring the vital social functions of open space (Engwicht 1998; Gehl 2001).

Services in urban public transport networks must be frequent and offer viable alternatives to car use (Laube 1998; Mees 2000). At least during the day, frequencies should be high enough to eliminate the need to consult a timetable (with headways less than 12–15 minutes). Regular service should continue during evenings and weekends, preferably making some provision for use 24 hours a day, ensuring users a permanent choice (Nobis 1999). The network should connect well, with easy transfers between routes, and reflect a hierarchical settlement pattern of central places and corridors (Scheurer 2006; Vuchic 2005). In medium-sized and large cities, a spoked network of rail routes supported by local and orbital buses meet such requirements better than a bus-only system. Rail enables travel speeds that are more competitive with cars and facilitates market support for policies of land-use concentration and densification around transit stations (Newman and Kenworthy 1999; Scheurer et al. 2005).

The interspersion and density hierarchy of a neighbourhood and configuration of public transport networks are effectively *supply-side* parameters influencing mobility patterns. Managing *travel demand* is another avenue of policy intervention. Individual choices of travel mode and destination do not always follow strictly rational, functional or predictable criteria (Jahn and Wehling 1999; Sager 2005). Superior sustainability performance cannot be achieved only by alterations to urban form, infrastructure and neighbourhood design (Holz-Rau 2001). Mobility policies need to extend to engaging with transport users, to instigate changes in their practical decisions, habitual socio-cultural behaviour, and environmental awareness about mobility.

Parking Cars and Bicycles

Often the most pressing neighbourhood issue is the impact of residents' vehicles, particularly with respect to dwellings. Parking spaces and facilities for vehicular access add substantially to housing costs, take up valuable open space, and reduce residential density (Newman and Kenworthy 1999; Tönnes 1997). Over the last fifty years housing policy makers have been concerned to maximize parking space without compromising residential standards. However, recently, attempts have been made increasingly to substantially raise amenity and housing affordability by limiting the share of land dedicated to cars. Incentives to reduce or eliminate excessive car ownership include:

- Separating the marketing of units and parking spaces, thus making the costs of car parks more explicit.
- Concentrating non-dedicated parking facilities in neighbourhood perimeters, to create traffic-free interiors and to privilege access to centrally located public transport.
- Exempting non-car owning households or employees from mandatory parking provisions.
- Suspending parking provision requirements in planning schemes, to target residential developments exclusively for households without cars, improving housing affordability and open space, particularly in areas of high density.

While policy makers have paid attention to supplying increasing car parking space, they have been complacent towards accommodating bicycles (Hathway 2000). Where bicycle parks exist, they are often insufficiently sheltered against adverse weather conditions, theft and vandalism, too small, and located in areas such as basements not immediately accessible from the street. Overcoming such shortfalls, and providing adequate infrastructure for bicycle riders, can assist in reducing car dependence, particularly in areas with lower densities and less functional integration, where public transit and walking are inherently limited (Apel et al. 1997; Næss and Jensen 2000).

Car-Sharing and Mobility Services

Mobility services to facilitate lifestyles with low car use supplement disincentives for car ownership through fewer car parks. Originally initiated by informal networks, car-sharing is dominated now by professional and commercial organizations in many European cities (Wagner and Shaheen 1998). Membership in a car-sharing organization provides access to a pool of different-sized vehicles within a neighbourhood or distributed across the city and, in some cases, several cities. Instant bookings are made using telephone or Internet, and payment is per hour and/or per kilometre. All vehicle acquisition, maintenance, insurance and operation costs, including petrol, rest with the car-sharing organization, relieving users from private car ownership responsibilities.

Similar schemes are conceivable, and practised, for sharing bicycles, bicycle trailers and other non-motorized vehicles (Nobis 1999). Car-sharing schemes have begun to attract other industry players; in Switzerland vehicles are allocated to railway stations to enable rail travellers to reach dispersed destinations, and housing developers save costs by offering parks for shared vehicles (Bäumer 2004). Such collaborations challenge the prevailing paradigm of private car ownership and reduce the amount of vehicles in circulation yet offer similar mobility benefits (Jahn and Wehling 1999).

Other mobility services include providing discounted and free periodical public transit tickets and discounting rail passes with the purchase/lease of housing units or through neighbourhood associations. User-friendly, inexpensive or free, home-delivery services by retailers, deliveries to authorized concierges in multi-unit developments, and/or via luggage trolleys, are substitutes for shopping trips.

This summary of travel-conscious design and mobility management techniques in neighbourhoods exemplifies the significance of integration of supply and demand-side policy approaches, and of collaborations between decision-making organizations and housing and transport users. Obviously supply-side measures to improve urban design or transport infrastructure tend to lack depth if unaccompanied by programs to influence user behaviour. Similarly, attempts to raise mobility awareness and induce behavioural adjustments may be futile if users fail to find a supportive physical environment and sustainable level of transport services. Combining 'hard' and 'soft' policies is crucial to achieve better sustainability performance. There is an emerging consensus that viable transport policies require significant demand management components, indicating the beginning of a fruitful collaboration between social policy and transport policy.

Practical Implications

How can we integrate distinct, lifestyle-derived individual and collective motivations for travel behaviour into local strategies and start to overcome the traditional division of top-down regulatory planning and bottom-up user-responsive visions? During the last decade, steps have been taken in some cities to depart from indiscriminate and ubiquitous parking provision in new residential developments often mandated in local planning regulations. Such approaches use any combination of measures introduced above, such as: separate marketing to make car parking costs explicit; excluding motorized traffic from all or part of a residential area; and relaxing parking provision requirements generally, at a statutory level.

In successful examples, such as the new Freiburg-Vauban neighbourhood and Tübingen's French Quarter in Germany (Soehlke 1999, Sperling 1999), tangible reductions in car ownership resulted from effective social contracts between stakeholders, spelling out each party's rights and responsibilities. Governments receive guarantees that parking reductions will not generate spill-over effects elsewhere or result in deteriorating traffic conditions, developers obtain access to the market for car-reduced housing, and residents become confident that commitment to a car-reduced lifestyle will be supported by future governments and businesses (Bellaire 2000).

In the increasingly dense Australian inner suburbs, there is an emerging trend away from rigid numerical statutory mandates for parking provision to performance-based standards to strengthen the roles of developers and users. Typically, this is achieved in tandem with a blanket ban on additional developments accessing on-street resident-only parking permit schemes, which have reached capacity in many places (City of Melbourne 2005). Thus developers may choose to save costs by offering lower than average parking to buyers with lower than average car ownership. Users gain greater choice between housing units, with parking provisions matching their needs. Conversely, inaccessibility of on-street parking to new developments may encourage developers to increase on-site parking, providing an incentive for car ownership. It is too early to quantify such effects.

In European cities, marketing campaigns maximizing pro-public transport behaviour change often supplement public transport infrastructure projects. In Australia large-scale extensions of public transport systems have been less common recently (Scheurer et al. 2005), yet individualized marketing campaigns are still employed within 'TravelSmart', travel demand management programs funded by federal and State governments. Thus, TravelSmart is often effectively limited to mobilizing latent demand for existing public transport services or to supporting service, not infrastructure, improvements. TravelSmart has had well-documented successes (James and Brög 2003), but its scope to shift travel to non-car modes is limited (Scheurer 2005). There are concerns that some evaluations have overstated its impact (Morton and Mees 2005).

The potential and limitations of campaigns such as TravelSmart highlight the need for policy integration and constructive relationships between stakeholders to effect change from car dependence towards sustainable modes of transport. Policy measures in support of sustainable transport, at local, metropolitan, national and international levels, are unlikely to alter the workings of a city, its people and its culture, if pursued in isolation. They need to be part of broad policy packages where success in one area can breed further initiatives and support self-reinforcing, 'virtuous cycles' of reform (Kaufmann 2000) towards better sustainability performance in urban mobility.

94   *Steering Sustainability in an Urbanizing World*

References

Aalborg Universitet (ed.) (1999), *Byøkologisk Velfærdsudvikling: Livsstil, Arkitektur og Ressourcekredsløb* (Aalborg: Aalborg Universitet).

Apel, D., Lehmbrock, M., Pharoah, T. and Thiemann-Linden, J. (1997), *Kompakt, Mobil, Urban: Stadtentwicklungskonzepte zur Verkehrsvermeidung im Internationalen Vergleich* (Berlin: Deutsches Institut für Urbanistik).

Barton, H. (ed.) (2000), *Sustainable Communities: The Potential for Eco-Neighbourhoods* (London: Earthscan).

Bäumer, D. (2004), 'Come Together: Involving Housing Companies in Mobility Management Action', *Proceedings 8th European Conference on Mobility Management*, Lyon, France, 5–7 May. ECOMM [website], <www.epomm.org/ecomm2004/workshops/anglais/baumer.pdf>, accessed 12 January 2007.

Bellaire, N. (2000), 'Wohnen Ohne Auto. Planung und Realisierung Autofreier und Autoreduzierter Quartiere in Nordrhein-Westfalen', *RaumPlanung* 90: June, 123–7.

Brunsing, J. and Frehn, M. (eds) (1999), *Stadt der Kurzen Wege. Zukunftsfähiges Leitbild oder Planerische Utopie?* (Dortmund: Institut für Raumplanung).

Carmona, M., Heath, T., Oc, T. and Tiesdell, S. (2003), *Public Places – Urban Spaces: The Dimensions of Urban Design* (Oxford: Architectural Press).

Chandra, L. (2005), 'Modelling the Impact of Urban Form and Transport Provision on Transport-Related Greenhouse Gas Emissions' [Masters thesis] Submitted to the Institute for Sustainability and Technology Policy, Murdoch University (Western Australia).

City of Melbourne (2005), *Carlton Parking and Access Strategy* City of Melbourne [website], <http://www.melbourne.vic.gov.au>, accessed 12 September 2005.

Department of Infrastructure (2002), *Melbourne 2030: Planning for Sustainable Growth* (Melbourne: Department of Infrastructure).

Duany, A. (2003), 'Neighbourhood Design in Practice', in Neal (ed.).

Engwicht, D. (1998), *Street Reclaiming: Creating Liveable Streets and Vibrant Communities* (Annandale: New Society Publishers).

Friedrichs, J. and Hollaender, K. (eds) (1999), *Stadtökologische Forschung. Theorien und Anwendungen* (Berlin: Analytica).

Gehl, J. (2001), *Life Between Buildings: Using Public Space,* 5th Edition. (Copenhagen: Danish Architectural Press).

Gestring, N., Heine, H., Mautz, R., Mayer, H. and Siebel, W. (1997), *Ökologie und Urbane Lebensweise. Untersuchungen Zu Einem Anscheinend Unauflöslichen Widerspruch* (Braunschweig/Wiesbaden: Vieweg).

Götz, K. (1999), 'Mobilitätsstile – Folgerungen Für Zielgruppenspezifisches', in Friedrichs and Hollaender (eds).

Götz, K., Jahn, T. and Schultz, I. (1997), *Mobilitätsstile – Ein Sozial-Ökologischer Untersuchungsansatz* [Forschungsbericht Stadtverträgliche Mobilität, Band 7] (Frankfurt: CITY:mobil Forschungsverbund).

Gwiasda, P. (1999), 'Nutzungsmischung – Stadt der Kurzen Wege für die Bewohner?', in Brunsing and Frehn (eds).

Hathway, T. (2000), 'Planning Local Movement Systems' in Barton (ed.).

Hesse, M. and Trostorff, B. (2000) *Raumstrukturen, Siedlungsentwicklung und Verkehr – Interaktionen und Integrationsmöglichkeiten* [Diskussionspapier] (Erkner: Institut für Regionalentwicklung und Strukturplanung).

Hjorthol, R. (1998), 'Reurbanisation and Its Potential for the Reduction of Car Use: An Analysis of Preferences of Residence, Activity and Travel Pattern in the Oslo Area', *Scandinavian Housing and Planning Research* 15, 211–26.

Holz-Rau, C. (2001), 'Bessere Organisation Statt Mehr Infrastruktur', *Verkehrszeichen* 17: 1, 12–17.

Holzapfel, H. (1997), *Autonomie Statt Auto: Zum Verhältnis von Lebensstil, Umwelt und Ökonomic am Beispiel des Verkehrs* (Bonn: Economica).

Institut für Landes- und Stadtentwicklungsforschung NRW (ed.) (1997), *Planung und Realisierung Autoarmer Stadtquartiere: Anforderungen – Konzepte – Chancen der Umsetzung* (Dortmund: Institut für Raumplanung).

Jahn, T. and Wehling, P. (1999), 'Das Mehrdimensionale Mobilitätskonzept: Ein Theoretischer Rahmen für die Stadtökologische Mobilitätsforschung', in Friedrichs and Hollaender (eds).

James, B. and Brög, W. (2003), 'TravelSmart/Individualised Marketing in Perth, Western Australia', in Tolley (ed.).

Jensen, O. (1994), 'Ecological Building – or Just Environmentally Sound Planning?', *Arkitektur DK* 7, 353–67.

Jensen, O. (1999), 'Livsstilsrum – Udkast Til En Teori Om Livsform, Livsstil Og Stil', in Aalborg Universitet (ed.).

Kaufmann, V. (2000), 'Modal Practices: From the Rationales Behind Car and Public Transport Use to Coherent Transport Policies', *World Transport Policy and Practice* 6:3, 8–17.

Laube, F. (1998), 'Optimising Urban Passenger Transport' [PhD thesis] Submitted to Murdoch University (Western Australia).

Mees, P. (2000), *A Very Public Solution: Transport in the Dispersed City* (Melbourne: Melbourne University Press).

Morris W. and Kaufman, C. (1996), *Mixed Use Development: New Designs for New Livelihoods* (Brisbane: Queensland Department of Tourism, Small Business and Industry).

Morton, A. and Mees, P. (2005), 'Too Good to Be True? An Assessment of the Melbourne Travel Behaviour Modification Pilot', *Proceedings of the 28th Australasian Transport Research Forum*, Sydney, Australia, 28–30 September. PATREC [website], <www.patrec.org/atrf/papers/2005/Morton%20&%20Mees %20(2005).pdf>, accessed 16 January 2007.

Murray, A. and Wu, X. (2003), 'Accessibility Tradeoffs in Public Transit Planning', *Journal of Geographical Systems* 5, 93–107.

Næss, P. (1995), *Urban Form and Energy Use for Transport: A Nordic Experience.* [Doktor Ingeniøravhandling] (Trondheim: Norges Tekniske Høgskole).

Næss, P. and Jensen, O. (2000), *Boliglokalisering og Transport i Frederikshavn* (Aalborg: Aalborg Universitet).

Næss, P., Røe, P. and Larsen, S. (1995), 'Travelling Distances, Modal Split and Transportation Energy in 30 Residential Areas in Oslo', *Journal of Environmental Planning and Management* 38:3, 349–70.

Neal, P. (ed.) (2003), *Urban Villages and the Making of Communities* (London: Spon Press).

Newman, P. (2003), 'Building Sustainability into Metropolitan Planning', [Unpublished paper] Metropolitan Planning, Development and Design Summit, Melbourne, Australia, 23–24 October.

Newman, P. and Kenworthy, J. (1999), *Sustainability and Cities – Overcoming Automobile Dependence* (Washington: Island Press).

Nobis, C. (1999), 'Neue Mobilität', in Sperling (ed.)

Rudlin, D. and Falk, N. (1999), *Building the 21st Century Home. The Sustainable Urban Neighbourhood* (Oxford: Architectural Press).

Røe, P. (1999), 'Intra-Urban Travel and Spatial-Structural Constraints: An Investigation of Travel and Activity Patterns in 30 Residential Areas in Oslo', [Unpublished paper] 13th AESOP Congress, Bergen, Norway, 7–11 July.

Sager, T. (2005), 'Footloose and Forecast-Free: Hypermobility and the Planning of Society', [Unpublished paper] AESOP Congress, Vienna, Austria, 13–16 July.

Scheurer, J. (2001), 'Urban Ecology, Innovations in Housing Policy and the Future of Cities: Towards Sustainability in Neighbourhood Communities' [PhD thesis] Submitted to the Institute for Sustainability and Technology Policy, Murdoch Unversity (Western Australia).

Scheurer, J. (2005), 'Achieving Mode Share Targets in Australian Cities through Policy Integration: Are We on Track?' *Urban Policy and Research* 23: 4, 525–30.

Scheurer, J. (2006), *Moving People in Melbourne's North-East* (Melbourne: Metropolitan Transport Forum).

Scheurer, J., Kenworthy, J. and Newman, P. (2005), *Most Liveable and Best Connected? The Economic Benefits of Investing in Public Transport in Melbourne* (Melbourne: Metropolitan Transport Forum).

Snellen, D., Borgers, A. and Timmermans, H. (1999), The Influence of Urban Form on Activity Patterns: Aspects of Data Collection in Nine Dutch Cities, [Unpublished paper] 13th AESOP Congress, Bergen, 7–11 July.

Soehlke, C. (1999), *Stadt mit Eigenschaften. Tübingen – Städtebaulicher Entwicklungsbereich Stuttgarter Straße/Französisches Viertel* (Tübingen: Stadtsanierungsamt Tübingen).

Sperling, C. (ed.) (1999), *Nachhaltige Stadtentwicklung beginnt im Quartier: Ein Praxis- und Ideenhandbuch für Stadtplaner, Baugemeinschaften, Bürgerinitiativen am Beispiel des sozial-ökologischen Modellstadtteils Freiburg-Vauban* (Freiburg: Forum Vauban/Öko-Institut).

Taylor, D. (2003), 'Connectivity and Movement', in Neal, P. (ed.).

Tolley, R. (ed.) (2003), *Sustainable Transport: Planning for Walking and Cycling in Urban Environments* (Cambridge: Woodhead Publishing).

Tönnes, M. (1997), 'Weniger Kosten — Mehr Wohnen. Die ökonomischen Vorteile Autofreier Wohnquartiere', in Institut für Landes- und Stadtentwicklungsforschung NRW (ed.).

Vuchic, V. (2005), *Urban Transit: Operation, Planning and Economics* (Hoboken: John Wiley and Sons).

Wagner, C. and Shaheen, S. (1998), 'Car Sharing and Mobility Management: Facing New Challenges with Technology and Innovative Business Planning', *World Transport Policy and Practice* 4: 2, 39–43.

WAPC (2000), *Liveable Neighbourhoods. A Western Australian Government Sustainable Cities Initiative*, 2nd Edition (Perth: Western Australian Planning Commission).

Chapter 8

Indicators, Audits and Measuring Success

Richard Hyde, Richard Moore, Lydia Kavanagh,
Melinda Watt and Karen Schianetz

Introduction

An increasing number and widening range of environmental assessment tools
have been produced in recent years. However, there has been little discourse over
how successful these tools are in assisting policy makers to meet their objectives.
Building environmental assessment (BEA) tools aim to contribute to the successful
implementation of sustainability policies and initiatives in housing. This chapter
examines the utility of BEA tools for sustainability policy making by addressing a
series of questions:

- Why are BEA systems needed to progress sustainable development?
- What models underlie the main two principles-to-indicator approaches?
- What are the weaknesses of principles-to-indicator methods?
- How are BEAs applied to measure housing sustainability?
- How do BEAs reward best practice?
- What demonstration projects exist?
- What is the significance of BEAs in terms of evidence-based planning
  policy?

Barriers to Ecologically Sustainable Development

A UK study (Wheeler 2003) of sustainable housing revealed some social and
economic, as well as environmental, barriers to achieving ecologically sustainable
development (ESD) and identified six main barriers:

- Fiscal systems involve disincentives.
- Planning systems and regulations confuse rather than support green
  proponents.
- Lack of investor and developer interest.
- Perceived higher costs.
- No agreed standard or definition of sustainability.
- Lack of consumer demand for sustainable houses.

One of the main problems in the UK is lack of a common standard or definition for
sustainable houses, a fundamental starting point in addressing these barriers. Australia

(Wales and Meed 2005) has a similar problem. BEA schemes can offer common standards by promoting sustainable housing through measuring and assessing levels of sustainability. However, the large and increasing number of tools and systems have added complexity and confusion to emerging systems of assessment, begging the question: What are the roles and capabilities of BEA systems to address the barriers to sustainable housing?

Role of Building Environmental Assessment

Environmental assessment is a method to examine the impacts of human processes on ecological systems and has been integrated into numbers of systems and tools examining the built environment. Most environmental assessment methods essentially examine a process. For a building, this might be the design process before construction or the operational process after construction. Processes can be examined in terms of inputs, outputs, and the activities within the process.

Environmental indicators can be used to examine all these aspects of the process and to assist with measuring its performance. Such audits are usually done independently to ensure rigour. Indicators, manageable measures, are usually elements of audits. For example, the energy consumption of a house is used as an indicator of environmental performance because it is recorded in energy bills, which are relatively easy to access.

Nesting BEA in design is not easy because it involves linking all design aspects. Roaf (2004) argues for 'closing the loop': considering the design, construction, and post-construction evaluation. Feedback occurs at the beginning of the design process of the next project and for retrofitting and improving the building during its life cycle. Tools have been developed to address this complexity and assist in steering projects to sustainable outcomes. The models that underlie these tools indicate their capabilities. Discussions of two examples of the main BEA-related models follow: firstly, the ISO 14000 (based on a process-oriented model) and, secondly, the principles-to-indicator approach (based on an input–output model).

ISO 14000

ISO 14000 is a series of international standards on environmental management, and offers a framework for developing environmental management systems and the supporting audit. ISO 14000 evolved from the Rio World Earth Summit (1992) and a number of national standards, BS 7750 being the first. Subsequently, the International Organization for Standardization (ISO) investigated how such standards might benefit business and industry, and an international standard (ISO 14000, 2006) was developed. ISO 14001 is the key standard of the ISO 14000 series, specifying a framework of control for an environmental management system through which a third party can certify organizations. The approach is concerned primarily with improving the process.

Rogers (2002, 6) has summarized the limitations of the ISO 14000 standards as:

- Absence of links with and specific policy, such as Agenda 21, and sustainable outcomes.
- Emphasis on legal requirements as a basis for performance.
- Limited involvement of interested parties (stakeholders) in the setting of performance outcomes.
- Concentration on process improvement rather than on actual outcomes.
- Perceived application of the standard to industrial rather than service sectors.

By way of an example, in Sri Lanka, in promotion implying environmental achievements, asbestos sheeting was advertised using an ISO 14000 manufacturing process (Baggs 2003) but the product has not met a range of other sustainability measures. Hence, it is agued that more holistic models are needed.

Principles-to-Indicator Model

Environmental assessment models that address input, process and output factors are commonly called 'principles-to-indicator models', for example using input factors in the form of policy frameworks and/or principles. Here the process is examined through indicators, and output factors from the indicators are matched to benchmarks, to enable a comparison with similar processes. For a given process policy, sound environmental principles are defined, then indicators are developed and the process is assessed using 'best practice' benchmarks.

   Mawhinney (2002) argues that the chief limitation of this model is the process of determining best practice. The model can be criticized according to certain criteria:

- The extent to which sound environmental principles are used.
- The logical match between the indicator suite and its antecedent principles and policy framework.
- How the level of the benchmarks is derived to evaluate the indicators.

However, the principles-to-indicator approach has integrated a number of tools for use in evaluating buildings.

Building Environmental Assessment Tools

Many BEA tools use one or both models and are criticized in relation to:

- The theoretical bases of policies and principles arising from how 'sustainability' is defined.
- How principles and indicators are linked to policy and principles, and missing indicators.
- How best practice is defined and the rigour by which it is assessed.

How the tools define the success of a particular project links to how sustainability is defined. Organizations have their own measures of success, associated with how they define sustainable development and the principles they use to run their business. Blair et al. (2003) applied a 'balanced theory' perspective to examine housing, developing a monitoring assessment tool to measure the affordability and sustainability of greenfield suburban developments and master-planned communities in Australia. The tool included an indicator suite, which used economic, social and environmental criteria, with potential for use in longitudinal studies to track progress and provide evidence of achievements in meeting policy objectives and addressing principles. However, the tool requires further work to advance the triple bottom line principles that underlie this approach, particularly in developing the indicator suite.

Problems with such tools involve internal inconsistencies in the structure of the models on which they are based. Mawhinney (2002) points out that missing parameters in many systems can influence the results achieved. Tools can be mapped and analysed in terms of the development scale – city, precinct or building – and when the assessment is made: after construction, in the operational phase, or during the planning and design phase. Debate exists over the best time to make assessments. Advocates of collecting operational data argue that assessments based on actual performance are more valid. Advocates of the design phase of assessment argue that it important to predict performance at the design phase because it is hard to rectify problems after construction. Tools and standards currently emerging arise from a number of sources, and private sector industry groups are increasingly playing a role.

City, Precinct and Building Scales

An 'ecological footprint' is a measure of how much productive land and water is required to produce all the resources consumed and to absorb all the waste generated using existing technology. Ecological footprints can be calculated for an individual, a city, a country, or humanity. The unit of measurement is land, a global hectare or one hectare of biologically productive space of world-average productivity. This type of tool assesses progress towards, or away from, a sustainable way of living given certain assumptions and limitations and offers a monitoring tool for cities.

Precinct-level tools are less common and tend to utilize a broader set of indicators that can be linked to principles or policy initiatives. For example, the BRE Sustainable Development Rating tool (Roaf et al. 2000) contains environmental, economic and social indicators. The Green Globe 21 Precinct Planning and Design Standard has a similar direction, aligning indicators with the master planning and design processes of mixed-use developments (Hyde et al. 2005). These tools include indicators that can be aligned to developers' and planning authorities' policies and strategies, with the potential to support sustainable developments.

Government and industry sectors have developed tools at the building level (Reardon 2005, Section 10.1). BEA rating tools have been developed for specific countries and building types. The Property Council, through the Green Building Council of Australia (2007), has been developing a voluntary standard and tool for sustainable building development, Green Star. Australian government tools include the National Australian Building Environmental Rating Scheme (NABERS), a federal initiative, and BASIX, the New South Wales government rating tool. BASIX is a mandatory tool linked to the design approval process for houses. NABERS HOME compares the environmental performance of a home with a theoretical average home in the same area, using tools such as the Energy Smart Home Rating. The Green Star Rating aims to compare energy bills complemented with a Virtual Home Audit, which investigates ways to reduce energy waste and provide the owner with a personal Energy Action Plan. (Hyde forthcoming)

Finally, there are a few 'international' tools, for example, with respect to the travel and tourism industry. Voluntary standards Green Globe 21 and Earthcheck have been developed for the design, construction and operation of tourism-related buildings (Hyde et al. 2005). Industries such as tourism share a common set of objectives that are part of the globalization of the industry and sustain a global system of principles and indicators. In this case, a strong link has been forged between international policies for sustainability founded by Agenda 21 and the indicators and standards used in the system. Consequently, this approach provides a level of rigour. The policy measures can be logically connected to the indictors in the system and linked to the way benchmarks are measured.

Rigour produces a conundrum for this type of approach. Highly rigorous tools comprehensively match the principles and/or policy frameworks with the indicators. Indicators require information that can be easily collected and yield valid data. Best practice standards are not biased or based on impractical levels of performance. Very often highly rigorous tools are data hungry and expensive to service, making them impractical to use in the schema of some organizations. However, lack of rigour makes the tools useless.

As rigour is often traded against practicality of use, tools usually include a checklist for pre-assessment, which allows potential users to quickly check to what extent their project engages with environmental criteria. Green Globe 21 has a pre-commitment questionnaire, which assesses the potential of a project to meet its standards. The advantages of these systems include saving time in collecting and validating data, but experts apply the criteria best. An example is the NABERS (2007) tool for housing, which started as a comprehensive environmental assessment approach, and has been simplified for use by laypersons through a web-based system.

Measuring Success

Tools have been applied to measure the success of projects in a number of innovative ways, generally through 'push' or 'pull' strategies.

Pull strategies encourage voluntary standards for developers. Developers can be rewarded for 'best practice' sustainable development through incentives, such as marketing advantages, ecolabels and branding. Demonstration and flagship projects in sustainable design are seen to pull the market towards improved performance and bring reputability to participating developers. At the other end 'base-line' building developers need pushing to improve the environmental performance of their buildings. Government based tools, such as NABERS HOME and BASIX, can achieve this goal.

Tools can facilitate the development process in the planning and design phases or, better, governance in the operational phase. Examples of policy initiatives being examined through an environmental assessment method are not common but can yield information on the effectiveness of policy decisions. Such studies compare housing development types to assess the merit of policy decisions. Best practice can be measured and rewarded by combining and integrating a number of assessment tools to meet legal requirements.

The Novotel Hotel, located in the Novotel/Ibis complex at Olympic Park in Homebush Bay (Sydney) provides an example of rewarding best practice. Built as part of the infrastructure for the 2000 Olympic Games, the Sydney Olympic Park Authority continued sound environmental policies after the Games ended by engaging a number of strategies to ensure continual improvement of its facilities. Legislation governing the Sydney Olympic Park Authority (2006) focused on ensuring best use and management of the precinct at Olympic Park, mandating sound master-planning, good environmental performance of the hotel, and involving 'green lease arrangements' that included sustainable goals in the brief and in the post construction ISO 1400 Environmental Management system.

This green design process was supported by environmentally appropriate infrastructure, such as the Olympic Park grey-water main, which provided a fifty per cent reduction in potable water use in the building. Numerous small eco-efficient environmental strategies significantly reduced the environmental footprint of the building, such as solar hot water, maximizing daylight and operable windows. By purchasing green power, the hotel became effectively net carbon neutral. The hotel has performed well in assessments against international standards, thus gaining rewards for 'best practice' compared to international industry standards.

In this project assessment tools functioned to demonstrate best practice and the fulfilment of requirements in the green lease arrangement. Would best practice have been achieved without the latter? Both pull and push drivers are needed to address barriers to sustainable housing.

Whilst this project primarily used existing technology and systems, other developers seek to use new technology and innovative social and economic strategies to improve sustainability. Such demonstration projects tend to define sustainability in their own terms, requiring different assessment tools.

Creating Demonstration Projects

Beddington Zero (BedZED) in London is an example of a sustainability demonstration project. This 1.7 ha brownfield residential and commercial development was designed to meet a number of environmental, social and economic goals. High benchmarks included carbon-neutral energy efficiency and taking account of social sustainability, such as facilitating use of public transport and economic needs (BRESCU 2002). Conventional housing does not meet such targets and required innovative design and green technology, such as passive solar heating through natural light, solar panels to generate electricity, materials with strong thermal properties and a whole-of-site rain collection system. BRE assessment systems assisted in validating the design and the scheme was assessed after construction using the BRE EcoHomes design phase tool.

Whilst the EcoHomes tool gave the BedZED scheme an excellent rating, it failed to identify additional issues revealed since it developed, including the need for a broader definition of sustainability in the precinct design, the need for ongoing assessment after the design phase, and the importance of qualitative aspects of sustainability (drivers for value adding).

Precincts such as BedZED emerge from a housing delivery process unique to the UK. Use of housing trusts, as in the case of BedZED, allows for a high degree of control over the delivery process, the administration of tenure, and the ongoing operation of the development. The crux of the problem lies in the master-planning approach taken: whether there are environmental goals used in this process and whether there is a sufficiently experienced multidisciplinary team to implement these goals.

A community consultation plan for social improvement is often missed in master-planning processes. The BedZED project used community consultations to create a neighbourhood renewal agenda that ranged from creating private and public green spaces for sun to community facilities and healthy lifestyles (BRESCU 2002, 26). Social progress was only one of a range of master-planning strategies, particularly relating to architectural design and landscaping, and formed the basic model for the precinct. Economic strategies were implemented to improve income streams associated with the proportion of housing reserved for low-income families to reduce their reliance on government subsidies. Mixed-use buildings with industrial functions were incorporated. Often mixed use involves incompatibility and conflicts between the interests of business and house owners. In the BedZED project, this was avoided through selecting compatible businesses, careful planning, and design. BRESCU (2002) argues that the BedZED planning and design approach forms a model for sustainable housing development for use in other circumstances.

There is a strong need for ongoing assessment after the design phase. The benefit of demonstration projects is that they identify positives and negatives. Reports of the operation of BedZED have identified a number of issues in the use of green technology, such as reports (Slavin 2006) of the failure of the Biomas CHP system, which is central to achieving the zero fossil fuel energy target. Yet, from the social perspective, user feedback was positive. Residents like the light and airy quality of the scheme and roof terraces, despite reporting some overheating of spaces for sun in summer. Their property values are higher than adjacent housing, suggesting lower operating costs.

In summary, BedZED is a successful demonstration project yet has not made full use of assessment systems to help measure this success. Without a systematic approach to ongoing monitoring, and use of broader assessment methods, evaluation is ad hoc and left to the media. Lack of systematic post-occupancy evaluation creates further barriers to implementing sustainable housing. Pull strategies for implementing sustainable housing must be complemented by government push measures.

Supporting Evidence-Based Planning Policy

Assessment tools, such as the Building Code of Australia (BCA) that emerged to support governmental planning and regulatory processes, represent push strategies for sustainable housing. Currently, the BCA is being transformed from a health-and-safety and fire mitigation standard to a code highlighting environmental standards. These environmental standards have focused mainly on energy efficiency as a criterion, which leaves local councils and developers to deal with other environmental standards.

The failure of planning processes to fully support moves to sustainable housing has been a major barrier (Wheeler 2003). Can we nest an effective assessment process in the current planning and development system? Would this assist in measuring the sustainability success of projects? In discussing these questions, the Currumbin Ecovillage located on the Gold Coast, Queensland, provides an example of assessment applied to support the planning and development processes.

The delivery of housing in Australia tends to be fragmented and is largely a developer-led system. A developer purchases the land, forms a subdivision and then sells parcels of the land to subdevelopers, who use the land to build houses, hotels, retail buildings and so on. Local governments assume control of the legal title of a precinct or it remains under the control of the developer and subdevelopers or owners as 'community title'.

While the Gold Coast Council controls the process, a range of federal, State and local government initiatives to promote sustainability influence developments. State legislation is dominated by the Integrated Planning Act, which promotes ESD through integrating State and local planning systems. Local planning responds to Desirable Environmental Outcome statements in the form of policies and codes. Community input and environmental impacts are assessed.

Input is obtained on environmental principles and strategies used in a development, methods and procedures for assessment depending on many factors, most importantly, the scale, complexity and sensitivity of the development to sustainability issues (Thomas 2005, 123). Planning system outcomes can be achieved by intervention at a number of levels. The Currumbin Ecovillage was a significant development in terms of local social, environmental and economic sensitivities, including: conflicts in defining sustainability with respect to the development and sustainability standards, lack of clarity in procedures (the compliance process was expensive, time consuming and exhaustive), and lack of a common metric for the regulatory system and the developer.

The ecovillage at Currumbin was a 110 ha site on the Gold Coast hinterland providing for 144 ecohomes in a variety of residential configurations, together with community facilities, including a small village centre. The ecovillage proposal incorporated a wide range of sustainability features, including: autonomy in water, waste water and energy; 80 per cent open space; more than 50 per cent environmental reserve; negligible vegetation loss and extensive native plant regeneration; edible landscapes and permaculture; and waste minimization and recycling. The developers claimed that it exceeded international and Australian sustainability best practices and it was hailed by government and industry as a leading example of housing sector ESD.

Substantiating these claims to best practice are very different definitions of sustainability within the international community and within Australia. McManus (2005) argues for a uniquely Australian definition of ESD, mostly concerned with retaining ecological systems. Whilst useful at one level, it is hard to apply this definition to urban development. Hence it can be argued that the Integrated Planning Act, which has its foundation in ESD, should be augmented through new definitions of sustainability dealing with urban contexts and international practices. Conflicts over definitions increase the complexity and ambiguity of procedure and assessment.

Thomas (2005) reports a lack of clear procedures for the implementation of the Integrated Planning Act. Currumbin code compliance meant extensive work. The documentation needed to gain planning approval proved costly, time consuming and exhaustive (Walton 2006). Environmental criteria for autonomous energy, water and waste services for the site meant council conditions on a range of additional measures in the approval process. A range of codes was needed to cover the biophysical aspects of designing and building houses. Ecohomes imply a reduced demand for services. By-laws were needed to cover social and management issues, to ensure efficient use of resources, and to minimize demand for services. Procedures for this type of sustainable development sit outside normal code compliance processes and are not assessable under regular planning codes, creating a need for new metrics to support assessment procedures.

Shane and Gracdle (2000) and McManus (2005) point to the importance of metrics to demonstrate environmental efficiency measures for environmental impact assessment. It is argued that metrics cannot fulfil all the needs of planning assessment because metrics are generic and require interpretation in the local context. However, metrics could form an aspect of the process. In the case of Currumbin, a metric was created from a range of authorities, including Gold Coast Water for the water benchmarks and the Environmental Protection Agency for waste treatment. A common metric between regulators and developers would expedite the compliance process, carrying forward the intent of the Integrated Planning Act and offering simpler procedures for implementing planning approvals for sustainable developments.

Research to apply the Green Globe Precinct Planning and Design Standard at Currumbin (Moore et al. 2006) aims to provide a definition of sustainability grounded in Agenda 21 and drawn from a definition of sustainability appropriate for such communities to reconcile environmental, economic and social factors. The metric is being offered to developers, planners and other stakeholders to reduce confusion in the application of sustainable development in practice.

Conclusion

Using metrics that follow the ISO 14000 and principles-to-indicator approach for BEA tools provides a logical structure to deal with the complexity of environmental management and assessment. The application of such tools demonstrates ways to address barriers to sustainable development. At Olympic Park the lack of an agreed standard or definition of sustainability was addressed by applying the ISO 14000 as a method of assessment at the master-planning and design stages to improve the predicted environmental performance of the precinct and the buildings and ongoing monitoring of the precinct in its operational phase ensured continual improvement of performance. In the BedZED project, the barriers were financial disincentives to green design particularly in the area of green technology. Government subsidies were needed to apply photovoltaic systems for electricity cogeneration. High benchmarks required ramping up engineering capabilities and addressing costs in the renewable energy sector. However, technical reliability and economic barriers were mitigated by mixed-use development and drawing on other sources of income to subsidize rentals. Qualitative aspects of sustainable design, such as light and airy buildings, sun spaces and private open space seemed to drive an unusual level of private investor interest. Barriers of perceived higher costs were addressed by value adding and encouraging consumer demand.

The importance of using assessment metrics based on sustainable planning and design principles was also demonstrated in the case of Currumbin Ecovillage. Creating a generic metric for all stakeholders in such community housing projects is crucial to address barriers to integrating sustainability in the planning process. Metrics support evidence-based planning by reducing barriers related to lack of clarity over defining sustainability, but cannot address all criteria in the planning assessment process.

References

Baggs, D. (2003), 'Materials in Context: Design Decision Making for Sustainable Materials', Ecospecifier Seminar, Brisbane, Spring.

Blair, J., Prasad, D., Judd, B., Soebarto, V., Hyde, R., Zehner, B. and Kumar, A. (2003), *Affordability and Sustainability Outcomes of 'Greenfield' Suburban Development and Master Planned Communities – A Triple Bottom Line Assessment* [Final Report] (Sydney: University of New South Wales–University of Western Sydney Research Centre of the Australian Housing and Urban Research Institute).

BRESCU (2002), *BedZED-Beddington Zero Energy Development Sutton* [General Information Report 89, Energy and Efficiency Best Practice in Housing], <http://www.est.org.uk.>, accessed 3 September 2005.

Green Building Council of Australia (2007), [website] <http://www.gbcaus.org>, accessed 15 January 2007.

Hyde, R. (forthcoming), *NABERS HOME – Applications in Teaching and Practice* Green Island [website], <http://www.greenisland.net.au>, accessed 17 January 2007.

Hyde, R., Moore R., Kavanagh, L., Watt, M., Prasad, D. and Blair, J. (2005), *PPDS Handbook*, Green Globe 21/Earthcheck online at Earthcheck [website], <http://www.earthcheck.org>, accessed 6 January 2007.

McManus, P. (2005), *Vortex Cities to Sustainable Cities: Australia's Urban Challenge* (Sydney: University of New South Wales Press).

Mawhinney, M. (2002), *Sustainable Development: Understanding the Green Debates* (Oxford: Blackwell Science).

Moore R., et al. (2006), 'Another Tool' in Skates (ed.).

NABERS (2007), National Australian Building Environmental Rating Scheme [website], <http://www.nabers.com.au/nabershome.aspx>.

Reardon, C. (ed.) (2005), *Your Home Technical Manual,* 3rd Edition. (Canberra: Commonwealth of Australia, Department of the Environment and Heritage, Australian Greenhouse Office).

Roaf, S. (2004), *Closing the Loop: Benchmarks for Sustainable Buildings* (London: RIBA).

Roaf, S., Yates, A., Brownhill, D. and Howard, N. (2000), *EcoHomes: The Environmental Rating Tool For Homes* (Walford: BRE Bookshop).

Rogers, S. (2002), *Green Globe – Beyond ISO 14000 for the Travel and Tourism Sector* (Australia: Avteq Consulting Services).

Shane, E. and Graedle, T. (2000), 'Urban Environmental Sustainability Metrics: A Provisional Set', *Journal of International Planning and Management* 43:5, 643–63.

Skates, H. (ed.) (2006), *Fabricating Sustainability. Proceedings of the Australia New Zealand Architectural Science Association Conference, Wellington, New Zealand,* Victoria University of Wellington [CD and website], <http://www.vuw.ac.nz/cbpr/conferences/anzasca/index.aspx>, accessed 17 January 2007.

Slavin, T. (2006), 'Living in a Dream', *Guardian,* 17 May, Guardian [website], <http://environment.guardian.co.uk/energy/story/0,,1845692,00.html>, accessed 17 January 2007.

Sydney Olympic Park Authority (2006) [website], <http://www.sydneyolympicpark.nsw.gov.au>, accessed 24 November 2006.

Thomas, I. (2005), *Environmental Impact Assessment in Australia: Theory and Practice* [4th Edition] (Annandale: Federation Press).

Wheeler, J. (2003), 'One Million Sustainable Homes', WWF [website], <http://www.wwf.org.uk/sustainablehomes/>, accessed 17 January 2007.

Wales, N. and Meed, E. (2005), 'Barriers to Sustainable Suburbs', Transactions of the Wessex Institute [website], <http://library.witpress.com/pages/PaperInfo.asp?PaperID=15606>, accessed 17 January 2007.

Walton, C. (2006), 'The Ecovillage At Currumbin', Ecovillage [website], <http://www.theecovilage.com.au/>, accessed 17 January 2007.

Chapter 9

Sustainable Water Systems and Household Practices

Joe Hurley and David Mercer

Introduction

The fundamental challenge for urban water management today is unsustainable consumption. Water is essential to earth's living creatures and central to maintaining the earth's ecosystems. If we do not respect the environmental processes that provide clean water, and use water wisely, we undermine the earth's basic building blocks of life (Postel 2005). The environmental impacts of inefficient water use highlight the critical importance of designing and implementing sustainable water management practices.

In part, this chapter seeks to redress an imbalance in current literature (Heathcote 2005), emphasizing the importance of agricultural, rather than urban, water consumption. While acknowledging that large complexes such as hospitals and casinos consume disproportionately large amounts of water (*Age* 2006), this chapter focuses on domestic water use in Australian cities, where most homes are connected to, and reliant on, metropolitan-wide distribution systems. We examine ways that water is used in such settings, review various programs and policies aimed at changing urban water use behaviour, analyse methods for (and barriers to) achieving change, and propose future directions for sustainable domestic water consumption. The Melbourne case studies discussed have relevance for all urban environments.

Urban Water Systems

In many Australian cities, large, centralized infrastructure systems that have provided high quality water to households are meeting their limits (Auditor-General of New South Wales 2005). Australia has a population of around twenty million, which might well reach thirty million by 2050. Over many years rainfall patterns in many parts of Australia have steadily declined. In Perth, a 21 per cent drop in rainfall has translated into a 64 per cent reduction in water flows into the main water storages. In south-east Queensland, which welcomes 50,000 new residents each year, annual precipitation has been falling since the 1980s. However, there are entrenched barriers to implementing alternative decentralized models of water delivery and treatment, dramatically highlighted in Toowoomba in July 2006, when a local referendum overwhelmingly rejected a proposal to augment the city's supply through the indirect reuse of waste water for potable (drinking) water (Brown 2005; *Sydney Morning Herald* 2006). Notwithstanding that recycling sewage is a common practice elsewhere, including Singapore and Washington DC, this decision jeopardizes the uptake of such technology in other parts of Australia.

Most river and aquifer systems providing water for Australia's major cities are highly stressed and degraded, affecting ecosystem health as well as agricultural, industrial, and tourist water users. Policy responses, and senses of urgency, have varied between cities. For example, Dr John Marsden is quoted (House of Representatives Standing Committee on Environment and Heritage 2005, 86) as strongly critical of the tardy response in Sydney: 'Perth knows that it is on a cliff. In fact, it is on the cliff face...and it is scaling it...whereas in Sydney...it has been wandering around in a fog denying that there might be a cliff anywhere.' In Australia, 75 per cent of harvested water is used by irrigators and there is increasing conflict between urban and rural consumers. In many rural areas – predominantly Aboriginal communities –the quality of drinking water does not meet minimal World Health Organization standards.

During most of the twentieth century, urban Australians assumed unlimited access to cheap and plentiful water (Mercer and Lloyd 1986). Over the last two decades this understanding has been seriously challenged, with increasing recognition of the limits to resource availability and importance of ecosystem health. A recent Business Council of Australia (2006) report pointed out that water costs Australians around half of what water costs in Europe. Growing evidence of climate change has been particularly significant, encouraging changes to urban water practices. To preserve the natural environment, citizens and institutions are recognizing that they must radically alter perceptions, management and use of water for sustainable consumption.

Historically, large infrastructure developments – dams, reticulated supply and sewerage systems, and waste-water treatment plants – have contributed to vast improvements in life expectancy, health and safety, and living standards. Limits to urban water supplies have been addressed by big infrastructure projects, while ecological impacts were ignored or downplayed (Johnson and Rix 1993). However, opposition to new dam construction has been gathering pace around the world (WCD 2000) along with calls to find alternative solutions to water supply problems, which increasingly involve moving from outmoded linear systems to circular systems of conservation and reuse (Pausacker and Andrews 1981). New approaches recognize that large centralized water supply and disposal systems have had extensive detrimental effects on the environment and have allowed wasteful consumption based on the belief that water resources are limitless.

Victoria's *Draft Central Region Sustainable Water Strategy* (DSE 2006) supports policies involving a water conservation target of 25 per cent by 2015 rather than supplying more water from new or expanded reservoirs. This is not a universally held view. For example, controversially, the Queensland Government has committed to a program of new dam construction for its rapidly growing south-eastern region. Desalination is on the agenda, including in Sydney and Perth, as a supply-side 'solution', even though US experiences provide ample evidence that this option is deeply flawed.

Continued concentration on supply-side solutions fails to address either environmental consequences or entrenched excessive consumption. Building dams, reservoirs and other water storage facilities, and diverting or extracting water from natural systems, results in altered flow regimes and habitat destruction, as well as diminished water quality in the remaining flows. Disposal of urban sewage and stormwater also affects water quality through altered flow regimes, increased nutrient loads, salinity, toxicants, and temperature pollution. In Victoria, the condition of one-third of the State's rivers and two-thirds of its estuaries are classified as 'poor' or 'very poor' due to water extraction and disposal (DSE 2004). Moreover, the use of large-scale urban water supply and waste-water removal systems has encouraged service expectations and patterns of use which assume limitless sources.

In 2001, the average Australian resident used 315 L of high quality drinking water per day in the home (ABS 2004), 30 per cent higher than the average in Organization for Economic Cooperation and Development countries. Less than 28 per cent of this water was used for human health and hygiene (ABS 2004), and less than 1 per cent was used to drink! When a householder turns on a tap, the water is always there, and hasn't ever cost much. Once used, it disappears down a hole. Most citizens never see or experience the impacts of water consumption. Can we realistically expect them to meaningfully engage with its management as a scarce resource?

Clearly, significant changes and new approaches are required to reduce the impacts of water consumption. An emerging 'new paradigm' has seen governments and the water industry acknowledge real limits to this essential resource and attempts to reconsider our consumption values have had some success.

Sustainable Urban Water Systems

There have been two pivotal moments in the evolution of sustainability thinking. *Our Common Future*, the World Commission on Environment and Development (WCED 1987) report, gave the first wide exposure to the concept of sustainable development. Subsequently, Local Agenda 21, a product of the 1992 Rio Earth Summit (United Nations 1992), began making the principles of sustainable development operational on a world scale. Girardet (2004:6) usefully modified the Brundtland Commission definition of sustainable development for cities: 'A "sustainable city" enables all its citizens to meet their own needs and to enhance their well-being, without degrading the natural world or the lives of other people, now or in the future.'

In applying sustainability principles to urban water use, the State of Victoria (DSE 2004) has aimed to: provide reliable and safe urban water and sewerage services into the future; maintain healthy rivers, aquifers, floodplains, estuaries, and catchments; and engage communities to make considered choices about consumption to conserve water. To seriously address current consumption behaviour and move to more sustainable practices, Cullen (2002) has argued that Australians need to reflect on water use and to develop new ethics for its use, as well as practices respecting and valuing water. Sustainable water systems will minimize consumption, provide fair and just access, draw only within sustainable yields (leaving sufficient environmental flows to maintain ecosystem health), maintain and improve ecosystem health, pay for mitigation and restoration measures, engage all citizens in water education programs to minimize negative impacts of water consumption on ecosystems and, most significantly, maintain all of the above for future generations.

Such actions are essential features of the emerging Integrated Urban Water Management (IUWM) paradigm. In a wide-ranging review and critique of IUWM as currently practised in Australia, Mitchell (2006, 589–90) describes IUWM as a management philosophy that 'takes a comprehensive approach to urban water services, viewing water supply, drainage and sanitation as components of an integrated physical system, and recognizes that the physical system sits within an organizational framework and a broader natural landscape', enunciating five core principles of IUWM:

1. Consider all parts of the water cycle, natural and constructed, surface and subsurface, recognizing them as an integrated system.
2. Consider all requirements for water, both anthropogenic and ecological.
3. Consider the local context, accounting for environmental, social, cultural, and economic perspectives.
4. Include all stakeholders in planning and decision-making processes.
5. Strive for sustainability, aiming to balance environmental, social and economic needs in the short, medium and long term.

We highlight Principle 4 as particularly relevant to our arguments advanced here. In the past, large infrastructure developments were planned and developed 'top down', mainly by engineers. Consumers were not active participants in the decision making, resulting in a focus on supply-side asset management rather than demand management. Neither suppliers nor consumers have understood how much water individuals consumed, and to what end. Under the new paradigm, ideally consumers gain accurate information and timely feedback about consumption patterns and can monitor and take more responsibility for their individual behaviour in terms of its cumulative consequences.

Reducing Water Use in the Home

Given cheap, reliable supplies of high quality water to Australian homes, consumption can be reduced through behavioural and technological changes. Changing behaviour related to showers, washing machines and toilets, which typically account for over 75 per cent of indoor use, can easily result in significant overall reductions in water use.

Table 9.1 summarizes some common initiatives, highlighting the role of end uses and pointing to areas of potential greatest saving. For example, use of quality potable water for domestic irrigation is extensive yet makes little sense.

Alternative Urban Water Supplies

Most urban areas face a shortage of high quality potable water, rather than water shortages per se. As the technical ability to treat water improves, options for both

Table 9.1   Reducing water use in the home

Domestic End-Use: % of Total Consumption (Roberts 2005, 4)	Consumption Change Initiatives
Garden irrigation, including filling swimming pools and car washing: 25%	Substitute exotic plant species requiring large amounts of water with more suitable plants, such as indigenous species.
	Mulch garden beds to increase water absorption and retention.
	Install targeted irrigation systems (such as drip irrigation) and water garden at cool times of the day.
Shower: 22%	Biggest indoor user of water in most households, so simply shortening shower time will save significant amounts of water.
	Install water-efficient showerheads (can halve shower water consumption).
Clothes washing machine: 19%	Water-efficient clothes washers use less than half the amount used by some inefficient machines.
	Only wash full loads.
Toilet: 13%	Old toilet cisterns use up to 12 L per flush while modern, dual-flush models use around 3/4.5 L for half/full flush.
Taps: 12%	Aerators or flow restrictors on kitchen, bathroom and laundry taps can reduce water use from 18 L to 2 L per minute.
Leaks and other: 11%	Leaks can often be easily fixed but, meanwhile, waste water.

decentralized and centralized treatment of water for reuse become more feasible. Most urban stormwater and waste water is disposed to rivers and oceans. While not fit to drink, such water can be used for non-drinking purposes, particularly when treated (City of Sydney 2004). Urban water managers must give due consideration to hierarchies of multiple supplies and assess the suitability of each supply for meeting the particular water service required. Table 9.2 summarizes issues associated with alternative water supply options.

The use of multiple supplies of water to meet different needs can greatly reduce domestic reliance on existing reticulated potable water systems. However, matching a range of water supplies – with varying levels of quality, quantity and temporal availability – to a range of demands challenges individual householders.

Table 9.2   Issues associated with alternative urban water supplies

Water Supply	Characteristics and Issues
Rainwater Tanks	Urban rainwater tanks commonly supply particular domestic demands (for example garden) combined with reticulated supplies.
	Temporal variation in rainfall means matching supply with demand.
	Tank can become contaminated, causing water quality concerns.
	Requires householders to manage collection, storage and supply.
Direct Re-Use of Grey Water	Most commonly diverted to garden in dry periods. Some divert shower water for reuse in toilet flushing.
	Provides a consistent supply, as an ongoing by-product of showering and clothes washing.
	Highly variable quality, from almost drinkable to very polluted, presenting health concerns.
	Demands significant behaviour change, requiring householder awareness of impacts of substances washed down the plug hole.
On-Site Recycling of Waste Water	Collection, treatment and reuse uncommon due to reticulated sewerage systems.
	Technology exists to treat water to varying levels of quality, even up to potable standard, but tends to be costly and energy intensive.
	Use of energy intensive water treatment is questionable from holistic sustainability perspective.
Regional 'Third Pipe'	Regional waste water treatment plants feeding reticulated treated water supply systems are increasingly considered.
	Require substantial piping infrastructure, thus limiting feasibility to new developments.
	Reticulated treated waste water, usually suitable for garden irrigation and laundry use, but existing technology to treat to potable standard.
	Reticulated treated waste water systems require householders to deal with two supplies of two levels of water quality suitable for distinct end uses. Accidental misuse could have health consequences.
Stormwater Harvesting	Harvesting urban surface water runoff is uncommon at household level but increasingly used for urban irrigation.
Desalination	Technology exists to convert sea water to potable water but process is costly and 3–5 times more energy-intensive than reclaiming water (House of Representatives Standing Committee on Environment and Heritage, 2005, 95).
	Energy intensity greatly diminishes holistic environmental benefits.

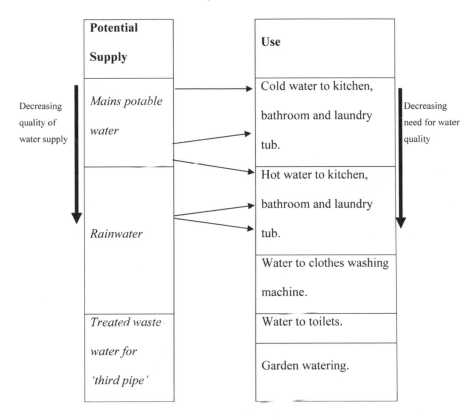

Figure 9.1   **Hierarchy of supply for the Aurora estate**

For instance, it is controversial whether the quality of shower water is appropriate for flushing toilets. Also poor supply–demand matches develop, such as if using a small rainwater tank for suburban garden irrigation, periods when water is available (when it rains) do not match well with periods water is required, through dry summer months. In this case, substantial storage is required for a successful supply–demand match.

Case Study, the Aurora Estate

New urban developments are beginning to integrate multiple water supplies into planning and design. The planned Aurora residential development of 8500 dwellings on Melbourne's northern fringe is incorporating three supplies to meet domestic demands: mains potable water, local area centralized recycled waste water and household rainwater tanks (see Figure 9.1 and McLean 2004). The highest quality (potable mains) water will service uses demanding the highest level of quality and security of supply. In addition, each dwelling will be connected to a reticulated supply of treated waste water for use in washing machines and for garden watering.

An optional rainwater tank will supply hot water to the house – the hot water system diminishing risks of bacterial contamination (Coombes et al. 2000). Along with demand-reduction measures Aurora residents are expected to use 72 per cent less mains water than other suburban Melbourne households (McLean 2004).

Urban Water Report Card

At both federal and State levels, there has been an intensive focus on water management issues in recent years, with significant inquiries and policy documents released, including: the *Sustainable Cities* inquiry (House of Representatives Standing Committee on Environment and Heritage 2005); the *Intergovernmental Agreement on a National Water Initiative* (COAG 2004); the *Inquiry into Sustainable Communities* (Environment and Natural Resources Committee 2005); and *Securing Our Water Future Together* (DSE 2004). Many different programs to improve water management and use focusing on domestic use of water have been established. Governments, the water industry, non-profit organizations and the private sector have implemented initiatives, many with government financial assistance. These can be categorized according to the method used to effect change: social (voluntary), regulatory (compulsory), and economic.

Intense public focus on water resources has resulted in initiatives to reduce domestic consumption. Table 9.3 highlights a representative selection of advertising campaigns, education programs, industry and community award schemes, demonstration projects, visitor centres, household audit and retrofit programs, and rebate schemes. For example, the Sustainable Schools Program presents an innovative, comprehensive approach to sustainability education in schools. However, many well-designed experiments compete for a place in the curriculum rather than complementing each other. Larri's (2004) evaluation of the Sustainable Schools Program highlights the need for collaboration between government agencies, NGOs and other actors developing and delivering such innovations.

While abundant social initiatives encourage householders to reduce water consumption, few regulatory and economic initiatives exist. The Water Efficiency Labelling and Standards scheme recently introduced by the Australian Government is long overdue, but it does not go far enough, having mandatory performance standards for toilets only. Mandatory standards should apply to showers and clothes washing machines, which use most domestic water. Victoria's permanent water-use rules demonstrate one State government's willingness to tell consumers to use water in measured ways but such restrictions are relatively minor and have much scope for extension.

How successful are such schemes in reducing overall domestic water consumption? Have we become more responsible domestic water users? The most recent Water Account (2000–01) from the Australian Bureau of Statistics (2004) shows a 12 per cent increase in average domestic water consumption from 1996–97, extending an historical pattern of increasing consumption. However, studies since then show a trend of reduced water consumption in most major cities. Adelaide has reduced its domestic consumption by 10 per cent and Perth by 12 per cent (ABS

Table 9.3   A selection of existing programs for better urban water management

Social initiatives	
Sustainable Schools Program (Larri 2004)	Developed by two Melbourne-based NGOs, works with schools to improve their sustainability performance, while creating a complementary integrated sustainability curriculum for the school.
Water Smart Bills (Environment and Natural Resources Committee 2005)	Water agency, Yarra Valley Water, introduced benchmarking information on bills to allow customers to compare their water consumption with a water-efficient household of the same size.
Regulatory initiatives	
Five Star Standard (Department of Sustainability and Environment 2006)	All new homes built in Victoria must meet the 'Five Star Standard'. This means including a rainwater tank, solar hot water service, or connecting to a dual-pipe reticulated supply, and installing low-flow shower heads and dual-flush toilets.
Permanent Water Restrictions	The Victorian Government has introduced permanent water saving rules, placing certain restrictions on water use.
Labelling and Performance Standards (Australian Government 2005)	The Water Efficiency Labelling and Standards scheme introduces consistent Australia-wide mandatory labelling of products and some minimum performance standards.
Economic Initiatives	
Water Pricing – Melbourne (Yarra Valley Water 2005)	Rising block tariffs for water pricing, to reward water conservation. Initial charges of $A0.78 per kL for first 40 kL; $A0.92 per kL for next 40 kL; and, over that, $A1.36 per kL.

2005). Melbourne has been very successful, with recent water consumption 22 per cent less than the 1990s average (DSE 2006).

Clearly a combination of initiatives, such as those in Table 9.3, and the thought provoking effects of prolonged periods of drought, are having significant results. However, such reductions must be maintained and improved to achieve sustainable levels of urban water consumption. Fundamental to this challenge is understanding the ways people consume water (better measurement and analysis of water use) and how existing initiatives affect behaviour (relative successes of different approaches, interactivity of different approaches, connection between initiatives and specific reductions). Such insights need to be applied continuously to the development of policy and programs to best target future efforts to achieve sustainable water consumption.

Achieving Social Change

The know-how and technology available to save water and improve water quality
are far in advance of common practice. There is a wide gap between people's
concerns for the environment and their practices. Studies (Environment and Natural
Resources Committee 2005) show that concern for the environment does not
necessarily translate into significant action. Effective policy responses will build on
understandings of drivers of, and barriers to, change.

The Victorian *Inquiry into Sustainable Communities* (Environment and Natural
Resources Committee 2005, 101–8) identified significant barriers to changing water
users' practices:

- *Cost:* people resist paying a higher price to buy 'green' products.
- *Underpriced resources:* the cost of water is very low and potential economic
  savings from better resource use rarely financially justify time and effort
  invested in making the savings.
- *Disassociation from the environment:* consumers of water in urban
  environments are physically and mentally disconnected from the natural
  environment, making it difficult to understand the consequences of their
  resource use and the necessity for behaviour change.
- *Disassociation from others:* many who do take action become disheartened
  and discouraged when the government or their peers don't take action.
- *Information overload:* environmental messages compete with other messages
  in the marketplace.
- *Entrenched attitudes and behaviour:* people often do not question habits.
- *Policy and regulation:* existing policy makes water-saving initiatives difficult
  (e.g. grey-water reuse), resulting in mixed messages, with information
  campaigns encouraging water saving while some regulations discourage it.
- *Cultural barriers:* such as attachment to European-style gardens, requiring
  irrigation.

Often the 'bell curve of social change' is invoked to explain the time dependency
of social change programs. The curve groups people according to their likelihood
of taking up a social change initiative: from innovators, through the bulk of people,
to laggards. In reality, many attempts at social change result in part-adoption only,
and it is not certain that, once implemented, a social change initiative will permeate
through all of the target population. Applied to water conservation behaviour, such
a curve would spread practices from a few excessive users, through the majority in
the middle, to leading water conservers. Indeed the results of many well-conceived,
voluntary programs suggest that they are most successful in helping to empower the
actions of 'innovators' and 'early adopters'. Such programs raise awareness within
the majority, creating vital potential for change, but this does not necessarily translate
to shifts in their behaviour. Instead, such programs tend to lead innovators and early
adopters to greater achievements through access to better information, resources
and/or other incentives yet leave the majority behind. More desirable changes will
rely on a substantial shift of the majority group to reduce water consumption.

The Organization for Economic Cooperation and Development (in Environment and Natural Resources Committee 2005) suggests social tools alone are unlikely to achieve change and governments need to focus more on developing economic and regulatory approaches to sustainability rather than rely so heavily on acceptable, but less certain, social instruments (Dalhuisen et al. 2003). While each policy instrument that governments use to influence sustainable behaviour has strengths and weaknesses, none is sufficiently flexible to address all sustainability issues in all contexts. Regulatory, economic and social measures work together holistically to influence behaviour, whereas exclusive reliance on one or a few measures yields limited results.

Conclusion

New approaches to managing our urban water systems, and significant changes in domestic water use behaviour, are required to secure supplies and protect the environment now and into the future. Unsustainable water use continues to be wasteful and environmentally irresponsible. As such, systems used for allocating, financing and pricing, as well as arrangements for managing demand and supply infrastructure, are failing to resolve competing needs (Barton Group 2005).

Maintaining and improving water reduction will require understanding better how households use water and how specific initiatives result in change. There has been a major focus on education, awareness and voluntary engagement programs, initiatives crucial to placing change on the community agenda and establishing common visions. However, substantial and lasting change requires brave and bold policies (Martin and Verbeek 2006). When the local referendum in Toowoomba rejected the well-tried technology of indirect potable reuse of waste water, a debate (ABC Radio National 2006) arose around two crucial questions: Was the educational campaign too hurried and not well enough resourced? Should the government have avoided a referendum and mandated introduction of the technology?

Governments and water utilities need a comprehensive package of policy measures designed to optimize the multiplier effects between initiatives, including the well-considered use of regulation and economic measures alongside social change methods. The political opportunity exists to implement enforceable minimum performance standards (particularly for toilets, showerheads and washing machines), extensions to permanent water-saving rules and new pricing policies. Such measures are necessary to change entrenched cultural habits and create a substantial shift in most of the population to more sustainable domestic water consumption.

References

ABC Radio National (2006), 'Toowoomba's Vote on Sewage', The National Interest [program], 30 July.
ABS (2004), *Water Account Australia 2000–2001* (Canberra: Australian Bureau of Statistics).

ABS (2005), *Household Water Use and Effects of the Drought* Australian Bureau of Statistics [website], <http://www.abs.gov.au/ausstats/abs@.nsf/0/a0b004e8941b6 fbfca25702f007a793b?OpenDocument>, accessed 17 January 2006.

Age (2006), 'Crown, Chadstone on secret "top 200" list of water users', 10 October.

Auditor-General of New South Wales (2005), *Planning for Sydney's Water Needs: Performance Audit* (Sydney: Audit Office).

Australian Government (2005), 'About the WELS Scheme', Australian Government, [website], <http://www.waterrating.gov.au/about/index.html>, accessed 28 January 2006.

Barton Group (2005), 'Australian Water Industry Roadmap', Barton Group [website], <http://www.bartongroup.org.au/AWIR_FINALV10.pdf>, accessed 10 August 2005.

Brown, R. (2005), 'Impediments to Integrated Urban Stormwater Management: The Need for Institutional Reform', *Environmental Management* 36:3, 455–68.

Business Council of Australia (2006), *Water Under Pressure: Australia's Man-Made Water Scarcity and How to Fix It* (Melbourne: Business Council of Australia).

City of Sydney (2004), *State of the Environment Report 2003–04* (Sydney: City of Sydney).

COAG (2004), *Intergovernmental Agreement on a National Water Initiative*, Council of Australian Governments [website], <http://www.coag.gov.au/meetings/250604/ iga_national_water_initiative.pdf>, accessed 17 January 2006.

Coombes, P., Argue, J. and Kuczera, G. (2000), *Figtree Place: A Case Study in Water Sensitive Urban Development,* Water Sensitive Urban Design in Sydney [website], Water Sensitive Urban Design and Sustainable Water Management Literature [webpage], <http://www.wsud.org/downloads/Info%20Exchange%20 &%20Lit/FIGTREE%20LAST21.pdf>, accessed 17 January 2006.

Cullen, P. (2002), 'Living With Water – Sustainability in a Dry Land', [Paper] Adelaide Festival of Arts Getting It Right Symposium, 11–12 March.

Dalhuisen, J., Rodenburg, C., de Groot, H. and Nijkamp, P. (2003), 'Sustainable Water Management Policy: Lessons from Amsterdam', *European Planning Studies* 11:3, 263–81.

DSE (2004), *Securing Our Water Future Together* (Melbourne: Department of Sustainability and Environment).

DSE (2006), *Draft Central Region Sustainable Water Strategy* (Melbourne: Department of Sustainability and Environment).

Environment and Natural Resources Committee (2005), *Inquiry into Sustainable Communities* (Melbourne: Parliament of Victoria).

Girardet, H. (2004), *Cities, People, Planet: Liveable Cities for a Sustainable World,* (Chichester: Wiley-Academy).

Heathcote, R. (2005), 'Review of: L.C. Botterill and D.A.Wilhite (eds), From Disaster Response to Risk Management: Australia's National Drought Policy', *Geographical Research* 43:4, 439–41.

House of Representatives Standing Committee on Environment and Heritage (2005), *Sustainable Cities* (Canberra: Parliament of the Commonwealth of Australia).

Johnson, M. and Rix, S. (eds) (1993), *Water in Australia: Managing Economic, Environmental and Community Reform* (Sydney: Pluto Press).

Larri, L. (2004), *Evaluation: Victorian Sustainable Schools Project* (Melbourne: Department of Education and Training).

Martin, P. and Verbeek, M. (2006), *Sustainability Strategy* (Annandale: Federation Press).

McLean, J. (2004), *Aurora – Delivering a Sustainable Urban Water System for a New Suburb*, Coomes Consulting Group, Water Sensitive Urban Design in Sydney [website], Water Sensitive Urban Design and Sustainable Water Management Literature [webpage], <http://www.wsud.org/downloads/Info%20Exchange%20&%20Lit/WSUD_04_Conf_Papers/WS040035.PDF>, accessed 17 January 2006.

Mercer, D. and Lloyd, D. (1986), 'Planning Melbourne's Water Supply', *Australian Geographer* 17:1, 51–64.

Mitchell, V. (2006), 'Applying Integrated Urban Water Management Concepts: A Review of Australian Experience', *Environmental Management* 37:5, 589–605.

Pausacker, I. and Andrews, J. (1981), *Living Better with Less* (Ringwood: Penguin Books).

Postel, S. (2005), 'From the Headwaters to the Sea: The Critical Need to Protect Freshwater Ecosystems', *Environment* 47:10, 8–21.

Roberts, P. (2005), *2004 Residential End Use Management Study*, Yarra Valley Water [website], <http://www.yvw.com.au/yvw/Home/AboutUs/ReportsAndPublications/ResearchPublications.htm>, accessed 18 January 2006.

Sydney Morning Herald (2006), 'Toowoomba Says No To Recycled Water', 30 July.

United Nations (1992), *Agenda 21*, United Nations [website], <http://www.un.org/esa/sustdev/documents/agenda21/english/Agenda21.pdf>, accessed 15 October 2005.

WCD (2000), *Dams and Development: A New Framework for Decision-Making* [Report of the World Commission on Dams] (London: Earthscan).

WCED (1987), *Our Common Future* [Brundtland Report, World Commission on Environment and Development] (Oxford: Oxford University Press).

Yarra Valley Water (2005), *Pricing Handbook 2005–06* [Final document] (Melbourne: Yarra Valley Water).

Chapter 10

Integrated Waste Management and Zero Waste

Glenn Eales and Nutana Donaldson

Waste management will be one of the greatest sustainability challenges for the global economy and environment in the twenty-first century. Due to the availability of land, Australians have continued to rely on landfill as a waste disposal method while many other countries have been forced to implement other waste management strategies. Meanwhile, Australia has become established as a high producer of waste, second only to the USA at the turn of the century (OECD 2001), and still amongst the top five waste producing OECD nations five years later (OECD 2005; Productivity Commission 2006). Landfills have grown at an unprecedented rate with pressure on suitable land increasing. Although easy and convenient, the landfill method of waste disposal is not sustainable.

All governments have been forced to consider sustainable waste management practices and systems to protect both environmental and human health. Actions to minimize and avoid waste – by encouraging the reduction, recovery, reuse, and recycling of waste – are essential to sustainable waste management. As a result, Australian governments have identified a need for 'zero waste', moving away from landfills towards integrated waste management to encourage materials efficiency and the recovery of as wide a range of resources as possible.

This chapter highlights global issues and management solutions before discussing Australia's waste management and policy options. Problems with landfills are highlighted, practices constituting the waste hierarchy are analysed, policy options related to integrated waste management are reviewed and, finally, issues associated with litter and recycling are examined. As with water management (see Chapter 9), the area of waste management highlights the importance of sustainable household practices, which are critical for collective waste management systems to succeed.

Global Waste Management Profiles

Sweden, Japan and India demonstrate contemporary urban solutions to waste management.

Sweden is an international leader in sustainable waste management. More than 90 per cent of domestic waste was recycled and less than 10 per cent of industrial (excluding mining) waste is disposed of as landfill (Swedish Environmental Protection Agency 2005). Swedish waste policies increase *producer responsibility* and *eco-efficiency*, including strong regulation of landfill operations and waste transport, a landfill tax, and prohibition on directing combustible or organic waste to landfills (Schönning 2006). The *producer responsibility* principle supports companies collecting waste from production and recycling in the best available ways. *Eco-efficiency* refers to an environment-oriented policy to prevent and reduce the negative impact products have on the environment and on human health throughout their entire life cycle (see Chapter 5).

Sweden's policies support more recycling and energy extraction of products and materials in order to decrease landfills. Waste materials are separated at source, where recyclable and combustible materials are recovered. At recycling stations, items are separated into four main forms of treatment: recovery of reusable and recyclable materials, combustion of bulk materials, special processes for hazardous materials and disposal of non-combustible bulk materials in landfills. The combustible materials are incinerated under controlled conditions, to reduce harmful greenhouse gas emissions, then recovered and converted into energy for heating and electricity. The residual ash is sent for disposal at a landfill along with non-combustible bulk materials. Some areas compost organic waste on a large scale and recover gases produced from decomposition to provide energy for heating (Sahlin et al. 2002; Schönning 2006; Swedish Environmental Protection Agency 2005).

In Japan, domestic waste amounts to over 51 million tonnes per year, an average of 1.114 kg per person per day, which compares favourably with the waste generation of the average Australian, over 2 kg per day (Fuller et al. 2000). As with the Swedish model, domestic waste is separated into general waste and recyclable waste, collected and treated separately. Incineration occurs under controlled conditions to reduce harmful greenhouse gas emissions and most heat generated is recycled into usable energy. The waste is reduced to ash and disposed of as landfill. However, waste generation levels are increasing along with a scarcity of suitable landfill sites. Fuller et al. (2000) estimated that, if current domestic generation patterns continued, Japan's landfill sites would only last another several years. Therefore, Japanese waste management systems focus on recovering various materials for recycling. Kerbside recycling collection recovers recyclable ferrous metals from bulky waste items and electrical appliances, such as television sets, refrigerators, washing machines and computers. Manufacturing companies are urged to develop reusable or recyclable goods and there is a large market for recyclable plastic products (Fuller et al. 2000).

In India, rapid and haphazard urban growth has resulted in a scarcity of suitable waste disposal sites. Urban Indians generate over 30 million tonnes of solid waste each year, 0.1–0.6 kg per person per day, 30–75 per cent organic waste and up to 20 per cent recyclable (van Beukering 1999). Uncontrolled waste dumping on urban outskirts, and overflowing landfills, are impossible to manage and pose serious implications for groundwater pollution while contributing to global warming. As the more developed countries eliminate outdated forms of incineration, which involve high costs associated with higher emission control standards, obsolete technologies are dumped on India and other developing countries. Also energy recovery from such incineration is often not successful because the composition of the waste is deficient in fuel for profitable energy consumption. India illustrates global challenges for waste generation and management: increasing levels of population and consumption; growing land shortages; and high economic, environmental and health costs.

The Landfill Challenge

Australians are generating an average of 800–1000 kg waste per annum (Beeton et al. 2006) sourced from natural resources: oil and gas to make plastics, trees and wood chips for paper, and minerals and ores to make metals. While some resources are renewable, for instance most contributing to foods and textiles, many are not. Thousands of tons of coal, gas and oil are fuel for making and transporting products that eventually become wastes. Indirect costs of waste production are often overlooked yet impact heavily on global sustainability issues, such as the generation of greenhouse gases. The energy used to mine, collect, manufacture and transport materials is a large contributor to greenhouse gas emissions, matched by contributions of carbon dioxide and methane generated from rotting organic matter in poorly managed landfills. Spreading urban populations demand that landfills are located distant from cities. This increases fuel costs and time moving waste, further contributing to greenhouse gas and resource use. High tech solutions such as incineration are imperfect although future technological advances might improve emissions.

In Australia, most urban household waste is placed in domestic bins, collected by trucks and transferred to landfills for disposal. Waste was originally buried in large holes, usually old quarries, referred to as 'dumps' or 'tips'. Today, at great cost, landfill areas are sited and designed so that buried waste is completely contained to minimize environmental impacts. Once waste is deposited, it is compacted, then covered with layers of soil and clay. One by one, filled cells (sections) are capped and sealed with clay, then covered with topsoil to grow grass and finally, the site is closed.

Waste materials breaking down inside a landfill cell produce 'leachate' (rainwater and other contaminated liquid run-off) that is dangerous if it soaks through the soil, enters groundwater and travels into waterways, carrying contaminants and pollutants. Landfill cells are lined with clay and geotextile fabric to prevent leachate soaking into groundwater reserves. A network of pipes is constructed at the bottom of the cell to remove leachate for treatment or to continuously recirculate it through the landfill ('polishing'). Australian landfills are the second highest contributor of methane, the greenhouse gas so harmful to our atmosphere. Therefore, a further network of pipes is constructed inside landfill cells to remove methane gas to be burnt off, to reduce its potency, or to be collected and used as a power source for on-site facilities. Some larger landfills make so much methane gas that it is collected and fed into the electricity grid to power local homes.

Urban Australians seek out pre-packaged, pre-prepared and single-use items but disposing of the waste produced by our modern convenience-oriented lifestyles implies more and larger landfill sites. Increased waste implies greater demand for virgin natural resources for substitutes as well as more landfills. Uncontrolled disposal of waste is unsightly, unhygienic and potentially disastrous to the environment. Conveniently locating environmentally responsible landfill facilities is expensive. Residents object to landfill sites established close to their homes due to concerns about litter, pollution, odour and negative impacts on home values. Authorities strictly regulate the formation and management of landfill sites to protect public health and local environments. Therefore Australian governments are moving away from landfill as the central waste management method towards zero waste and integrated waste management.

A zero waste approach to sustainable waste management both slows down the rate at which we use resources and focuses on using resources in cleaner ways (Government of South Australia 2006; Department of Environment Western Australia 2004; Environment Victoria 2003). 'Eco-efficiency' means producing more goods and services with less energy and fewer natural resources, resulting in less waste and pollution. In a 'materials efficient world' or 'closed loop economy', waste creation is minimized by clever product and package design and delivery, and through production processes that exclude wastes (see Chapter 5). Discarded materials are recovered for their inherent value and reused, recycled and reprocessed to optimize their qualities.

The Waste Hierarchy

Minimizing waste involves analysis of waste in the home, school and office. Integrated waste management reduces waste at source. Waste avoidance means buying a minimum of products and packaging and buying goods that can be recovered to use again. Waste materials that cannot be recovered for reuse and recycling must be disposed of using environmentally sound landfills above current environmental protection licensing standards (Productivity Commission 2006; Environmental Protection Act Qld 1994 2000; Government of South Australia 2006).

The 'waste hierarchy' prioritizes practices from the most to the least preferred. It is based on the following criteria: avoid, reduce, reuse, recycle, recover energy, and dispose. At the heart of integrated waste management, the waste hierarchy illustrates a behavioural, attitudinal and action-oriented process designed to minimize the total volume of waste going to landfill. Reduce, reuse and recycle are also referred to as the '3 Rs'. Discussion of these household strategies demonstrates the complexities of informing householders about waste generation and management. Householders need to think about each daily purchase: Is it necessary? What quantity is ideal? Can it be reused or recycled to contribute to sustainable and integrated waste management nationally?

The first and second preferred options are to *avoid* purchases and to *reduce* consumption – buying only what is necessary, considering hiring instead, buying more durable items, and so on. Manufacturers package goods to protect them in transport and storage and to protect consumers' health. However, packaging can be excessive. Consumers should choose lightly packaged items. With small, single-serve items the ratio of packaging to product is usually high compared with bulk purchases. However, buying in bulk can cause wastage depending on the use-by date and household needs.

The third option is to reuse or pass on for reuse – 'one person's trash is another person's treasure' – through the likes of a second-hand dealer. Items can be repaired or combined with another material to make new, functional products. Waste paper can be reused as scrap paper. Old clothing and curtains can be donated to charity or used as rags. Old toothbrushes can be reused as cleaning tools. Egg cartons can become seedling trays.

The fourth option is recycling: the process of recovering, reprocessing and using reprocessed resources to make new materials or products. Thus manufacturers use fewer natural resources and less energy. Recycling schemes are provided through local council waste collection and treatment. Individuals have two tasks in recycling processes. First, they need to present materials for recycling by putting only the right plastics, glass, paper, steel and aluminium items in the recycling bin and, when away from home, investigate what recycling services are available and materials accepted. (The complexities of these processes are discussed further below.) Second, individuals need to purchase new products made from recycled materials.

Householders can support recycling in their backyards too, by establishing and managing a compost bin or worm farm. Composting replicates the recycling of materials that occurs in natural systems, i.e. 'nutrient cycling', which maintains soil nutrients and plant communities and sustains ecosystems. In nature, matter is neither destroyed nor created, it simply changes form; recycling resources is very important in natural systems. The mass of organic waste constitutes almost half of the average domestic household's waste stream: typically, fruit and vegetable scraps make up about one-third and the rest is from the garden.

Deposited in a landfill, organic material breaks down underground to release methane and carbon dioxide, major contributors to the greenhouse effect. Organic waste is easily diverted from landfill by using compost or worm farms in homes, schools, work places and on large commercial sites. The process is essentially the same, but large-scale systems demand faster composting times for economic sustainability, shredding all materials as finely as possible before starting the composting. Compost is beneficial for creating kitchen gardens and other domestic vegetation.

The final option of 'last resort' is disposal. Often the only choice to councils without landfill sites in their municipality is to transport waste to a landfill site elsewhere, which will involve the labour and material costs of building a facility where waste is off-loaded into pits, transferred to large trucks and transported to landfill. This issue raises broader questions such as population policies. Most manufactured materials persist in the environment for a very long time. Landfills take up space that is important for natural habitat (see Chapter 18). As outlined above, by-products from the decomposition of our waste include leachate and methane gas, which endanger the wider environment and require management, especially to protect catchments and the atmosphere. Integrated waste management is a holistic policy response to the social and environmental implications of waste.

Integrated Waste Management

Guided by the waste hierarchy, Australian governments, businesses, organizations and individuals are developing strategies and programs for integrated, sustainable waste management. See Table 10.1 for a representative range of approaches and examples. Aside from these efforts, many community-based programs focus on litter and recycling. Both issues indicate the significance of community education. Waste management cannot succeed without well-informed residents and sustainable household practices. Waste-education facilitators can introduce community members to the mysteries of recycling and show them how to set up and manage compost bins and worm farms. For instance, Queensland's Logan City Council Watch Out Waste community education program offers:

* Community presentations explaining how recycling is collected and processed, and teaching residents waste minimization skills such as establishing a worm farm.
* Tours and open days of the local waste management facility.
* Special events, such as the annual Waste Awareness Week, which raises awareness of waste minimization at various venues throughout Logan.

Table 10.1   Waste management principles and strategies

Waste Management Principles and Strategies	Practical Examples
Polluter Pays: A principle stating that those who cause industrial pollution should offset its effects by compensating for the damage incurred, or by taking precautionary measures to avoid creating pollution (Evolution Markets 2005).	A common example of polluter pays for householders is a landfill tip fee, where the waste generator is directly responsible for the cost of material disposal and treatment, rather than the entire community bearing landfill management costs through municipal rates or levies. The States have adopted polluter pays approaches to business, controlling pollution through economic incentives: the South Australian Marine Environment Protection Act 1990 established effluent fees for discharges to marine and coastal waters, and Victoria has a load-based licensing system for effluent discharges. In these cases, instead of a fixed licence fee, payments are linked to distinct economic activities, kinds of pollutants discharged, levels of discharge and the sensitivity of receiving environment (Australian Government 2006).
User Pays Principle: Cost sharing principle, whereby the end user of a product or resource is charged for the full supply cost (Mallee Catchment Management Authority 2004).	Mosman Council (NSW) offers residents a choice of bin sizes for waste collection based on the principle of user pays; less waste means a smaller bin and a lower waste charge (Mosman Municipal Council 2006)

Extended Producer Responsibility (EPR): a policy whereby producers accept significant direct or financial responsibility for treating or disposing of products. The distinguishing features of EPR policies are to shift responsibility upstream to the producer and to provide incentives for producers to consider environmental implications when designing products (OECD 2006).	The National Packaging Covenant is a self-regulatory agreement between industries in the packaging chain and all spheres of government, a leading instrument for managing packaging waste in Australia. The covenant aims to minimize environmental impacts of consumer packaging waste throughout the entire life cycle of the packaging, closing the recycling loop and developing economically viable and sustainable recycling collection systems (Australian Government 2006).
Waste Stream Analysis: determination of the quantity and qualities of individual components present in a waste stream (Standards Australia 1998).	Information on waste-stream analysis, including data from around Australia, can be found at the Australian Waste Database (CSIRO and Department of Environment and Heritage 2006).
Resource Recovery: recovery and reuse of materials or energy.	Local government kerbside recycling systems are familiar examples of resource recovery.
Resource Exchange: works on the principle that 'one man's trash is another man's treasure'. Resource exchange facilitates business-to-business exchange of waste or unwanted materials (Global Presence 2000).	The Waste Exchange Database, developed by the Victorian Environment Protection Authority and the Victorian Waste Management Association, brings waste generators and potential waste receivers together to identify reuse and recycling options for wastes otherwise disposed of to landfill. One can browse the database for wastes that are wanted or available for reuse or recycling or simply register on-line to place a free advertisement (EPA 2006).
Plastic Bag Reduction Campaigns: designed to encourage reduction in use of plastic bags, often through providing alternatives.	The Bribie Island Chamber of Commerce 'Bribie Bag' and associated education and awareness campaign was initiated by the local Chamber of Commerce to help the island become a plastic bag free zone and reduce the impact of littered bags on the precious marine environment and national park. The project targets all island businesses, residents and visitors through the local media, town and retail signage, and an annual festival (Keep Australia Beautiful Queensland 2006).

Litter

Litter is an issue for every city in Australia. Litter includes: cigarette butts, plastic straws, bottle caps and rings, fast and snack food packaging, broken glass and plastic, large furniture, electrical appliances, tyres and car bodies. Litter is 'rubbish on the run' – refuse escaped from overfull or open bins, rubbish left in gutters or on the ground in public spaces, or materials found floating in waterways. New sources of litter emerge with lifestyle changes, such as: increasing sales of takeaway food, increased production of advertising ('junk mail') and automatic teller machine slips. Although it might seem trivial and superficial compared with business and household waste, a discussion of litter clearly illustrates the environmental impacts and community-wide responsibilities for waste.

Many manufactured materials, such as plastics, do not assimilate into the environment well and persist for a very long time. Litter affects the immediate environment or travels to impact on surrounding catchments and flora and fauna. Addressing litter has become an environmental priority because of negative affects on:

- Wildlife (choking and strangling birds and animals).
- Water quality (diminished).
- Open spaces (streets, parks and waterways becoming dirty and unsightly).
- Drains (blockages).
- The community purse (costs).
- People (hazards, such as broken glass).
- Landscape (likelihood of fire).
- Valuable and recoverable resources and materials.

A study undertaken by Community Change Consultants for the Beverage Industry Environment Council (BIEC 1997, 7–8) found that:

- More than half of all littering occurred within 5 metres of a bin.
- There is no such thing as a littering 'type'. People of all ages and social backgrounds were observed littering and using bins inappropriately.
- Australians of all ages are more likely to use bins than to litter.
- The people least likely to litter were those aged under 15 years.
- There is no clear line between 'litterers' and 'binners'. Many people both littered and used bins in the same hour.
- Cigarettes are three times more likely to be littered than binned.
- A high proportion of littering occurs in locations where the rubbish can be hidden or in places resembling litter bins.
- Factors affecting disposal include: the person's attitude, their skill in monitoring their own behaviour and the disposable objects, the type and placement of bins at the site, the nature and distance of other 'bin like' objects near the person, the type of object and the context in which disposal occurs.

Such findings demonstrate the importance of informing individuals and households of the impacts of their practices and creating policies and strategies to counter inappropriate practices. Anti-litter legislation has been developed and anti-littering organizations, such as Clean Up Australia (2006) – now a global movement – and Keep Australia Beautiful (2005), have been formed to run campaigns urging people not to litter.

Recycling Challenges

Australian city dwellers are expected to sort domestic waste according to its destination, to landfill or for recycling. To minimize costs and maximize the benefits of recycling, householders need to understand recycling processes, what can be recycled. Plastics include a range of compounds made from non-renewable oil and gas and not all are recyclable. Householders must know which items can be and how to identify them.

Householder ignorance and apathy results in complex difficulties for recycling. Glass, made from non-renewable resources such as silica (from sand), soda ash and limestone and wholly recyclable, offers an example. In south-east Queensland many tons of sand for glass is mined from Stradbroke Island (eastern Moreton Bay) every day. The more glass that is recycled, 'post consumer glass', the less sand that needs to be removed from this popular recreation island to manufacture replacement bottles and jars.

Although all glass is recyclable, window glass, glass light bulbs and pyrex are made from different ratios of the same basic ingredients to produce glass with different characteristics. Manufacturing processes are altered to produce glass with different characteristics – glass that can be heated, does not shatter or is stronger. Only glass bottles and jars wholly compatible with remanufacturing processes are acceptable. Therefore, successful glass recycling relies heavily on householders presenting the correct materials for recycling and on the materials recovery facility carefully sorting recycling materials.

The biggest difficulty in glass recycling is contamination from small pieces of other glass and non-recyclables, such as window glass, pyrex, stones, coffee cups, crockery, crystal, light bulbs, or heat-proof oven and cookware. A small piece of window glass or pyrex in the furnace used to manufacture glass will not melt fully. Impurities form lumps in the finished item, such as a bottle, which is then dramatically weakened and likely to break under stress. The most common stress for glass bottles is during filling and transport or when exposed to temperature changes, such as storing or removal from the fridge. In these contexts breakages can be dramatic, even explosive. Therefore quality standards regarding recycled cullet are stringent. For example, loads of recycled glass cullet discovered to contain as little as 250g (the equivalent of one coffee cup) may result in the entire load (up to 18 tonnes) being rejected (Schmidt 2005).

Recycling results in huge environmental savings. Using cullet in the manufacture of glass reduces the energy needed for melting by up to 25 per cent, saving fuel as well as raw materials. Paper products are made from 'pulp' produced by crushing plants, normally trees. Recycling paper conserves trees and saves water and electricity. A ton of paper produced with recycled materials saves 17 trees and uses half of the water required to make paper from virgin materials (AMCOR Limited 2005).

Almost any paper can be recycled, except for paper used for hygiene purposes, greasy or food-contaminated papers, waxed cardboard and paper products containing other non-paper materials (such as envelopes with transparent address windows). If householders diligently sort papers, recycling is shortened and more efficient.

Pure metals are made from non-renewable minerals and ores by melting and extraction processes, which use large amounts of energy. However, metals are recyclable through melting and reshaping. Large steel items are not recycled through the bin collection system due to health and safety risks, damage to collection and sorting equipment, as well as destruction of other potentially recyclable materials. Australia is one of the largest sources of the mineral bauxite. Bauxite is made into aluminium by an energy intensive process called electrolysis. Five tons of bauxite is required to produce one ton of aluminium, but recycling aluminium saves energy. Producing twenty drink cans from recycled materials uses the same amount of energy as making one can from raw materials (Visy Pty Ltd 2004).

Conclusion

Waste management strategies in Australian cities will continue to be premised on the principles outlined in the waste hierarchy – emphasizing avoidance and reduction as the preferred options and minimal disposal to landfill. If Australia is to move down from the top of the table of nations producing the most waste per capita, new waste services and technologies will need to be introduced coupled with an informed, active community prepared to adopt waste minimization principles in production, consumption and disposal.

Sustainable waste management is the responsibility of the three key groups involved in generating and managing waste in Australia: the producers, through extended producer responsibility; the generators, including the household through polluter and user pays approaches, waste minimization, participation in resource recovery processes, and participation in reuse/exchange programs; and the legislators, who provide economic and other legislative instruments to catalyse individual and organizational behaviour change.

References

AMCOR Limited (2005), AMCOR: Leading Through Innovation [website], <http://www.amcor.com/default.aspx?id=529>, accessed 20 December 2006.

Australian Government (2006), National Packaging Covenant [webpage], Department of the Environment and Heritage [website], <http://www.deh.gov.au/settlements/waste/covenant/index.html>, accessed 20 December 2006.

Beeton, R., Buckley K., Jones, G., Morgan, D., Reichelt, R. and Trewin, D. (2006), *Australia State of the Environment 2006* [Independent Report by the 2006 Australian State of the Environment Committee to the Australian Government Minister for the Environment and Heritage] (Canberra: Department of the Environment and Heritage).

BIEC (1997), *Understanding Littering Behaviour in Australia* (Sydney: Beverage Industry Environment Council).

Clean Up Australia (2006), [website, home page], <http://www.cleanup.com.au>, accessed 1 July 2006.

CSIRO and Department of Environment and Heritage (2006), *Australian Waste Database* [website], <http://awd.csiro.au/default.aspx>, accessed 20 December 2006.

Department of Environment Western Australia (2004), *Statement of Strategic Direction for Waste Management in Western Australia* Zero Waste WA: Live the Vision [website] (2005), <http://www.zerowastewa.com.au/ourwork/strategypolicy/>, accessed 20 December 2006.

Environment Victoria (2003), Zero Waste [webpage], <http://www.envict.org.au/inform.php?item=6>, accessed 20 December 2006.

Environmental Protection Act Qld 1994 (2000), *Environmental Protection (Waste Management) Policy 2000,* Reprinted as in force on 4 October 2004, Reprint No. 2B, Office of the Queensland Parliamentary Counsel.

EPA (2006), Waste Exchange Database, How To Turn Your Waste into a Valuable Resource [webpage], Environmental Protection Authority Victoria [website], <http://www.epa.vic.gov.au/waste/database.asp>, accessed 20 December 2006.

Evolution Markets Incorporated (2005), Glossary of Terms [webpage], <http://www.evomarkets.com/ghg_glossary.html>, accessed 20 December 2006

Fuller, P., Smith, G., Wright T. and Zoi, C. (2000), *Report of the Alternative Waste Management Technologies and Practices Inquiry April 2000* [Independent Report by the Alternative Waste Management Technologies and Practices Inquiry Committee to the State Government of New South Wales Office of the Minister for the Environment] (Sydney: Government of New South Wales).

Global Presence (2000), Resource Exchange Information System: For Regional Exchange Operators [GP website], About Resource Exchange [webpage], <http://www.globalpresence.com.au/exchange/about.htm> accessed 20 December 2006.

Government of South Australia (2006), Zero Waste SA [website], <http://www.zerowaste.sa.gov.au/>, accessed 20 December 2006.

Keep Australia Beautiful (2005), Keep Australia Beautiful National Association [website], <http://www.keepaustraliabeautiful.org.au>, accessed 1 July 2005.

Keep Australia Beautiful Queensland (2006), Programs and Campaigns: Plastic Bags [webpage], <http://www.keepaustraliabeautiful.org.au/qld/01_cms/details.asp?ID=205> accessed 20 December 2006.

Mallee Catchment Management Authority (2004), Mallee CMA [website], Glossary: Common Malleee CMA Terms [webpage], <http://www.malleecma.vic.gov.au/glossarymcma.asp>, accessed 20 December 2006.

Mosman Municipal Council (2006), MMC [website], Waste and Recycling Services [webpage], <http://www.mosman.nsw.gov.au/environment/waste.html>, accessed 20 December 2006.

OECD (2001), *OECD in Figures: Statistics on the Member Countries*, Organization for Economic Cooperation and Development Publications, <http://www.oecdbookshop.org/>, accessed 19 December 2006.

OECD (2005), *OECD in Figures 2005: A Supplement to the OECD Observer; Statistics on the Member Countries*, Organization for Economic Cooperation and Development Publications, <http://www.oecdbookshop.org/>, accessed 19 December 2006.

OECD (2006), *OECD Environmental Policies and Instruments: Extended Producer Responsibility* [webpage], <http://www.oecd.org/document/19/0,2340,en_2649_34281_35158227_1_1_1_1,00.html>, accessed 20 December 2006.

Productivity Commission (2006), *Waste Generation and Resource Efficiency*, [Draft Report 23 May 2006] (Canberra: Productivity Commission).

Sahlin, J., Unger, T., Olofsson, M., Ekvall, T. and Sundberg, J. (2002), 'Heat and Power from Waste Incineration in Sweden – How Will it Develop Under Future CO2 Commitments?', *Waste Management World Magazine* January–February 2002: 27–33.

Schmidt, A. (2005), 'Gold Coast City Council: Taking Recycling to a New Level', *Waste Disposal and Water Management in Australia* 32:3, 5–10.

Schönning, M. (2006), *Integrated Waste Management in Sweden,* Integrated Waste Services Association [website], <http://www.wte.org/docs/060510_Waste-mgt-Sweden.pdf >, accessed 19 December 2006.

Standards Australia (1998), *Australian/New Zealand Standard*^{TM}*: Waste Management Glossary of Terms,* AS/NZS 3831:1998 (Homebush/Wellington: Standards Australia/Standards New Zealand).

Swedish Environmental Protection Agency (2005), *A Strategy for Sustainable Waste Management* Sweden's Waste Plan [agency website], <http://www.naturvardsverket.se/bokhandeln/dse/620-1249-5>, accessed 19 December 2006.

van Beukering, P. (1999), 'Analysing Urban Solid Waste Developing Countries – A Perspective on Bangalore, India', *Warmer Bulletin* July 2006: 12–20.

Visy Pty Ltd (2004), *Visy Recycling* Visy [website], Aluminium and Steel [webpage], <http://www.visy.com.au/divisions/category_page.aspx?did=1&sid=3&cid=89&scid=93>, accessed 20 December 2006.

Part III
Community and Civil Society

Chapter 11

Community Action and Engagement for Sustainability

James Whelan

Introduction

Community action shapes the urban landscape of Australian cities and towns. Our urban future will be just as much determined through vigilant and resourceful action by residents' groups and environmentalists as by the innovative policy work, solutions-oriented research and clever design outlined in other chapters of this book.

Vigorous community action is clearly an important element of planning processes in Queensland's South East region. This rapidly growing coastal area and its hinterland struggle to reconcile population growth with maintaining and restoring a mega-diverse natural environment. Community groups in the region have responded to this challenge with creative and tenacious strategies to conserve and restore habitat, minimize waste and consumption, educate, entertain and protest. On the Gold Coast and in the rural village of Maleny on the Sunshine Coast community action has generated involvement, awareness and sustainable enterprises, as well as averting some of the more destructive development tendencies and proposals.

Civic and conservation groups in such Australian cities and towns participate actively in government-initiated community involvement activities but often find engagement and consultation has minimal impact on planning decisions. As a result, residents with clear priorities for urban futures rely on community action, organizing and mobilizing, to influence decisions. Their experiences suggest local and State government authorities struggle with deliberative, inclusive and iterative decision-making processes. Campaign anecdotes recounted here through an activist lens shed light on decision-making processes for a sustainable urban future.

Community Action: Vital to Sustainability

Community action is vital to sustainability. Without the active involvement of community members in shaping towns and cities, development is unlikely to follow a sustainable pattern. This conclusion has been consistently drawn in sustainability blueprints, at least since the World Commission on Environment and Development Report (WCED 1987) *Our Common Future*. International and domestic sustainability plans, including Agenda 21, the consensus action plan that emerged from the 1992

World Earth Summit, reinforce this conviction. Broad public participation in decision-making and genuine partnership between community, government and industry are prerequisites for the achievement of ecologically sustainable development (ESD). The practical benefits of community involvement are now accepted at all levels of Australian government. Through active self-determination, citizens mobilize resources (including funds and volunteerism that may not have been available otherwise), generate and share knowledge, contribute to better decisions and create community solutions in tune with community needs (Wates 2000, 4–5). Public participation also has the potential to accomplish a more equitable distribution of environmental risk or even diminish risk (Schlosberg 2002, 13).

The 'sustainable community' narrative comprises a set of assumptions or beliefs: firstly, decisions ideally are made through equitable, deliberative and inclusive processes that allow community members a range of options for involvement; secondly, these processes encourage and support social learning, negotiation, and community building (a positive feedback loop); and, thirdly, the resulting decisions are ones that everyone can live with, and that steer the community toward sustainability. A fourth thread is that subscription to the narrative is universal and in the public interest. This narrative motivates elected representatives and planners to actively involve stakeholders in decision making, and encourages community members to participate in civic life. However, some contemporary examples of activists in Australian cities demonstrate the consequences of overwriting the storyline of environmental democracy with top-down, decide-announce-defend governance arrangements.

Two Australian communities – a booming coastal city and a small rural community – provide the backdrop for this discussion. Few Australian cities illustrate the dilemmas of sustainable urban development better than the Gold Coast. This sixth-largest city in Australia expects to grow by one-third to 700,000 in the next fifteen years. Having started life as a holiday resort village, the Gold Coast now extends along almost 70 km of coastline and is rapidly extending into the coastal hinterland, one of Australia's fifteen biodiversity 'hotspots' (DEH 2005). The Gold Coast City Council (GCCC) considers this city the most biologically diverse in Australia. The protection of the region's flora and fauna and institutions that support community involvement in the burgeoning city clearly warrant urgent government and community action. This is equally true of Maleny, a rural village of roughly 1,700 located on the Maleny Plateau, which has a dispersed population of around 4,500. Such hinterland towns and villages and coastal cities of the Sunshine Coast are all experiencing rapid population growth and consequent pressures on both the biophysical and social environments.

Empowered Communities, Powerful Women

The Gold Coast City Council's on-line community directory lists more than 2,000 non-profit community groups, including fifteen environment groups. The diversity, resourcefulness and tenacity of community action is revealed by looking closely at one of these groups, the Gold Coast and Hinterland Environment Council (Gecko 2006). Six local environment groups founded this umbrella organization in 1989.

Gecko House, on the banks of Currumbin Creek, is a hive of voluntary activity. As well as doing advocacy and community building work, Gecko has created three non-profit businesses. Gecko Regen coordinates tree planting and revegetation projects including the rehabilitation of landfill sites, and employs thirty people to manage its nursery, field projects and training. Gecko Recycle is modelled on successful reverse garbage enterprises in Brisbane and Sydney, and redirects resources from the waste stream. And Gecko Ed helps schools and other educational institutions engage qualified environmental educators. Volunteers also provide a free information service and website. Gecko is perhaps best known for community events, including the Gold Coast's annual World Environment Day 'Do' and the 'Clean Up Australia Day'. Both events provide opportunities for thousands to participate in environmental learning and action and have been recognized through awards and sponsorship. Gecko creates further community involvement opportunities with regular information nights, conferences, seminars, a monthly meeting of member groups, Walk With Wildlife guided bushwalks and artGecko participatory cultural events.

For a small village, Maleny has a remarkably strong community sector. An on-line directory (*Sunweb* 2005) lists almost seventy diverse community organizations in the town, from a recorder group to nursing mothers, film society, Landcare and hospital auxiliary. Jordan and Haydon (2003) interviewed members of almost one hundred and fifty village groups. The City of Caloundra, of which Maleny is a satellite settlement, boasts more than twenty-three voluntary community-based environmental organizations (CC 2001b). A striking feature of community life in Maleny is the more than twenty cooperatives established since the 1970s. Their objectives include the coordination, provision and support of housing, whole foods, social and cultural activities, education and learning, artistic and publishing enterprises, conservation and waste minimization, credit, finance and business incubation. Maleny's cooperative sector has received international attention, contributing to the town's spirit of cooperation and enterprise (Schwarz and Schwarz 1997) in a time when Australian rural communities have been declining. Cooperatives have created, directly, at least one hundred and thirty jobs (Jordan 2000; 2003) and, indirectly, hundreds more. Maleny's Local Energy Transfer System (LETS) facilitates the exchange of 'bunya', a non-cash 'currency' named after the edible nut prized by the region's traditional owners, in return for labour services, the first of its kind in Australia (Douthwaite 1998).

In researching Maleny, it is impossible to ignore the narrative of an empowered community seeking to determine its own sustainable destiny. This shone through in radio interviews (ABC 2003) in which Maleny locals spoke of their community having a high level of social capital and cohesion, comparing it to a 'tribe', an intentional community, and suggesting these attributes provide a degree of resilience in a time of rapid change. For this reason, the unsuccessful community campaign examined here is of particular interest.

Another feature of community action in Maleny, the Gold Coast and other Australian cities is the pivotal role of women. Lois Levy and Sheila Davis have been the public faces of Gecko for fifteen years. Lois's profile on Gecko's website

(2006) communicates her belief that 'an educated community plays a vital role in protecting and caring for nature'. As well as being a full-time TAFE instructor and social worker, she received an Order of Australia medal in 2001 for services to the environment. Sheila is widely recognized as a tenacious battler and community builder. She juggles being Gecko's Campaign Coordinator with raising two children, as well as writing and volunteering for several other community groups. Jill Jordan is arguably Maleny's best-known community activist. During the last thirty years, Jill helped found and steer cooperatives locally and around Australia. In the early 1990s she served as a councillor for the rural division of Caloundra City, encompassing Maleny.

Jill, Sheila, Lois and the many, many women involved in community actions described here are part of a bigger picture. Women often drive grassroots campaigns in Australia and internationally. This is seen in Kathleen McPhillips's (2002) collection of activists' accounts of community toxics campaigns in Australia, Lois Gibbs's leadership against toxic waste dumping in Love Canal (USA), and women leading the demand for justice in Bhopal, India, where Union Carbide released poisonous chemicals in 1984, and opposition to nuclear power stations in Europe (Miles and Shiva 1993,14).

Eisler (1987: 189) attributes women's dynamic contribution to community life to socialization processes that encourage men to 'pursue their own ends, even at the expense of others' whereas women are socialized to 'see themselves primarily as responsible for the welfare of others, even at the expense of their own well-being'. Milbrath (1989: 54) concludes that 'women have a much better chance of saving the world than men'. Gender forms an additional element to the narrative: women occupy positions of leadership in healthy communities on the path toward sustainability.

Government Initiated Community Engagement

Local government, the form of government closest to communities, has better opportunities than State and national governments to engage, involve and mobilize communities around sustainability objectives. This is affirmed in 'Local Agenda 21', the international campaign endorsed at the 1992 Rio World Earth Summit, which 'promotes a participatory, long-term, strategic planning process that helps municipalities identify local sustainability priorities and implement long-term action plans' (ICLEI 2005). Ten years after Rio, 6,400 local government authorities in 113 countries had implemented Local Agenda 21 initiatives, including establishing stakeholder groups to develop and implement local sustainability plans. The Local Government Association of Australia and Gold Coast and Caloundra city councils embrace Local Agenda 21.

This commitment to active community participation and to the sustainable communities narrative permeates government discourse. Caloundra City Council's Corporate Plan (CC 2001a, 6) set an objective for 2006, to 'be a City and a community which has created its own destiny and which continues to refine and redefine its future on a regular basis'. Elected representatives express this vision in the city's corporate and strategic plans and *State of the Environment* reports. Caloundra's

Mayor, Don Aldous (Local Government Focus 2004), said the council 'cannot' meet the challenges of governing a rapidly growing and changing city 'in isolation' but 'needs the enthusiasm and participation of its community'.

The GCCC claims to take a consultative approach to decisions about flood mitigation, catchment management, rates, beach and harbour management, transport, tourism, crime and safety. The importance attached to community involvement in decision-making is evident in the Harbour Planning Study, which GCCC (2003) refers to as having reconciled 'traditionally competing interests to construct a long-term mechanism for area management' that integrates 'broadly-based community, environmental and business interests'.

Conservationists were active in this policy-setting exercise and the parallel Waterfuture Strategy, which examined water quality and quantity options for this drought-prone city. In developing the Waterfuture Strategy, GCCC used a range of community engagement processes. Following initial research, the council disseminated a discussion starter that outlined problems and possible solutions and held community information sessions, workshops and focus groups. A newsletter and survey were distributed throughout the city, generating 9,000 responses. To develop a strategy that would 'create a feeling of joint ownership' (GCCC 2005a), the council identified and addressed questions of community trust and confidence in the council to ensure the strategy did not 'ignore community opinion' (GCCC 2005b). This council is not unique in experiencing distrust and criticism concerning provision for community involvement in governance. Woolcock et al. (2003) note these concerns are widespread and substantial. The council also remains open to community opinion year-round through its on-line consultation panel, which provides regular opportunities for community members to contribute to decisions through surveys and focus groups.

Community groups value such opportunities. Their vision for a sustainable region and members' wide range of interests motivates Gecko to participate in up to a dozen advisory and consultative committees with State and local government authorities at any one time. Lois Levy would like to see Gecko even more involved in making policy.

Conflict: Competing or Complementary Narrative?

Despite strong expressions of support for community involvement to steer sustainability, Maleny and the Gold Coast have generated headlines nationally and internationally for sustained conflict over development decisions. The high level of engagement suggested in local government plans and strategies, and described by community activists interviewed for this chapter, has been a backdrop to urban planning decisions characterized by rancorous conflict, litigation and allegations of secrecy and corruption.

In Maleny, conflict has been triggered by the construction of a supermarket beside picturesque Obi Obi Creek, which crosses the village's main street. On the Gold Coast, a controversy is raging around a proposal to develop a terminal for cruise ships on The Spit, a strip of dunes separating the city's harbour (The

Broadwater) from the ocean. Both developments are contrary to local area plans developed through extensive community consultation. These disputes communicate a contrasting narrative including the following threads:

1. Community action is an essential safeguard against solely economic interests that are, by nature, unsustainable.
2. Government-initiated community engagement practices have strictly limited capacity to counteract these economic interests, especially when local government is overtly influenced by the development industry or overridden by the Queensland Government.
3. Community action that builds power to confront government and industry is an essential part of the mix.

The suggestion that a large supermarket may be built in Maleny has brewed for years and the town's history of cooperative enterprises and buying locally has consistently generated opposition to the notion. Community members participating in the development of the town's Local Area Plan (1999–2001) ensured that the planning scheme explicitly ruled out this possibility. Naturally, locals were up in arms when a supermarket development in the heart of the village was subsequently proposed. Community spokesperson, Michael Berry (*Range News* 2002), urged Caloundra City Council to 'exercise its duty of care' by protecting 'the retail and social heart of this town', noting, as visitors do almost immediately, that Maple Street embodies the village community's spirit. Conducting interviews with locals at footpath cafés on Maple Street – the source of all the quotes and background information without specific reference in this chapter – I was continually interrupted by greetings and connections typical of a close-knit town. This spirit was spectacularly demonstrated when the village's existing independent supermarket celebrated its centenary and almost 2,000 people turned out.

Even before Woolworths secured its site, community organizing began in earnest. People were galvanized by concerns about traffic generated by the proposed supermarket's 180 parking spaces, stormwater and trade-waste management, anticipating impacts on the town's economy and character, the loss of open space and impacts on a recognized platypus habitat. (Maleny is one of the very few towns where these shy monotremes can be regularly observed in the heart of an urban area.)

Another significant point of community opposition to the proposal was the decision-making process. Community members felt left out, and expressed outrage through a long series of community meetings, rallies and publications. As the development approval processes gained momentum, so did the community campaign. The council's failure to embed the wishes of the community into its 2004 strategic plan (the local town planning scheme) allowed the State government to take the supermarket decision out of the community's hands. A petition asking for the decision to remain the council's responsibility was signed by 2000 Maleny residents but failed, which prompted Michael Berry (*Range News* 2002) to note:

We are locked out of the process and Council has no duty to take heed of resident objections. In other words, a developer living in Melbourne can decide to fundamentally change the character of the Maleny township without ever having been here and without the township having any say in that change.

In the ensuing conflict, councillors, town planners and community leaders pointed the finger at each other, while Woolworths moved closer to realizing its intention. One councillor suggested that community representatives in the local area planning group were responsible for failing to include provisions against such a proposal in the council's planning scheme. Jill Jordan was quick to point out, however, that the voluntary committee members:

> gave up their nights and Sundays for three years to do a great job on developing a plan that the community wanted and had 'signed off' on, and they shouldn't be castigated for not doing what the Council Planning Department, whose planners are being paid $80,000 per annum, should have done!

Community action (2004–2005) culminated in a series of well-attended rallies and protest actions. There were regular community-initiated negotiations involving Woolworths, the construction company and the council. The Deen Brothers, who had come to fame for their part in the midnight demolition of several heritage buildings in Brisbane, were hired to clear forty large trees on the site in April 2004. Heavy machinery rolled into town at night. The community's condemnation was palpable. Over two hundred people attempted to stop the work despite the lack of warning. With the support of local Aboriginal groups, approximately seventy protestors occupied the site chanting, 'We won't shop there,' and, 'We shall overcome' (*Courier Mail* 2005a). Around twenty of them erected tents and marked out the platypus burrows they believed would be destroyed. Maleny local, Daniel Jones, climbed one of the remaining bunya pines, where he stayed for 100 days. His supporters in the community (including local businesses) provided warm meals and solidarity throughout the winter months, further demonstrating the depth of community support for the protest.

In May 2004, the Woolworths developer, Cornerstone Properties, offered to sell the site to the council and community for $A1.89 million (considerably more than the $A600,000 paid nine months previously). A petition with 5,300 signatures – more than the town's entire population – contributed to the council's effort to acquire the land as a community asset. Despite extraordinary community fundraising efforts and a part commitment by the council, the asking price was not achieved. The whole scenario was replayed in July 2005 when an eleventh hour deal was brokered with the new Woolworths developer, Uniton Pty Ltd, to purchase the site. By mortgaging their homes and pledging donations, the small community raised $A2 million within 48 hours. The developer spurned the cheque on the grounds that Woolworths had not agreed to the deal. The opportunity for a win-win conclusion was lost, and construction commenced. Even so, creative and vociferous community opposition to the supermarket continued. In July 2005, Maleny residents lay head to toe in a nearby park, spelling out anti-Woolworths slogans and, in August, Daniel Jones, dressed in a platypus suit, re-entered the construction site to lock himself to heavy machinery.

It was difficult to imagine Woolworths succeeding in Maleny, where placards, stickers, t-shirts and banners reading, 'Don't shop there', 'Support small business', 'Spare Maleny from bad planning', and 'Keep Maleny's character', urged shoppers to boycott the supermarket. On-line activists were encouraged to register opinions on the <http://www.WeWontShopThere.com> website. The gate of the construction site was decorated with ribbons as a reminder of local opposition and locals spoke with conviction about ensuring the business failed. Jill Jordan swore that the community would 'frustrate them at their own game' and 'teach them about economics'. 'At the beginning,' Jill says:

> it was really just the radicals. As the campaign's gone on, it's just grown and grown. As Woolworths have shown themselves to be the bullies they are, it's drawn more and more the conservative community who are now contributing to the strategic options of how we can make this thing fail.

Around the country, people sympathetic to the community's battle abandoned shopping trolleys filled with non-perishable items in Woolworths supermarkets in solidarity.

On the Gold Coast, a similar battle was raging. Community groups, including Gecko, contributed to the Gold Coast Harbour Study, which identified The Spit, a peninsula of sand dunes and open space immediately to the north of the city centre, as an important asset to be retained and enhanced. Specifically, the study (GCCC 2003) resolved that there would be no further private or commercial development on The Spit. Lois described the consultative processes that led to this policy as 'exhausting'. Gecko submitted written responses to the council's monthly drafts and proposals, and eventually 'carried the vote'. Despite the policy, a terminal for large cruise ships and associated on-land development was placed on the drawing board. Community groups identified a range of concerns about this proposal, including: loss of open space, amenity and recreational access on land and water; pollution; economic impacts; waste management; and impacts on marine habitat and biodiversity.

As in Maleny, the dialogue between the community and its local government became somewhat irrelevant as the development decision was placed in the hands of the State government. The project was declared a significant project, championed by the Department of State Development, acting as both proponent and assessor. The cruise terminal was exempted from the State coastal policy. Having decided the area north of Sea World would be a port, the State government was not obliged to recognize the council's planning guidelines. This top-down approach, combined with secrecy surrounding a State government study of liner movements in the seaway, compounded Gecko's lack of confidence in the modes of consultation and engagement on offer. Lois, Sheila and other community leaders declared the foreshadowed Environmental Impact Statement a 'rubber stamp for development' and called for more meaningful dialogue. Gecko (2005) said that the 'Premier and his Government have failed the accountability and transparency test by refusing to provide the community with any information', and warning (*Courier Mail* 2005b):

'They're going to override our town plan. If they do it once what's to stop them doing it again. It sets a precedent.'

A forgiving appraisal of these two scenarios might let government agencies off the hook. Local government authorities cannot be held responsible for planning decisions and methods adopted by State agencies, and vice versa. Some conservationists blame Queensland's Integrated Planning Act for State government decisions that contradict prior community consultation by local government. From a community perspective, however, such justification is unconvincing. Citizens who have actively contributed to policy decisions at either level will naturally react with disappointment, if not outrage, if jurisdiction is subsequently assumed by other agencies.

Having exhausted the usefulness of community delegations and submissions, Gecko and their allies soon turned to alliance building and mobilization. The Save Our Spit (SOS) alliance was formed to pursue the shared concerns of over twenty groups, including conservationists, residents, ratepayers, surfers, divers, recreational fishers and local businesses. In April and July 2005, the alliance held rallies of more than 2,000 people in the Doug Jennings Park on The Spit and collected 6,500 signatures on a petition subsequently carried on a surfboard by local surfers into a meeting of State government ministers and parliamentarians in July 2005.

These two struggles seriously test the 'sustainable community' narrative. Community members participating in consultative policy-setting exercises in Maleny and the Gold Coast speak of being out-voted by pro-development interests, having their input ignored, receiving little or no support for their participation while generous allowances are available to others, and of 'burning out' their voluntary delegates.

Jill considers the council's community engagement activities are 'rigged' and outcomes that might impede development are ignored. Despite maintaining positive relationships with council planning officers and working solidly to facilitate collaboration, Lois Levy says that 'the lines are drawn' between Gecko and GCCC and that relations with developers are worse. During the last five years Gecko noted with concern the termination of the environmental advisory committee and the current mayor's 'lack of interest in community engagement'. Their experience was at odds with the *State of the Environment Report* (CC 2001b, 2), where the mayor acknowledges 'the achievements of the many individuals and community groups who have generously committed their own time to sustain the environment which benefits all of us.' Community groups in both cities consider secrecy is a regular feature of decision making.

It is tempting to suggest a discontented minority fuels such disputes, and to suggest that more effective or creative engagement processes can overcome the conflict by creating a deliberative space for all views to be heard and integrated. But the observations and interviews that inform this chapter suggest that, in these and other communities, planning decisions are infrequently made through satisfactory engagement and consensus-based decision making. Basic standards of transparency and inclusiveness were not adhered to.

During the conflicts described here, a probity audit was launched to investigate Caloundra City Council's decisions as developer and assessment authority for a golf course and residential development in Maleny. Simultaneously, the GCCC was embroiled in a Crime and Misconduct Commission inquiry into allegations of misconduct and election bribery in the 2004 council elections, when a secret developer-backed election campaign fund was established to support a majority of 'like-minded' (pro-development) councillors. The inquiry would also pursue allegations that a subdivision of one of the region's last cane farms 'ignored Council officers' advice and state government planning regulations' (*Sunshine Coast Daily* 2005). Lois Levy said, 'It won't matter what happens now with the Crime and Misconduct Commission. That Council is dead and buried. Nobody will ever believe them again.'

In terms of democratic legitimacy, voluntary community groups enjoy broad and resilient foundations. Citizens trust and rely on community groups more than government or industry, especially with respect to environmental information (NSW EPA 1994; 2004). Citizens are highly responsive to the rallying calls of conservation groups. Gecko's rallies to conserve The Spit have attracted growing numbers, and their membership is strong. The Maleny protests were well attended and, when it looked like the supermarket site could be bought, $2 million was raised within 48 hours.

Reconciling the Two Narratives

From the experiences of community activists in Maleny and the Gold Coast, it is easy to conclude that polite discussion about the future of Australian cities and towns are unlikely to steer us toward sustainability. Even though government, community and industry almost universally embrace dialogue and deliberation and attempt creative mechanisms for this dialogue, there are compelling reasons for conservationists to rely on mobilization and grassroots politics rather than community engagement.

Conservation victories achieved outside the deliberative space are impressive. In the recent past, community groups on the Gold Coast prevented construction of a cableway through the Springbrook World Heritage Area and cabins in an adjacent conservation area, they attempted to prevent further development on the city's major flood-prone area, the Gurungumbah flood plain, and successfully opposed building the Eastern Tollway through koala habitat. At the same time, they have seen prevailing decision-making approaches result in the incremental erosion of parkland and remnant vegetation – what Lois calls the 'nibble syndrome' – and the wholesale destruction of areas of remnant vegetation for housing development. Community action also prevented a cement batching plant from being established in Maleny. It seems unlikely that the spirit reflected in these campaigns will be diluted or defused. Even as bulldozers cleared the Woolworths site, one Maleny local predicted the campaign loss 'will actually strengthen the idea of Maleny as being an independent community which stands up for its rights and what it believes in' (ABC 2005).

However, there are long-term consequences of failing to provide satisfactory mechanisms for deliberative planning, of forcing conservationists and other community groups to choose between dialogue and oppositional community action that may outstrip short-term gains. Lester Milbrath (1989) suggests the 'dominator society' is incapable of sustainability and that social learning through approaches involving partnership and collaboration is urgently required. Community activists in Maleny and the Gold Coast know this. Despite years of 'hard slog' on committees where they are 'hopelessly outnumbered by rednecks with no idea about environmental planning', Lois, Sheila and Gecko remain committed to dialogue. Jill Jordan is similarly committed to fixing, rather than rejecting, engagement practices. 'Conflict can be magic,' Jill assured me, 'but only when people are genuinely willing to listen, and to change their position on the basis of what they've heard.'

References

ABC (2003), 'Re-Imagining Utopia 5: Alternative Economics', ABC [website], Radio National Life Matters [webpage] 2 June [broadcast], http://www.abc.net.au/rn/talks/lm/stories/s853654.htm>, accessed 15 November 2005.

ABC (2005), 'Police Move in on Maleny Platypus Protest', ABC [website], Radio National PM [webpage] 12 July, <http://www.abc.net.au/pm/indexes/2005/pm_20050712.htm>, accessed 15 November 2005.

CC (2001a), *Corporate Plan: Creating Our Future*, Caloundra City Council [website], <http://www.caloundra.qld.gov.au/website/cityOnline/forms_publications/forms_pubs_home.asp#corporate>, accessed 15 November 2005.

CC (2001b), *State of the Environment Report*, Caloundra City Council [website], <http://www.caloundra.qld.gov.au>, accessed 15 November 2005.

Courier Mail (2005a), 'Protestors Closed Ranks at Woollies Site', 6 May, <http://www.malenyvoice.com/obiobi/media.htm>, accessed 15 November 2005.

Courier Mail (2005b), 'Coast Cruise Terminal Goes Ahead', 16 September, <http://www.ncws.com.au/story/0,10117,16616325-1248,00.html>, accessed 15 November 2005.

DEH (2005), *Australia's 15 National Biodiversity Hotspots*, Department of Environment and Heritage [website], <http://www.deh.gov.au/biodiversity/hotspots/facts.html#3>, accessed 15 November 2005.

Douthwaite, R. (1998), *Strengthening Local Economies for Security in an Unstable World*, 'Epilogue' [webpage, updated February 2003], Foundation for the Economics of Sustainability [website], <http://www.feasta.org/documents/shortcircuit/index.html?epilogue.html>, accessed 15 November 2005.

Eisler, R. (1987), *The Chalice and the Blade: Our History, Our Future* (San Francisco: Harper and Row).

GCCC (2003), *Gold Coast Harbour Study* [Council Report 22], Gold Coast City Council [website], <http://www.goldcoast.qld.gov.au/t_standard2.aspx?PID=3167>, accessed 15 November 2005.

GCCC (2005a), *Gold Coast Waterfuture Strategy 2006–2056*, Gold Coast City Council [website], <http://www.goldcoast.qld.gov.au/t_gcw.asp?PID=3840>, accessed 15 November 2005.

GCCC (2005b), *Gold Coast Waterfuture Community Engagement Report*, Gold Coast City Council [website], <http://www.goldcoast.qld.gov.au/t_gcw.asp?PID=3840>, accessed 15 November 2005.

Gecko (2005), 'Media Release Time for Terminal Accountability', Gecko [website], <http://www.gecko.org.au/Media_Releases/mrTimeForTerminalAccountability0 40705.doc>, accessed 15 November 2006.

Gecko (2006), [website], <http://www.gecko.org.au/>, accessed 25 November 2006.

ICLEI (2005), *Local Agenda 21 (LA21) Campaign* [webpage], International Council for Local Environmental Initiatives Local Governments for Sustainability [website], <http://www.iclei.org/index.php?id=798>, accessed 15 November 2005.

Jordan, J. (2000), 'Focus on the Future: Workshop 2, Jill Jordan on Community Building, Workshop at Rosneath Ecovillage', Rosneath [website], <http://www.rosneath.com.au/resources/jordan-essay.html>, accessed 15 November 2005.

Jordan, J. (2003), 'The Co-operative Movement in Maleny, Queensland', [Case Study No.11. Paper] Co-operative Federation of WA Inc. Conference.

Jordan, J. and Haydon, S. (2003), *Maleny Working Together* (Canberra: Commonwealth Department of Family and Community Services).

Local Government Focus (2004), *Engaging the Community in Tailored Consultation*, <http://www.loc-gov-focus.aus.net/editions/2004/february/engcomm.shtml>, accessed 15 November 2005.

McPhillips, K. (2002), *Local Heroes: Australian Crusades from the Environmental Frontline* (Sydney: Pluto Press).

Milbrath, L. (1989), *Envisioning a Sustainable Society: Learning Our Way Out*, (Albany: State University of New York Press).

Miles, M. and Shiva, V. (1993), *Ecofeminism* (Melbourne: Spinifex).

NSW EPA (1994), *Who Cares About the Environment? A Benchmark Survey of the Environmental Knowledge, Skills, Attitudes and Behaviour of the People of New South Wales.* (Sydney: New South Wales Environmental Protection Authority).

NSW EPA (2004), *Who Cares About the Environment in 2003? A Survey of NSW People's Environmental Knowledge, Attitudes and Behaviours* (Sydney: New South Wales Environmental Protection Authority).

Range News (2002), 'People Power: Residents Vow to Fight Development' 13 December, <http://www.hinterlandgrapevine.com/RNStories03/ShoppingCent-13.12.02.html>, accessed 15 November 2005.

Schlosberg, D. (2002), *Environmental Justice and the New Pluralism: the Challenge of Difference for Environmentalism* (London: Oxford University Press).

Schwarz, W. and Schwarz, D. (1997), 'Culture of Cooperation', *Resurgence* 184, Resurgence [website], <http://www.resurgence.org/resurgence/184/schwarz. htm>, accessed 15 November 2005.

Sunshine Coast Daily (2005), 'Caloundra's Audit Report Stays Shrouded in Mystery' 28 September, *Sunshine Coast Daily* [website], <http://www.sunshinecoastdaily. com.au>, accessed 15 November 2005.

Sunweb (2005), 'Groups and Organisations', Sunweb [website], <http://sunweb. com.au/groups/contacts.html>, accessed 15 November 2005.

Wates, N. (2000), *The Community Planning Handbook: How People Can Shape Their Cities, Towns and Villages in Any Part of the World* (London: Earthscan Publications).

Woolcock, G., Renton, D. and Cavaye, J. (2003), *What Makes Communities Tick? Local Government & Social Capital Action Research Project, Pilot Study in Queensland* (Brisbane: Local Government Association of Queensland and University of Queensland 'Boilerhouse' Community Service & Research Centre).

WCED (1987), *Our Common Future* [Brundtland Report, World Commission on Environment and Development] (Oxford: Oxford University Press).

Chapter 12

WestWyck: An Urban Sustainability Demonstration Site

Mike Hill and Lorna Pitt

Introduction

Sprawling suburbia is the net result of the developer-driven layout of our cities. As western cities sprawl they leave a trail of social, economic and environmental devastation: isolated and disconnected people, decaying infrastructure, motor vehicle worship and domination, and dramatic declines in qualities of design and construction. This chapter describes how a small private enterprise swam against the tide, yet discovered support and success in changing the dominant paradigm of urban development. When a group purchased an inner suburban Melbourne primary school to prevent its demolition they were delivered a rare opportunity to create a demonstration model that saved buildings, respected the environment and built a new community.

WestWyck

WestWyck is sited in West Brunswick, Victoria, Australia (WestWyck 2007). It looks south to the central business district of Melbourne, across Royal Park, and west to the Moonee Ponds Creek with the famous Moonee Valley racetrack, a ten-minute walk away. It is 7 km from the Melbourne Town Hall and twenty minutes, at most times of the day, from the Melbourne airport. It is situated in a designated urban village and has many local facilities on its doorstep.

The WestWyck building has been listed on the National Estate and is within one of Moreland City Council's designated heritage areas. The area contains a mixture of single-fronted Victorian terrace homes, larger hilltop Edwardian houses, some intact Californian bungalows and some more modern infill housing.

WestWyck occupies the building and grounds of the former Brunswick West Primary School. The school ran out of students in the 1980s, just one example of quality urban infrastructure that had lost its purpose and faced the bulldozer as a result of the changing demographics of inner Melbourne. As inner city population levels fell, cash-strapped governments attempted to meet the needs of the sprawling outer suburbs by selling off underused urban social and physical infrastructure.

In 1993 a consortium of five people bought the old school, wanting to save quality infrastructure from demolition and bring to the building a new and vibrant life in its traditional setting. The consortium undertook a feasibility study, which considered its possible uses as housing, a performance venue, backpackers' accommodation and a seminar or conference centre. Initially it operated as a performance venue and occasional seminar facility, becoming well known locally for some high-quality and accessible performances.

Gradually, it became clear that, whichever direction WestWyck took, it would require a high level of investment. At this point, when some members of the original consortium gave notice that they wished to sell out, Lorna Pitt and Mike Hill – the authors of this chapter – committed themselves to buying their partners' shares. They felt that the building was likely to be demolished if placed on the open market.

Subsequently, in 1997, Lorna and Mike dedicated themselves to creating WestWyck as an integrated showpiece of ecologically sustainable development (ESD) and living, a model preservation of quality building stock, and demonstration of high-quality design. To this end, they set out to create a cohesive community by building new dwellings within the former school building and on the former playground.

At the end of the completion of Stage One (2007) the WestWyck development comprised a communal (shared) housing area, five new town houses on the school grounds, and seven warehouse-style apartments skilfully designed into the old classrooms and corridors of a Victorian era school building. By late 2006 four of the schoolhouse apartments were already occupied by new owners, two further apartments were on the market and construction work had commenced on the five townhouses. Marketing was undertaken by a partnership between a local agent and a real estate company specializing in environmental property projects.

Demonstration, Advocacy and Education

A key aim of the WestWyck project had been to create a 'demonstration ecovillage' in an urban location. WestWyck had a mission to influence. Through provision of a demonstration model, it wanted to support and facilitate the evolution of sustainability policies and practices that relate to the built form within urban communities. It targeted change at all associated levels: State government, local government, water and energy authorities and private sectors.

WestWyck has been educational, aiming to raise standards and increase the knowledge base for future residential developments through demonstration and leadership, with a long-term aim to conduct tours to promote issues associated with sustainable housing development. The WestWyck developers consciously set out to make contact and retain relationships with like and related projects in Australia and overseas (see Table 12.1).

ESD the WestWyck Way

WestWyck has developed a residential site according to key sustainability principles of materials efficiency, energy efficiency and water efficiency.

Table 12.1   Examples of projects with aims similar to WestWyck

Project	Website
Australia	
Somerville Ecovillage	<http://www.greenedge.org>
Christie Walk	<http://www.urbanecology.org.au/>
The Sustainable House	<http://www.sustainablehouse.com.au/house.htm>
The Green Building, 60L (60 Leicester Street, Carlton)	<http://www.60lgreenbuilding.com/
Szencorp Building, 40 Albert Rd, Melbourne	<http://www.ourgreenoffice.com/>
CERES, Brunswick	<http://www.ceres.org.au/>
Merri Co-housing & Eco-village, Moreland	<http://members.optusnet.com.au/~cohousing/merri/HOME>
Solar Dwellings	<http://www.solardwellings.com.au/>
Moreland Energy Foundation	<http://www.mefl.com.au/>
WestWyck	<http://www.westwyck.com>
United Kingdom and Republic of Ireland	
Hockerton Housing Estate	<http://www.hockerton.demon.co.uk/>
Beddington Zero Energy Development	<http://www.bedzed.org.uk>
The Village, Cloughjordan	<http://www.thevillage.ie/>

Materials Efficiency

The WestWyck development uses materials efficiently, reusing and recycling at every opportunity, making careful decisions about the sourcing of introduced building products and minimizing materials going to landfill. Healthy building principles have guided its development.

As a starting point, the reuse and recycling of the former school building was the basic objective of the project. 'Normal' practice would have seen truckloads heading for a landfill site and new materials being brought in for replacement buildings. WestWyck worked to a different set of rules altogether, believing that the high quality materials in the beautiful old building could be recommissioned for a new use. So, materials harvested from the demolition of outbuildings and within the school building were either reused within the project or, where possible, sorted and sent for further processing. The reuse of materials included timber floor and lining boards, steel and timber beams, bricks and even former school science laboratory basins.

WestWyck has been able to source recycled, salvaged or second-hand materials, including a generous donation of reclaimed steel windows from Geelong's Ford factory by the family of the company that had originally fabricated them in the 1920s.

Energy Efficiency

At WestWyck, energy efficiency is designed into all dwellings. The same principle of emphasizing reduction applies. Maximum use has been made of solar orientation opportunities, natural ventilation and natural lighting. To achieve reduced consumption of energy, WestWyck has included high-rating insulation, full double-glazing and energy efficient lighting and appliances. A communal gas-boosted solar hot water system was integrated into the hydronic heating for the initial batch of apartments and the new townhouses have been designed to generate some of their own power from a photovoltaic array.

Water Cycle

WestWyck's key water objective has been to reduce usage of potable mains-supplied water. A subsidiary objective was to reduce the discharge of used water from the site via the stormwater and sewerage systems. Water-saving devices (flow restrictors, efficient appliances and efficient fittings) were installed and roof water harvested to replace as much of the mains water as possible (mainly to supply the solar hot water system).

Behavioural objectives have priority too. A CSIRO research project (Grant et al. 2005) found that occupants in two apartments on the site used around two-thirds less water than an average comparable local house. Covenants on the title require that residents maintain the use of water-efficient appliances. The body corporate collects water usage data and discusses these results at its meetings. It also assists in the choice of soap powders and detergents that have minimum impact on soil and ground water.

Treatment and reapplication of used water has further reduced reliance on mains supply. The grey-water treatment plant receives bathroom and laundry water, and subjects it to bacterial, membrane and ultraviolet treatment to create 'Class A' water for reuse in toilet flushing and gardens and, potentially, the laundries.

A key innovation at WestWyck that could be adopted by a wide range of other urban dwellers, including municipal authorities, is a grassed car park which serves as an evapo-transpiration bed. A system of subsurface agricultural piping beneath a layer of crushed rock allows treated water to pass through and seep to the surface, maintaining a grassed surface and allowing excess liquid to transpire and evaporate. The fully lined carpark is surfaced with a proprietary material (Grasspave), which can bear the load of medium-weight vehicle traffic and has suitable grasses planted into it.

WestWyck treats its own black water too. Organic waste, including human waste, as well as food scraps and garden waste, is treated on site in two 3,500 L vermiculture pits under the car park. Solids are processed by worms and the liquid waste pumped through to an evapo-transpiration bed, where it is absorbed and processed by selected plants, such as woolly ti-trees and locally found grasses and river mints, before any residue is pumped to a sewer. This process only occurs if seasonal weather conditions prevent total absorption on site. A generous concession has been gained from the local water authority, Yarra Valley Water, reducing water charges in acknowledgement of the reduced quantity and enhanced quality of discharge.

Collecting roof water for use in the solar hot water system and removing or minimizing impermeable surfaces, such as bitumen and concrete, has reduced the amount of stormwater that needs to be discharged from the site and a system has been designed to retard the passage of stormwater through the site. Swale drains have been constructed and planted out in reeds as a key landscape feature, which partially retards, absorbs and cleans the stormwater before releasing any residual to the stormwater drains. This reduces the impact on local drainage infrastructure and, eventually, waterways.

The plants at WestWyck have been chosen to do jobs. Some are part of the complex process involving transpiration beds so they have to breathe hard to pump out excess moisture. Other plants are designed to hold the water in the stormwater reed beds and slow its flow, purifying it as it moves along and producing an attractive landscape up against the building without causing any structural damage to it. Generally speaking, local indigenous plants have been preferred because they work just by being there. Local indigenous plants attract insects and birds and provide habitat corridors to neighbouring parklands. The local indigenous plant is always a good option in a dry country. It is accustomed to survival without human watering. There are water-loving plants at WestWyck but precious potable water does not quench their thirst. Instead they are fed through the stormwater systems or transpiration beds. An example is the use of *Tristaniopsis laurina* (Kanooka, or Water Gum), a beautiful streamside tree that frequents the rivers of East Gippsland, as a transpiration plant around the car park.

During 2005 and 2006, WestWyck was one of the sites that Museum Victoria selected to participate in its Water Smart Homes project, exposing large numbers of people to water efficiency principles. In 2006, around two hundred people visited on Open Day, with many more learning about WestWyck and water saving through Museum Victoria's written material and website.

Motor Vehicles

WestWyck reduces vehicle intrusion on the site in accordance with the Moreland City Council urban village objectives. The council has acknowledged WestWyck's heritage and environmental commitments with its significant street frontage and has required only one on-site car park per dwelling. The saved space has been dedicated to productive communal food gardens and reed beds.

WestWyck is constructing a communal bike storage facility and has entered into discussions with a local car-share company to locate a vehicle on site for use by neighbours as well as WestWyck residents. Perhaps an ultimate indicator of success would be the conversion of the grassed car park into a village green!

WestWyck – Building Community

WestWyck aims to create 'community' within and to be an active part of the surrounding community. At WestWyck there are many components to 'community'. A new community of 'owners' is forming as people purchase dwellings being built on the site. These people join those already living at WestWyck in the shared accommodation segment of the building and those who still feel an involvement through previous contributions to the project. Other facets of the community involve the designers, the builders, the neighbours and the broader Moreland community.

WestWyck had originally aimed to become a co-housing project by involving interested people early in the design phase of the project and its dwellings. However, WestWyck had limited capacity to pay holding costs on its investment while interested people were located elsewhere and a meaningful decision-making process started. Financing was difficult, with advice from lending and marketing interests to the effect that Australians did not live in shared housing, which was a northern European model. Thus, co-housing objectives were scaled back and stored away for future exploration.

However, one vestige of the co-housing concept is the dedication on a building block to a shared productive garden for the community. The shared bike storage area, a productive food garden and an outdoor recreational space are all part of the design.

A commitment to building community remains a key WestWyck focus, the notion of an ecovillage entailing people being brought together to address environmental issues and share in the development of solutions.

Designing Shared Facilities

The design layout encourages interaction within the development. Each residence opens onto a curved landscaped pathway linking communal spaces such as the shared outdoor recreational areas, the productive garden, the bicycle storage facility, the clothes drying area and the grassed car park. Sharing resources and sharing support needs are vital elements of traditional communities. WestWyck aspires to be a place of sharing.

Communal Household

Already there is a body of people that feel part of the WestWyck community. Since 1993, many communal households formed and re-formed in the northern WestWyck classrooms. While the recent WestWyck development has been unfolding, Lorna and Mike have lived in the northern communal section of the building as part of a large shared household. Artists and activists, students and professionals, employed and unemployed, travellers and others requiring temporary accommodation, musicians, unionists and small business people, retirees and job market entrants have all been part of WestWyck households since it began.

New Owners

As mentioned, a new community of owners has been forming as people purchase new dwellings being constructed on the WestWyck site. There is a high level of integration between the new owners of apartments and those who live in the communal household, involving shared parties, weddings, celebrations and broader involvement in Melbourne's political life. Sharing of resources, interests, transport and skills can be a fundamental way of achieving a conserver society and providing for all our lifestyle requirements. People are attracted to living at WestWyck, or buying into the new dwellings, by the thought of living closer to other people than is the norm in twenty-first century urban areas. The project design, its infrastructure and its protective covenant provide frameworks for the organic growth of this new community. Community decision-making through the body corporate will guide the future direction and management of the WestWyck community and its shared areas and facilities.

Market Model of Community

The community that arrives at WestWyck has been self-selecting and largely delivered by the marketplace. It is very difficult to control who purchases the newly created properties and even harder to apply a filter to the second and third and subsequent generations of purchasers.

Most residents at WestWyck have been committed to a low impact on the environment and have been actively involved in external community activities ranging from political campaigns to arts and culture. WestWyck residents are involved in various community projects. They are physically active as bike riders, soccer players, yoga devotees, campers and bushwalkers. There is a strong interest in gardening of one form or another and it is expected that the shared productive garden will be heavily used.

Building Team

The early residents and first purchasers, those who built the dwellings and the landscape, as well as technical advisers that allowed the concept to grow into a reality, all feel a distinct and integral part of the WestWyck community. Their involvement has entailed strong personal commitments.

WestWyck aspired to provide a place of learning employment for the building team and has benefited, in return, from the strong commitment and clever ideas of the builders and consultants associated with the project. The building team extended its skills through on-the-job training and support, attending courses and learning from project consultants such as a landscape artist.

Local Economy, Local Community

WestWyck aims to be an active part of the broader community, influencing sustainability outcomes, being involved in local environmental activities and campaigns and participating in local council decision making. This includes participation in local high-profile environment groups, such as the Moreland Energy Foundation and CERES (see Chapter 4). WestWyck seeks collaborations with like-minded local sustainable housing projects to develop activities, such as a joint visitors' program promoting ecohousing.

WestWyck has supported the local economy, using local trades people and sourcing local products, making use of and sustaining local infrastructure and services, as well as contributing to the neighbourhood. Many local trades people responded enthusiastically to the WestWyck environmental brief. WestWyck is included in the council map, *There's More to Moreland* (MCC 2005a), which highlights key features of the municipality and it appears in the council's *Inside Moreland* (MCC 2005b, 24) community guide.

Pushing the Boundaries, Learning the Hard Way

WestWyck has been one of the pioneers in creating clustered ecological residential developments in urban settings. The urban context has been the greatest environmental challenge. In cities, land is scarce and highly valued. The lending institution frequently expressed frustration with the slowness of the project. But pioneering work involves a large amount of research and development.

WestWyck has needed to seek out and engage highly innovative consultants to provide site-specific solutions. In 1998, when the sustainability project started, much of the technical advice WestWyck required was simply not available or was unproven. Retrofitting a significant old building like a Victorian era school is time consuming and expensive. The fire separation work alone took months to complete. The builders disappeared into the ceiling cavities for what seemed like months on end!

WestWyck experienced all those vagaries common to the building industry. Every tradesperson seemed to leave Victoria at certain times, such as after the damaging hailstorm in Sydney and during the construction phase for the Olympic Games, also in Sydney. The same factors generated severe materials shortages. At another crucial point, our dedicated and indispensable builder decided it was *the* time in his family's life to take a well-earned sabbatical holiday. Also, having to decontaminate a site used for the previous century as a school had not been expected.

Initially the local water authority placed barriers in the way of on-site sewerage treatment and grey-water systems. There was certainly no offer of support or even any advice about the steps we might be able to take to achieve our objectives. At the time WestWyck finalized its subdivision, the water authority was reluctant to approve it specifically because of the alternative on-site sewerage and grey-water systems.

How things change! An extended drought, a change of management within the water authority, a change of government and the same authority is now encouraging and supporting WestWyck, providing a ready source of advice. As mentioned, WestWyck has even arranged for a significantly reduced water service charge to take account of its minor but partially treated contribution to the sewerage system. Yarra Valley Water even dedicated a page to WestWyck and this special arrangement in its *Sustainability Annual Report* (YVW 2006).

Moreland City Council publicly welcomed an environmentally sustainable development within its municipal boundaries and now includes the site on its tourist map of prominent local sustainable features. However, it is doubtful that WestWyck could have proceeded under most other planning regimes in Victoria. The council had a number of policy positions that supported sustainable building practices. The council designated a precinct containing WestWyck as an urban village (MCC 1997). In an effort to strengthen small viable and local business activity and public transport nodes, the council has encouraged walkable neighbourhood centres for shopping and other interactivity. Our local urban villages were created around such small shopping centres linked to strong public transport systems. WestWyck took advantage of this designation, and its commitment to low-car priority living, to receive some limited parking concessions (see Chapter 7).

WestWyck, Next Steps

Stage One of the WestWyck project ends in 2007. The intrepid developers are still afloat. They may be chastened and humbled but they are certainly wiser and extremely proud of the ecovillage unfolding around them. Stage Two is being pinned to the drawing boards. Stage One achieved such quality that it has added significant value to the site. Further innovative housing will be able to take full advantage of the knowledge acquired and of rapidly developing technologies.

WestWyck hopes that it has been part of the movement for stronger ESD application in buildings, to create new paradigms for addressing climate change. In the longer term Lorna and Mike are confident that WestWyck will become 'just another environmental village', no longer standing out as unique and different in a world where sustainable living has become the norm.

References

Grant, A., Gray, S. and Anderson, N. (2005), 'Sustainable Water Systems Schemes and Technologies: Monitoring Results from Melbourne Site 1' [Unpublished Report for the CRC for Water Quality and Treatment and CSIRO, Highett, Victoria].

MCC (1997), *Moreland City Council Urban Villages Policy* (Coburg: Moreland City Council).

MCC (2005a), *There's More to Moreland* [map] (Coburg: Moreland City Council Strategic Planning Unit).

MCC (2005b), 'An Ecofriendly Village' *Inside Moreland* 3 (Summer), 24.

WestWyck (2007) [website], <http://www.westwyck.com>, accessed 5 February 2007.

YVW (2006) *Sustainability Annual Report 2005–2006* (Melbourne: Yarra Valley Water) – available on-line at WestWyck (2007) [website], <http://www.westwyck.com>, News and Events [webpage], accessed 5 February 2007.

Chapter 13

The Role of Leisure Time in Achieving Sustainability

Richard Denniss

Introduction

Work–life balance has become a barbecue stopper, according to Australian Prime Minister, John Howard (2002). In recent years it has emerged as a topic of such importance that few domestic public policy debates are immune from its influence. Everything from the shortage of doctors and skilled workers to the 'crisis' of population ageing and the need for industrial relations reforms relates back, in one way or another, to the issue of work–life balance. This chapter attempts to extend the realm of work–life balance even further by arguing that it is inextricably linked to societal efforts to balance economic activity with environmental sustainability (Hayden 1999) and that increasing leisure time should be of central concern to those seeking to reduce the adverse impact of human activity on the natural environment.

The first section of this chapter provides an overview of the increasing amount of time that Australian households spend in market work as a result of longer working weeks, the rise of two-income families, and the declining uptake of paid holiday leave. The second section discusses the link between work, spending and environmental impact. It argues that societies organized around long hours of work and high levels of spending are inherently more wasteful and, in turn, environmentally harmful. The third section presents the case for linking increases in leisure time to reductions in environmental impacts. It argues that, while we are told regularly that increased income is desirable because it allows us to have more choices, we are actively discouraged from using our income to buy more time. The final section presents some conclusions. It is argued that the pursuit of increased leisure time would help address a wide range of emerging social and community issues such as isolation, disconnection from community and fear of others.

Working Out Our Lives?

Australians work the longest hours in the developed world (Campbell 2002; Denniss 2003; Gittins and Tiffen 2004) – see Table 13.1. Figures cited in Fagan (2004, 115) show that, by the late 1990s, Australia had the third-highest proportion (27 per cent) of people working more than 48 hours per week. Gittens and Tiffen (2004, 82) ranked Australia tenth within a list of 17 developed countries with respect to the percentage of employed working more than 40 hours per week (47.1 and 48.6 per cent respectively in 1990 and 2000). Among their top ten countries, only the proportions of those working more than 40 hours per week in Australia and the United States had increased between 1990 and 2000.

Table 13.1   Average hours worked per employed person per annum (2000)

Country	Annual Hours
Australia	1855
United States	1835
Japan	1821
New Zealand	1817
Canada	1767
Finland	1730
United Kingdom	1708
Ireland	1690
Sweden	1625
Italy	1622
France	1590
Switzerland	1568
Belgium	1530
Denmark	1504
Germany	1482
Netherlands	1381
Norway	1376
Mean	1641

Source: Adapted from Gittins and Tiffen (2004, 82).

In addition, although the number of public holidays enjoyed by Australians is around the European average, they are entitled to less than average paid annual leave, enjoying only four weeks' leave per year, compared to the European average of five weeks. Some countries currently provide workers with up to six weeks' paid annual leave per year – see Table 13.2.

Far from being the 'land of the long weekend' (Conway 1978), with a culture dominated by a predilection for a 'smoko' and a 'sickie', Australian culture is dominated by a work ethic. Informing a friend or colleague that you are about to take a holiday is more likely to be met with a sarcastic 'some of us are lucky' than a friendly 'me too'. As well as dominating the lives of individuals, these trends have come to dominate relationships and communities. Barbara Pocock (2003) refers to these trends as the 'work life collision'.

Table 13.2   International comparison of paid annual leave and public holidays

Country	Collectively agreed entitlement for annual leave – working days 2001	Minimum of annual leave – working days 2002	Number of public holidays (days)
Australia	NA	20	10–11
Austria	25	25	13
Belgium	NA	20	10
Denmark	30	25	9.5
Finland	25	24	12
France	25	25	11
Germany	29.1	20	9–12
Greece	23	20	10–12
Ireland	20	20	9
Italy	28	20–301	12
Luxemburg	28	25	10
Netherlands	31.3	20	8
Portugal	24.5	22	12–14
Spain	NA	22	12–14
Sweden	33	25	11
UK	24.5	20	8
EU average	25.7	22	10.8
Japan	17.82	10–203	15
US	9.6–21.74	No binding law	10

Source: Denniss (2003, 2).

Wasting Our Time?

In 2005 the Australian economy grew by around $A65 billion (ABS 2006). Every year it is likely to grow by even more, not because it will be a great year but because that is the way economies grow. We usually describe economic growth in percentage terms. For example, we might refer to the economy growing at an average of 3–4 per cent over the last decade. A constant growth in percentage terms means more and more growth in dollar terms. When the economy was half as big as it was now back in the 1980s, 4 per cent growth meant a lot less extra production than does today's 4 per cent growth, which requires twice as many natural resources to feed that growth as the Australian economy growing at the same rate needed back in the 1980s.

There is no escaping the link between all the work that Australians do and all of the pressures that our economic activity place on the natural environment. When more people work longer hours and take shorter holidays the direct result is that more factories use more energy and more resources to release more pollution into the environment. Regulation has played an important role in minimizing some of the harmful pollutants we release into the atmosphere and the water system. We have made some significant steps filtering the end of the 'pipe'. However, such efforts are inevitably overwhelmed by the ever-increasing size of the pipe.

Environmental damage is typically portrayed as the result of producers' decisions. Of course, producers are directly responsible for an enormous amount of harm to the environment. Logging old-growth forests can be nothing other than destructive, and using arsenic to help extract gold and then looking surprised when the arsenic leaks into a river system is simply irresponsible. Lobbying ceaselessly to prevent introducing laws to abolish such practices is, perhaps, the most reprehensible act of all.

But, while producers are responsible for the direct impacts of their manufacturing processes on the natural environment, consumers (especially wealthy consumers in wealthy countries) must take responsibility for a growing share of the damage being done. Only so much can be done to reduce the environmental impact of a particular production process. Admittedly, we are nowhere near the point where such efforts will be exhausted (pardon the pun). Once processes have been 'cleaned up', there is a direct relationship between increased consumer demand and increased environmental impact.

A good example is the tension between clean production and clean use of passenger cars. Car companies have made efforts to reduce the direct environmental impacts of manufacturing processes. Car interiors, for instance, are now commonly made from recyclable plastics to ensure that at the end of the car's life such material can be reused rather than sent to landfills. But these practices are irrelevant if wealthy consumers are inclined to buy a new car every two, instead of every ten, years. Australia's car sales have risen steadily in the past decade. Of greater concern is that more of cleanly produced cars are of the less safe and less fuel-efficient four-wheel-drive variety.

As Australians work longer hours and take fewer holidays their take-home pay continues to rise. For most people, higher pay means more expenditure and, in turn, an increase in the environmental damage caused by their consumption. While our incomes may have risen rapidly, our desire for more consumption has grown faster still.

One explanation for the rapid increase in consumption expenditure is the feedback mechanism. Demand for goods and services is not independent of time spent in the labour market. Rather, it is likely that the more time we spend in the labour market, the more money we spend.

An obvious example is the purchase of takeaway or restaurant meals to substitute for home-cooked meals, which are much cheaper than purchased food but take longer to prepare. Less obvious mechanisms may include the increased desire by those who work long hours to 'unwind' at expensive retreats or spas, or even for those working long hours to socialize exclusively with others with similar work and spending patterns.

It is possible that when people are considering new arrangements that they underestimate the amount of additional expenditure that their new 'lifestyle' will require. If working long hours is proportionately more expensive than working short hours, then trends described in the first section will not just be bad for individuals and their families. The indirect effects on the natural environment are likely to be severe.

The relationship between consumer expenditure and environmental impact has been described extensively, arguably beginning with Henry Thoreau's (1875) *Walden*. The linkage between environmental impact (I), population (P), affluence (A) and technology (T) is highlighted in the IPAT relationship (Erlich and Holdren 1971). Alternatively, individuals are urged to 'reduce, reuse and recycle'. However, there is little public debate, and even less public policy, focused on reducing affluence or consumption.

Rather than attempt to reduce consumption levels, most policy makers focus on possibilities of new technologies breaking the nexus between material consumption and environmental harm. This hope pervades public debate and public policy. The most recent manifestation is the emphasis on geosequestration technologies which, we are told, offer Australians the opportunity to continue increasing energy consumption if we can develop the tools to bury carbon dioxide emissions deep underground.

One of the most harmful forms of expenditure is on wasteful consumption, expenditure on products that are never even used. International evidence suggests that there is substantial expenditure on food that is never eaten, clothes that are never worn, and books that are never read. A study by Hamilton et al. (2004) replicated these studies for Australia and found that, in 2003, Australian consumers admitted spending over \$A10.5 billion on such wasteful consumption. Reducing wasteful consumption would benefit both consumers and the environment, but retailers would not appreciate it.

There are obvious reasons why policy debates focus on possibilities for mitigating environmental impact via technological change rather than on reducing incomes or expenditure. Political and personal challenges associated with reducing consumption do not diminish the need to do so. In time, we will have to grasp the nettle.

There is, however, one way of reducing the nettle's sting. Just as longer working hours are associated with higher incomes and greater environmental impact, reduced working hours are associated with an increase in leisure time and a reduction in environmental impact. That is, at present we focus exclusively on the 'costs' of working less, in the form of lower pay, rather than the benefits of working less, in the form of more leisure time. Given the culture of complaint that has arisen around the growing length of the Australian working week, and the subsequent impact of those working hours on personal relationships, it appears likely many Australians would be willing to swap a bit less money for a lot more time.

Your Money Or Your Life?

Most people in western countries believe that they cannot afford to buy everything that they need (Schor 1999). Studies in Australia (Denniss 2003) show that nearly 50 per cent of people living in the richest households agree that their needs outstrip their incomes.

While most people in developed countries, including Australians, do not believe that they have enough money to meet their needs, few believe that money is more important than health or families to their happiness. However, most people do not

168

make decisions about money, family and health in a coordinated way. People who take a promotion because they 'need' more money are unlikely to have decided that they 'need' to spend less time with their family or less time taking care of their health.

In fact, when confronted with a specific choice between time and money, most of the full-time employees in our study (Denniss 2003) opted for more time. That is, when asked whether they would prefer to have a 4 per cent pay rise or an additional two weeks' paid annual leave, 51 per cent of those surveyed preferred to have additional paid leave. Yet fewer than 1 per cent of employees act on such preferences.

Why do so few people purchase additional leave? Do actions speak louder than words? A wide range of evidence suggests that individuals experience both personal and structural barriers to pursuing additional leave. Many workers already struggle to use their entitlement to four weeks' annual leave either because they are too busy at work or their boss would not give them time off that suited their needs (Denniss 2003). Further, many workers believe, rightly or wrongly, that seeking additional leave signals a lack of commitment to either the organization or their peers.

For over twenty years Australian politics has been deregulating the labour market to make it more 'flexible'. It is ironic that, despite the rhetoric of flexibility and individual choice that has dominated public debats, individuals who express a choice for more leisure time are either derided as lazy or blocked from achieving their preferences by recalcitrant managers or structures designed to ensure that individual choices are only made within a highly constrained set of options.

Along with all developed countries, Australia began the twentieth century with no paid holidays. The progress towards four weeks' leave took seventy years, but in the last thirty years there has been no further progress. While most European countries continued the pursuit of leisure time, employees in the USA, for example, still have no statutory entitlement to holidays, with most workers negotiating ten days or less of leave each year.

At a national level such choices have major effects. Economists (Burda et al. 2006) have investigated the implicit benefits to Europeans of working shorter weeks and taking longer holidays. Results suggest that the differences in GDP per capita between the USA and Europe overstate the differences in labour productivity and quality of life between the two systems. But, in the context of this discussion here, such results suggest an entirely different implication: Europeans' preference for time rather than money implies that, on average, Europeans do less harm to the environment.

As we get richer, we can either buy more things or have more leisure time. Given the link between consumption expenditure and environmental impact outlined above, a shift in preferences away from buying 'stuff' and towards buying time is likely to yield significant environmental improvements or, at a minimum, significantly slow the rate at which we damage the environment.

It is important to note that 'leisure' is not used here to imply holiday travel. Like most human activities, leisure time has become highly commodified, with the result that, for many people, talk of increased leisure time elicits images of greater international travel, more four-wheel-drive cars towing caravans, and more people buying jet skis. Such outcomes are as unlikely as they are undesirable. The additional leisure time is associated with a reduction in income (or the forgoing of pay rises). Therefore, it is highly unlikely that most people would respond to an increase in leisure time and a reduction in income with a significant increase in recreational expenditure.

Once, the primary meaning of leisure was 'the pursuit of one's passions'. For many it has become 'the pursuit of time on the couch'. The purpose of encouraging more leisure time is to shift consumption patterns away from material-intense activities harmful to the environment. Therefore shifts must occur not just in the way we spend our money but also in the way we spend our time.

The pursuit of increased leisure time should be legitimated. The economic rationalists' case for labour market deregulation was based on prioritizing individual choice. The rhetorical line of conservative politicians in Australia is that we need to invest more in family relationships to preserve the 'Australian way of life'. The church sermon is that money does not buy happiness and that we need to search for deeper meaning. Yet individuals who seek to work less in order to improve their lives, their families' lives and the natural environment are likely to be met with calls from conservatives and economic rationalists that they are irresponsible and, most inconsistently, that they should instead put the needs of 'the economy' or 'the national interest' above their personal interest! When the economic rationalists start relying on socialist calls to act for the collective, you know their argument is beginning to fray.

What Can Individuals and Policy Makers Do?

We have argued that long work hours in Australia are harming the environment as well as personal relationships. This section begins with a discussion of the measures people can take to reduce their environmental impact through consuming more leisure. A discussion of community organizations that seek to facilitate such change is provided with a list of actions that policy makers and political leaders could take in order to encourage and facilitate such a shift.

Individuals

The simplest action for individuals to shift their consumption patterns away from stuff towards leisure is to pursue longer holidays instead of increased pay. Individuals can make it easier for themselves and their workmates to achieve this by talking about such preferences with each other, unions and management. Similarly, individuals in management positions must accommodate employees' desires and show leadership by pursuing such goals themselves. When a work culture is dominated by the notion that long hours are the best way to demonstrate commitment to the firm then it is more difficult for individuals to achieve the desired balance between time and consumption.

It is important for individuals to comprehensively analyse the cost of long working hours. It is taken for granted that people consider the benefits of returning to work after having a baby, having considered the costs of tax, child care and transport. It is less common for people to consider the costs of working long hours: expenditure on takeaway food, restaurant meals, house cleaning, dry cleaning, mobile phones and day spas to 'recharge'.

Community groups

There is a growing level of interest in the nexus between high levels of consumption, high levels of work time stress and adverse environmental impacts. In Australia and internationally, community groups are highlighting the dangers of overemphasizing material consumption or are extolling the benefits simple living – see Table 13.3.

Table 13.3   Community organizations promoting more leisure and less consumption

The Slow Food Movement	Slow Food is a non-profit, eco-gastronomic member-supported organization founded in 1989 to counteract fast food and fast life, the disappearance of local food traditions and people's dwindling interest in the food they eat, where it comes from, how it tastes and how our food choices affect others.
The Simple Living Network	Simple Living is not about living in poverty or self-inflicted deprivation. It is about living an examined life – one in which you determine what is important, or enough for you and discard the rest.
Buy Nothing Day	Originating in Vancouver, Canada, Buy Nothing Day draws attention to the harmful effects of over-consumption in industrialized nations that is detrimental to the rest of the world. International Buy Nothing Day is full of cheerful and peaceful actions and activities to confront shoppers in western countries with the consequences of over-consumption and influence of advertising.
Take Back Your Time	Take back your time is a major US–Canadian initiative to challenge the epidemic of overwork, overscheduling and time famine that now threatens health, families and relationships, communities and environment.

Government action

While the actions of individuals and community groups will play an important role in shifting the consumption patterns, significant change will require political leadership and sustained policy action. Unfortunately, the current emphasis on industrial relations reforms and the pursuit of economic growth in Australia means both political debate and policy reform are likely to exacerbate overwork and the associated environmental impacts. That said, how can governments promote increased leisure time and reduced material consumption? The following policy options would deliver the biggest benefits.

Federal government:

1. Increase the existing standard four weeks' annual leave to world's best practice of six weeks for all full-time workers.
2. Ensure that employers do not restrict employees from access to leave entitlements.
3. Ensure that all women are entitled to paid maternity leave.
4. Encourage job sharing.
5. Promote public awareness of the availability and desirability of leave-purchasing arrangements.
6. Ensure that all federal government employees are offered the option of six weeks' paid holidays per year.
7. Whenever federal government employees become entitled to a pay rise ensure that they are asked whether they would prefer increased pay or an increase in paid holidays.

State governments:

1. Ensure that State government employees are offered the option of six weeks' paid holidays per year.
2. Whenever State government employees become entitled to a pay rise ensure that they are asked whether they would prefer increased pay or an increase in paid holidays.
3. Ensure that infrastructure investment decisions, such as public transport, public parks and cycle ways, allow individuals who prefer lower incomes and more leisure time to participate fully in society.
4. Allow individuals to perform community service work in lieu of paying some State taxes and charges.

Local governments:

1. Ensure that local government employees are offered the option of six weeks' paid holidays per year.
2. Whenever local government employees become entitled to a pay rise ensure that they are asked whether they would prefer increased pay or an increase in paid holidays.
3. Facilitate consumers' capacity to reduce and reuse. For example, promote the sale of second-hand goods as a substitute to diversion to landfill. Ensure that all public spaces have drinking fountains, to reduce the need for bottled water.

Conclusions

Australians are working longer, earning more, spending more, borrowing more and, in so doing, placing increasing pressure on natural resources and fragile ecosystems. Most strategies for ameliorating these environmental impacts focus on either technological solutions or radical reductions in energy use and consumption expenditure. There is little that individuals or policy makers can do to ensure the development of 'saviour' technologies such as geosequestration, and there is little public or political appeal in suggesting that social and economic life as we know it must come to an end. However, there is a different path, not a middle ground, but a new direction for change.

Along with all developed countries, Australia has long since passed the point of delivering the necessities of life to its population. Historically such an achievement is the exception not the rule. However, having met our needs, we are simply expanding our material consumption. The impacts on our personal lives, health, families and communities are well documented. Awareness of environmental impacts is also growing.

The pursuit of leisure time rather than the pursuit of material consumption provides a unique opportunity to minimize the impact of human behaviour on the environment while delivering benefits, rather than costs, to those affected. Leisure time is a desirable good. High income earners should to aspire to consume more leisure. The data suggest that most full-time employees have such desires, yet find the pursuit of such options personally or structurally difficult.

Choice is central to the alleged benefits of a modern society. Yet, while individuals spend hours deciding what to wear and weeks choosing which Internet provider to register with, most believe that they have little choice in the way that their life is structured, the way that they balance work and leisure, and in investing time in relationships with family and friends.

As Australians work longer hours and spend more time with people making a similar choice, it is harder for individuals to compare the benefits of working longer versus the benefits of pursuing increased time ahead of increased material consumption. Those interested in solving environmental and social problems need to consider the importance of the scarcest commodity in a developed country – time.

To increase consumption of time and reduce consumption of material goods will require significant leadership from governments. Individual action is important but collective action delivered large increases in leisure-time throughout the twentieth century, achieving four weeks' paid annual leave and numerous public holidays. Policy reforms that would help shift the balance away from working and spending and towards leisure and reduced consumption include:

- Improved access to leave-purchasing arrangements.
- Improved access to maternity and paternity leave.
- The right to work part time and for employees to negotiate job-sharing arrangements.

While such reforms would assist in achieving the objective of reduced material consumption and increased leisure time, there are two important obstacles to overcome. First, the current thrust of federal government policy is designed to achieve longer work hours and shorter holidays. Whether such an approach represents the majority opinion of the electorate or the minority opinion of the government, there are large political barriers to change. The second major obstacle involves a combined lack of role models and legitimacy, associated with prioritizing time over money. The importance of 'family values' is often stressed in Australian political debate but 'financial values' dominate public debates about responsible citizenship. Those who work in businesses part-time are more likely to be decried as 'slackers' than applauded for contributing to family and community life.

Role models and political leadership help individuals to negotiate with managers and employers. At present, requests for additional paid leave, or the right to part-time work, is most likely to be perceived as a lack of commitment to work. Collective negotiation delivered four weeks' paid holidays in Australia, but individual negotiation, especially in the contemporary political climate, is unlikely to achieve further gains.

No doubt, policy mechanisms such as changes to the industrial relations system have an important role especially in overcoming disadvantages faced by part-time and casual workers. However, the real challenge is to create the political will for achieving changes to deliver individuals richer personal lives and healthier natural environments by reducing material consumption. If economic growth relies on increased personal and environmental inputs, it cannot deliver the work–life balance that most residents in developed countries seek.

References

ABS (2006), *Australian National Accounts: National Income, Expenditure and Product*, [Cat. No. 5206.0, June] (Canberra: Australian Bureau of Statistics).

Burda, M., Hamermesh, D. and Weil, P. (2006), 'Different but Equal: Total Work, Gender and Social Norms in the EU and US Time Use', Fondazione Rodolfo Debenedetti [website], <http://www.frdb.org/documentazione/scheda.php?doc_pk=10451&id=157>, accessed 18 January 2007.

Campbell, I. (2002), 'Extended Working Hours in Australia', *Labour and Industry* 13:1, 91–110.

Conway, R. (1978), *Land Of The Long Weekend* (Melbourne: Sun Books).

Denniss, R. (2003), *Annual Leave in Australia: An Analysis of Entitlements, Usage and Preferences* [Discussion Paper 56] (Canberra: Australia Institute).

Ehrlich, P. and Holdren, J. (1971), 'Impact of Population Growth', *Science* 26, 1212–1217.

Fagan, C. (2004), 'Gender and Working Time in Industrialized Countries', in Messenger (ed.).

Gittins, R. and Tiffen, R. (2004), *How Australia Compares* (Melbourne: Cambridge University Press).

Hamilton, C., Denniss, R. and Baker, D. (2004), *Wasteful Consumption in Australia* [Discussion Paper 77] (Canberra: Australia Institute).

Hayden, A. (1999), *Sharing the Work, Sparing the Planet: Work Time Consumption and Ecology* (Toronto/Melbourne/London: Between the Lines/Pluto Press Australia/Zed Books).

Howard, J. (2002), 'Speech Delivered to Aston Electorate Dinner', Melbourne, 16 July, Macmillan English Dictionaries [website], <http://www.macmillandictionary.com/med-magazine/June2005/31-New-Word-BBQhtm>, accessed 21 June 2006.

Messenger, J. (ed.) (2004), *Working Time and Workers' Preferences in Industrialized Countries: Finding the Balance* (Abington, Routledge).

Pocock, B. (2003), *The Work Life Collision* (Sydney: Federation Press).

Schor, J. (1999), *The Overspent American* (New York: Harper Collins).

Thoreau, H. (1875), *Walden – On Life in the Woods* (Boston: Ticknor and Fields).

Chapter 14

Local Multi-Stakeholder Partnerships for Sustainability

Tavis Potts, John Merson and Michael Kachka

Global Talk to Local Action

In June 1997 world leaders gathered at the United Nations (UN) headquarters, New York, to review achievements in meeting the environmental commitments made at the Rio World Earth Summit on Environment and Development in 1992. At the meeting five years earlier leaders of rich and poor states collectively focused on emerging global conflicts between demands for economic growth and development and the need to conserve the world's depleted natural resources, this resulting in the Rio Declaration on Environment and Development, the Statement of Forest Principles, the UN Framework Convention on Climate Change, the UN Convention on Biological Diversity and an ambitious program of more general environmental reforms known as Local Agenda 21 (LA21). The Earth Summit involved 172 countries and 108 heads of state or government committing to these ambitious programs and conventions and a number of associated environmental and development changes to implement over the following decade. To keep up the momentum achieved at Rio representatives from participating countries agreed to report back five years later.

The UN General Assembly gathered for a depressing week of duplicitous reports and an occasional honest confession of failure to meet commitments made at Rio. However, in the basement of the UN building, a very different and far more interesting meeting was taking place – the parallel meeting of the LA21 program (Cotter and Hannan 1999). In small crowded rooms, town and municipal authorities from around the world reported on what they had done to address environmental and development issues. From China and India to Brazil and Australia municipal representatives documented changes arising from local government working with local businesses and communities to improve environmental conditions. Local government delegations from Australia, Canada and Brazil spoke of results exceeding the national average.

Much of the general literature on urban development assumes that state intervention and market-based responses drive environmental change and ignore the extremely important role that local governments and community can play to create conditions for sustainable development. For instance in Curitiba (Brazil), enlightened leadership at a local governmental level has transformed the pattern of urban development to a model of sustainability (Hawken et al. 1999). This chapter reviews an Australian example of local government playing a significant role in bringing about a more sustainable pattern of urban development in partnership with local business, the community and the university sector.

Partnerships as a Sustainability Strategy

Many developments in sustainability have emerged from international policies. The instruments and commitments they contain aim to flow into decision making, policy and regulatory processes of states. For sustainability to succeed and shift everyday behaviour into more environmentally benign patterns, there must be a marriage between higher order government policies and local community action (Smith and Scott 2006). Effective policy requires the support of local communities and partnerships with public and private sector organizations.

Community and business ownership of environmental issues is essential for a synergistic societal approach, a model demonstrated in India with city-scale initiatives addressing serious pollution impacts (Prakash 2003). Mainstream acceptance of sustainability in the Australian national psyche has suffered from lack of integrated action involving community organizations, business, universities and local government.

Glass (2002) correctly surmises that, for sustainability to succeed, it must change the lifestyle patterns of production and consumption, the ecological footprint, and what we value as individuals and communities (Rogers and Ryan 2001). Local action, education and active engagement is critical for influencing the values of both towards sustainable lifestyles. Cumulative actions from individuals, households and communities contribute to major environmental issues involving transport, waste and so on. Catalysing change at this level is primarily the role of local and regional government through democratic processes (Armstrong and Stratford 2004). Creating a demand for sustainable products and services, and developing businesses that focus on sustainable development, require the support of individuals and broader communities. An example is the increasing community demand for certified organic produce and the subsequent increase in growers, suppliers and retailers in this sector.

Partnerships are tools that promote dialogue, cooperation and education across different sectors and stakeholders. They enable diverse and complementary competencies and resources to be applied and shared (Loza 2004). Gibson and Cameron (2001) identify partnerships as unifying or mobilizing devices regulating interactions between government and individuals, while Brand and de Bruin (1999) emphasize partnerships as an 'action lever' in the transition to sustainability. Local partnerships can complement and implement national and international policies. LA21 local initiatives aim to implement the mandate of Agenda 21 and the Johannesburg Plan of Implementation (UNCSD 2006). Successful partnerships involve cross-fertilization of ideas and knowledge from different actors, instilling a sense of common purpose and drive and attempting to harness a consensus in local and regional sustainability strategy.

Frame and Taylor (2005, 277) identify several core objectives for partnerships to achieve sustainability:

- Combine efforts and resources toward common aims.
- Share information and expertise.
- Understand different points of view.
- Make improved decisions.
- Create more 'win-win' outcomes.

Actions that specify a local sustainability partnership include:

- The involvement of a cross-section of community, business and government sectors.
- Focusing on a local or regional sustainability issue and generating a positive improvement in that issue.
- Considering the triple bottom line and increasing social capital.
- Encouraging mutual sustainability learning and dialogue across differing perspectives.
- Being open, accountable and innovative.
- Leverage of financial and human resources to address the issue.
- Encouraging participatory action, involvement, ongoing commitment and review.

Regulation to Partnership – Business and Universities

Literature on partnerships often discusses emerging and critical links between local government and communities (Armstrong and Stratford 2004; Kupke 1996; Feichtinger and Pregernig 2005; Frame and Taylor 2005; Potts 2004; Smith and Scott 2006). Public agencies are moving towards considering citizens as 'partners' rather than 'clients' or 'customers' and are experimenting with sustainability-focused collaborations with the private sector and universities (Martinez-Fernandez et al. 2005; Vigoda 2002).

One explanation for an increasing focus on collaboration is the frustration incurred from policy 'gridlock' and inefficiencies in solving certain environmental disputes. Conflict between stakeholders with differing values, viewpoints and interests can cause entrenched disputes with ongoing social, legal, regulatory and financial implications. While conflict and political risk can be an important driver of change (Newman 2004) it can also prevent the formation of mutually beneficial long-term partnerships.

Practice to date suggests that local sustainability partnerships are seeking greater participation from business and university groups in addition to traditional community organizations. Business groups are increasingly considering the triple bottom line and corporate social responsibility, viewing partnerships as tools to achieve this goal (Loza 2004). Spectacular public corporate crashes have eroded public confidence and led to measures of greater accountability. Although corporate citizenship practice is not embedded in Australia (Birch and Batten 2001) preliminary data (Martinez-Fernandez et al. 2005) suggest that attitudes toward regional partnerships are changing, especially in the context of environmental innovation and ecological modernization. A recent example is a regional cleaner production partnership between Newcastle City Council, the Hunter Business Chamber and local businesses in which local consultants and government work to reduce the water and energy inputs and minimize the outputs of waste and pollution. This program has engaged with 32 regional businesses and generated annual savings of more than $A1 million and an ongoing reduction of an estimated 30,000 tonnes in carbon dioxide emissions (Newcastle City Council 2005).

Universities and not-for-profit organizations are increasing their roles in sustainability partnerships. Universities can provide independent information, analysis and scholarship to address significant local and regional problems and can mediate and facilitate dialogues between disparate groups to positively influence regional development (Forrant 2001). Reasons why universities participate include: civic obligations to regional communities, educational experiences for students and research opportunities, intellectual and professional interest, research subjects, case studies and data (Fermen and Hill 2004). Partnering with a university can generate additional financial and human resources, information for product or service development, evaluations and access to networks, and increase the legitimacy of a partnership (Fermen and Hill 2004). Universities have clear roles to play in developing regional economies and promoting sustainable practices, disseminating and applying knowledge.

Macarthur Regional Environmental Innovation Network

A recent university–community research project, Innovation at the Edges, involved local businesses in the Macarthur region, south-west Sydney, assisting them to identify regional challenges to innovation. The project developed a broader than traditional innovation studies approach, highlighting critical but often overlooked environmental and social factors (Martinez-Fernandez et al. 2005). The conceptual framework was based on the view that economic or industry forces alone cannot explain why some regions are innovation intensive while others stagnate. The 'innovation ecosystem' approach argues that three critical systems for regional development coexist: knowledge intensity and partnerships, environmental drivers and regional issues, and a creative and productive social climate (Martinez-Fernandez et al. 2005). This triple bottom line approach to innovation allows regions to unlock their potential as 'smart regions'. The Macarthur region contained significant elements that contribute to an innovative and sustainable region: a regionally focused university (University of Western Sydney), a strong regional and community identity, increasing sustainability awareness amongst firms and regional business, and local government support to develop new programs and activities. However, the researchers identified regional limitations: few business networks, minimal use of knowledge-intensive services, little opportunity to progress environmental innovation and lack of cross-sector partnerships.

The research recommended forming regional partnerships. Late 2005, the Regional Environmental Innovation Network (REIN) was launched, aiming to build regional links and generate dialogue on environmental innovation between community groups, the university, local business and government. REIN provides a focal point and public forum for action by facilitating information sharing on the 'how to' questions that surround environmental innovation, developing collaborative research, and disseminating information on issues such as water conservation.

REIN is a partnership managed by the university and a local community environmental organization, the Macarthur Centre for Sustainable Living (2006). REIN has been successful in developing a series of information and networking evenings to discuss recent developments in energy efficiency, green building, and so on. Community members, academics, students, and local business and government representatives have participated in REIN workshops. The energy efficiency workshop, held on the winter solstice, attracted over a hundred participants in a mixture of practical and ideas-based seminars, emphasizing the 'how to do' aspects of energy efficiency and renewable energy in homes. Disseminating recent research, best practice, stories and policy development provides practical messages of environmental innovation. Linking researchers, students, businesses and local communities to discuss future partnerships and collaborative work, REIN is a 'partnerships and ideas incubator' that has attracted key national and international speakers to assist in improving regional business and civic engagement over environmental innovation and sustainable development.

Lawson and the Blue Mountains

The Blue Mountains region has a World Heritage listing. It is the catchment and 'lungs' of the basin of Sydney, the capital of New South Wales (NSW), and is a key tourist and recreational destination. Policy makers require better information flows to underpin policy development and implementation within and around the Greater Blue Mountains World Heritage Area associated with current and potential impacts of development, sustainable land use and to identify 'beyond boundary' socio-economic benefits.

The confluence of urban, industrial and agricultural development suggests potential for integrating human and natural systems. As a result, the Blue Mountains World Heritage Institute (BMWHI) was established in March 2004. Its founding partners reflected the growing recognition that strategic partnerships can better integrate knowledge and research with policy and management. The BMWHI involves three universities (Sydney, New South Wales and Western Sydney), three agencies concerned with the region's urban and environmental development – NSW Department of Environment and Conservation, Sydney Catchment Authority and Blue Mountains City Council (BMCC) – and additional research bodies (Australian Museum and Botanical Garden Trust).

Lawson is located in the Greater Blue Mountains area, 90 km west of the Sydney central business district, beyond the suburban sprawl. The original study area was the Lawson industrial estate south of the township, orientated towards manufacturing and service industries. Heavy industry is non-existent and there is minimal light industry. Small businesses generally employ less than ten people, while one in four is home-based (BMWHI 2005b).

In line with the BMCC vision for a sustainable region, the BMWHI established a partnership between the council, the community and business to investigate opportunities to incorporate ecologically sustainable development into the estate's planning and whole community. Its design required harmony with the surrounding World Heritage Area and economic and social benefits, lowering the ecological footprint whilst increasing employment opportunities. In response, the BMWHI proposed a model of 'ecologically sustainable urban development', which requires an entirely new approach to land zoning and ongoing council–business cooperation.

Energy, waste and water management were key issues and provided the baseline for future development of the estate as a showcase for sustainable industries and innovative companies (BMWHI 2005a). Opportunities to encourage existing businesses to promote and apply sustainability practices to operations and to market the estate as a leader in sustainable businesses were identified, a strategy which was planned to attract other small to medium sized enterprises and environmental technology based firms. Coordinated by the BMCC and local business groups, the Blue Mountains Business Advantage is a complementary program to train and certify local organizations in sustainable practices.

The BMWHI surveyed local firms to capture data associated with business services and operations, resource inputs and waste outputs, and to measure the level of understanding of sustainability within existing businesses. As a result the BMWHI identified waste synergies to help reduce waste production and costs; several businesses could use wastes produced by others and reduce overall waste across the estate. This process involved building on existing practices, such as recycling and community reuse of marble off-cuts and wood, and expanding business awareness and cooperation. This process led to improved communication between local business and the BMCC while previously dialogue had been rare. For example, in a recent major BMCC review of waste management, business attitudes to recycling facilitated by the partnership resulted in a council feasibility study of business recycling services.

Businesses were concerned with the lack of capacity of existing electrical infrastructure. Instead of advocating the expansion of electricity services (a traditional response), the BMWHI recommended incorporating ecologically sustainable energy generation within the estate to reduce network dependence and greenhouse emissions. Technologies such as photovoltaic panels are ideally suited to this application since industrial estates usually operate between 7 am and 5 pm, Monday to Friday. Integral Energy funded energy audits of the community centre and major businesses within the estate to identify potential energy savings to reduce the existing electrical load on the network, as well as questionnaires on energy usage distributed to Lawson residents to assess how greater efficiencies could be achieved. With the support of General Electric, free compact fluorescent light bulbs were distributed to residents to increase awareness of the economic benefits. An education program through the local school and community centre formed part of a wider awareness-raising process associated with this strategy. Similar complementary initiatives are being developed in relation to water use and waste water management involving resident groups, the local Chamber of Commerce and Industry and the BMCC.

To date, the results of this partnership for sustainability have been positive for Lawson businesses and community and there has been increased interest from businesses to participate in the Blue Mountains Business Advantage. Ecologically sustainable urban development is a long-term process and requires commitment by all stakeholders. The partnership has provided for a fresh dialogue between government, business and the community and has lifted awareness of new approaches to waste management and energy and water conservation, establishing groundwork for future reform and sustainable outcomes.

The BMWHI has acted as an independent broker in circumstances where many businesses in the industrial estate had become disillusioned with the council's ability to address their needs. Furthermore many residents felt powerless in the face of their town centre being obliterated to make way for a new highway. There was clearly a need to support this community to develop a new vision for the township. Here community cultural development workers are important to drive technical change. Where stakeholders in local government processes have become entrenched in positions of disillusionment, often based on past failures, it is difficult for partnerships to be effective. It is still very early in the process of Lawson's transforming itself into a model of sustainable urban development, but a high degree of enthusiasm remains for the ideal. The real test is for such partnerships to be sustainable in the long term, despite short-term failures and personality conflicts within and between partners.

The Future for Local Partnerships

Sustainability-based partnerships can provide a range of positive outcomes for local communities. Local decision makers gain fresh information on community and business activities, and partnerships enable exploration of different viewpoints and ideas. In the Macarthur region, REIN is networking local stakeholders around environmental innovation. In Lawson, the BMCC obtained valuable policy inputs and implemented energy efficiency projects. The partnership increased business and council dialogue and cooperation towards a common vision for Lawson.

Regional views on sustainable innovation converged, with business, community and local government developing agendas for action and improvement, highlighting how partnerships can lead to different forms of policy learning (Dovers 2005). Knowledge of business and community created through partnerships can assist government to evaluate the effectiveness of local administrative arrangements. New insights can increase community policy awareness and participation, and include critiques of local processes, feedback, review, and accountability.

A significant outcome of the partnership process was the generation and redistribution of financial and human resources. The Lawson case study highlighted the BMWHI as a facilitator between stakeholders. The contribution of an electricity agency towards energy audits and efficiencies was positive. Through REIN, dialogue is occurring about funding arrangements and sponsorship, collaborative research and knowledge diffusion. As partnerships mature, set and achieve goals, and gain legitimacy, they increasingly attract new financial resources, human capital and expertise for investment into local sustainability outcomes.

Partnership outcomes often increase the profiles of regions and the contributing stakeholders, considerably benefiting local government, business and participating organizations. Local networks improve along with community confidence in policy processes. Establishing sources of 'local pride' are important outcomes for communities, especially in regions aiming to encourage sustainable development.

Obstacles

Several obstacles appeared during the course of the initiatives. Like any policy process, partnerships are value laden and subject to contestation. One obstacle in the development of partnerships is tensions between short-term and medium to long-term objectives. Partnerships take *time* to organize, coordinate and achieve outcomes. They cut across different timescales, such as business cycles, policy planning, elections and community expectations, which places pressures on expectations of partnerships. It is difficult for a partnership to achieve all objectives in the short term, except establishing an effective process. This is particularly true in the evolving Lawson project. Stakeholders need to be aware of time scales, commitments and the evolving nature of partnerships. In evaluating partnerships, observing the process is critical, because a successful process itself provides positive outcomes.

The Lawson and REIN partnerships engaged a mix of community, business, university and government stakeholders. The make-up and mix of any partnership is essentially a function of the players within a particular sustainability issue. Determining the right mixture and quantity of players is critical and can change over time. It is important to note that there is no 'magic number' to determine the actors in a partnership.

The availability of relevant and reliable data and information remain obstacles to achieving the objectives of sustainability partnerships. The Lawson project demonstrated that micro-scale data about business waste and resource use is often absent. Protocols and a partnership over data collection have been developed to examine the key issues. The collection of data was a secondary concern to information dissemination for REIN. However, the lack of integrated regional data and publicly available indicators on sustainability and innovation were issues. Establishing what data requirements are necessary for local partnerships is essential. Keeping data for evaluation was also critical in both initiatives.

Often diverse multi-stakeholder processes lead to a 'talkfest', emphasizing dialogue rather than concrete action or policy change. Emerging partnerships must establish clear, practical and achievable objectives that do not paralyse. The benefits of joining a partnership must be clearly communicated and endorsed by the participants.

Policy Recommendations

Local government plays a key role in facilitating and supporting local partnerships, particularly through sustainability education, resource management and community action. Local government can provide resources and spaces for partnership discussions to evolve. The benefits will be particularly significant at the local level.

The following policy recommendations are targeted at local government officers to facilitate the partnership process and maximize the success of new and established initiatives:

1. *Resources for local partnership initiatives.* Local partnerships require human capital and financial resources to maintain effectiveness and deliver outcomes. When establishing a partnership, identify resources to support the process. This may involve a financial contribution from stakeholders, physical infrastructure such as meeting facilities, and dedication of time by stakeholders.

2. *Terms of reference/memorandum of understanding.* Establishing clear and succinct terms of reference is critical for the functioning of a partnership. The terms of reference create direction and clarity for the partnership, outlining its aims, objectives and outcomes. The terms of reference can outline or 'bind' the partnership to a specific sustainability issue and provide necessary focus. A memorandum of understanding clarifies the relationship between stakeholders and can establish the required commitment.

3. *Build support for the partnership.* A partnership will not function well if it is unknown in the community. A new partnership will require a 'spark' – a public launch, guest speakers, media, or a facilitator. A launch requires resources but provides benefits to all stakeholders and, if effective, often results in more members and resources. A launch adds momentum and commits a partnership to its objectives. Regular newsletters will ensure that the partnership stays in the public domain. Support of elected officials can strengthen the partnership and increase the legitimacy of its outcomes.

4. *Build the business case.* Getting business on board is a crucial component of a partnership and relies on building a 'business case'. Local businesses do not often participate in sustainability partnerships or engage with local government over sustainability issues. The business case includes access to new clients and networks, marketing the partnership, facilitating corporate social responsibility and triple bottom line (Potts 2004). A partnership needs to be efficient and to deliver outcomes for business operators. It is not a commercial activity, but should offer something to all stakeholders.

5. *Use partners' knowledge and skills to maximum effect.* Participants in a partnership bring skills, ideas, and sources of knowledge. Different skill sets provide important frameworks for debate, sustainability actions and stronger societal consensus. Cross-learning is a valuable approach and can help build empathy amongst stakeholders within and outside the partnership. Knowledge creation and diffusion is a key driver of sustainable innovation (Martinez-Fernandez et al. 2005).

6. *Document and evaluate the process.* Sustainability partnerships are a learning process. An adaptive approach should be taken where problems and outcomes feed into a regular review of the activities. Documenting the activities of the partnership and relevant data (participation, outcomes and so on) will be useful for future reviews and evaluation (Loza 2004). Documenting the approach facilitates the sharing of information and experiences with new organizations starting a partnership.

Conclusion

It is clear that sustainability partnerships are tools that practically implement the broader national and international objectives and principles of sustainable development. All stakeholders within a partnership can gain benefits. This discussion highlights particular benefits that can accrue to business and universities by participating in local sustainability partnerships and emphasizes that a structured approach to developing multi-stakeholder partnerships is necessary to achieve local outcomes and build sustainability into communities. At the present time local sustainability partnerships are not mainstream practice in Australian municipalities. With an increasing number of success stories and on-the-ground outcomes for government, universities and business, we hope that sustainability partnerships will spread in scope to become an important tool in implementing sustainable development.

References

Armstrong, D. and Stratford, E. (2004), 'Partnerships for Local Sustainability and Local Governance', *Local Environment* 9, 541–61.

Birch, D. and Batten, J. (2001), *Corporate Citizenship in Australia: a Survey of Corporate Australia* (Burwood: Corporate Citizenship Research Unit, Deakin University).

BMWHI (2005a), *Towards a Sustainable Lawson Estate – Issues and Options for Waste and Water Management* (Katoomba: Blue Mountains World Heritage Institute).

BMWHI (2005b), *Review of Lawson Industrial Estate* (Katoomba: Blue Mountains World Heritage Institute).

Brand, E. and de Bruin, T. (1999), 'Shared Responsibility at the Regional Level: the Building of Sustainable Industrial Estates', *European Environment* 9: 221–31.

Cheney, H., Katz, E. and Soloman, F. (eds) (2004), *Sustainability and Social Science Roundtable* (Sydney: Institute of Sustainable Futures and CSIRO Minerals).

Cotter, B. and Hannan, K. (1999), *Our Community Our Future: A Guide to Local Agenda 21* (Canberra: Environment Australia).

Dovers, S. (2005), *Environment and Sustainability Policy: Creation, Evaluation and Implementation* (Sydney: Federation Press).

Feichtinger, J. and Pregernig, M. (2005), 'Imagined Citizens and Participation: Local Agenda 21 in Two Communities in Sweden and Austria', *Local Environment* 10: 3, 229–43.

Ferman, B. and Hill, T. (2004), 'The Challenges of Agenda Conflict in Higher Education–Community Research Partnerships: Views From the Community Side', *Journal of Urban Affairs* 26:2, 241–57.

Forrant, R. (2001), 'Random Acts of Assistance or Purposeful Intervention? The University of Massachusetts Lowell and the Regional Development Process', in Forrant et al. (eds).

Forrant, R., Lyle, J., Lazonick, W. and Levenstein, C. (eds) (2001), *Approaches to Sustainable Development: The Public University in the Regional Economy* (Massachusetts: University of Massachusetts Press).

Frame, B. and Taylor, R. (2005), 'Partnerships for Sustainability', *Local Environment* 10:3, 275–99.

Gibson, K. and Cameron, J. (2001), 'Transforming Communities: Towards a Research Agenda', *Urban Policy and Research* 19:1, 7–24.

Glass, S. (2002), 'Sustainability and Local Government', *Local Environment* 7:1, 97–102.

Hawken, P., Lovins, A. and Lovins, L. (1999), *Natural Capitalism: The Next Industrial Revolution* (New York: Little, Brown & Company).

Kupke, V. (1996), 'Local Agenda 21: Local Councils Managing for the Future', *Urban Policy and Research* 14:3, 183–98.

Loza, J. (2004), 'Business–Community Partnerships: The Case for Community Organization Capacity Building', *Journal of Business Ethics* 53, 297–311.

Macarthur Centre for Sustainable Living (2006), [website], <http://wwwmcsl.org.au/index.htm>, accessed 16 November 2006.

Martinez-Fernandez, C., Potts, T., Receretnam, M. and Bjorkli, M. (2005), *Innovation at the Edges: The Role of Innovation Drivers in South West Sydney* (Sydney: University of Western Sydney).

Newcastle City Council (2005), *Cleaner Production* [factsheet] (Newcastle: Newcastle City Council, Hunter Business Chamber and NSW Department of Conservation).

Newman, P. (2004), 'On Climbing Trees: An Australian Perspective on Sustainability and Political Risk', *Local Environment* 9:6, 611–21.

Potts, T. (2004), 'Triple Bottom Line Reporting – A Tool for Measuring and Reporting Change in Local Communities', in Cheney et al. (eds).

Prakash, V. (2003), 'Combating Environmental Ills: Using the Synergy of Citizens, Governmental and Nongovernmental Agencies', *Local Environment* 8:3, 345–49.

Rogers, M. and Ryan, R. (2001), 'The Triple Bottom Line for Sustainable Community Development', *Local Environment* 6:3, 279–89.

Smith, G. and Scott, J. (2006), *Government and Sustainability in Australia: Living Cities, An Urban Myth?* (Dural: Rosenburg Publishing).

UNCSD (2006), United Nations Commission for Sustainable Development [website], Partnerships for Sustainable Development [webpage], <http://www.un.org/esa/sustdev/partnerships/partnerships.htm>, accessed 18 February 2006.

Vigoda, E. (2002), 'From Responsiveness to Collaboration: Governance, Citizens, and the Next Generation of Public Administration', *Public Administration Review* 62:5, 527–40.

Part IV
Transforming Suburbs

Chapter 15

Innovating for Sustainability in Estate Development: VicUrban in Melbourne

Tony Dalton and Geoffrey Binder

Introduction

For over three decades Australian States have had a public sector agency – sometimes referred to as a 'government business enterprise' (GBE) – which acquired, developed and sold freehold land allotments to households. By the late 1990s these agencies began to include 'sustainability' in their objectives, as governments responded to research and social campaigns concerned with urban resource demand and waste increasing ecological footprints, especially in low-density metropolitan cities. In this context sustainability became a 'wraparound term' referring to environmental performance and longer-term objectives: affordability, the financial viability of agencies, urban design and service provision. The State government land development agencies developed new ways of working with different groups – builders, contractors, designers, consultants, utilities and so on – in design and development processes and demonstrated that it is possible to innovate and pursue environmental performance objectives while remaining profitable.

This chapter describes and assesses the work of VicUrban, the Victorian Government's land development agency, focusing on the way it pursues sustainability through acquiring, developing and selling land on the fringes of metropolitan Melbourne. VicUrban has made the process for guiding the design and development of its projects explicit in a working document, *Sustainability Charter Making Our Communities Better (Draft)* (VicUrban 2006), herein referred to as the *Sustainability Charter* or 'draft charter'. This work evolved from considerable discussion and debate within the organization, since early 2004, over a succession of drafts. The draft charter was the subject of consultation with an external review panel comprised of experts from different disciplinary fields. As VicUrban (2006) states:

> The Charter is a living document, not a static one. The intent in developing it has been to define the essential priorities that underpin VicUrban's work, and to assess the Authority's performance in achieving the goals set. There has not been a model available to guide the preparation of this Charter, so the journey has been one of exploring many tracks and venturing down quite a few cul de sacs. But the document is a major achievement, and it may change shape as its users test it out.

The five measures that the draft charter identified for assessing projects – commercial success, community wellbeing, environment, urban design excellence, and housing affordability – are the focus of the analysis in this chapter. Significant revisions regarding the treatment of affordability were occurring at the time of this analysis, which is based on the performance of the charter in field trials. The charter's aim to encourage an industry-wide approach to sustainability is not considered here. Barton Williams (VicUrban) led the development of the draft charter and we gratefully acknowledge his support, advice and recommendations regarding this chapter.

This assessment of VicUrban's pursuit of sustainability objectives is organized into three sections. First, we identify policy problems that VicUrban seeks to address when speaking of 'sustainability': decline in housing affordability, the provision of services to new suburban areas, and reducing the environmental impact of low-density suburban development (key issues in contemporary outer suburban development). Second, the VicUrban draft charter is discussed as an innovation in performance planning, guided by triple bottom line accounting, which assesses project proposals against declared objectives. We review the objectives, performance measures and means used to assess projects. Third, we present an initial assessment of VicUrban's performance against the draft charter's measures and address the question: What is the contribution that a government-owned development agency can make to increase the long term sustainability of outer suburban metropolitan development?

Housing Affordability

During the late 1960s and early 1970s, high and rising land prices impacted on housing affordability (Sandercock 1975; Sandercock 1983a) – see Chapter 16 too. The federal Labor government (1972–75) cajoled State governments into establishing land commissions and funded them within its broader urban development agenda. The principal objectives were to counteract the monopoly aspects of metropolitan land markets, moderate land price increases and ensure a steady supply of new lots. Thus the Victorian Urban Land Council was established in 1975 to provide 'an adequate supply of fully serviced building blocks... at minimum cost, and in so doing provide a substantial measure of price stability' (Troy 1978, 305).

Improving housing affordability was achieved by pursuing two strategies. First, during periods of tight land supply and high demand, purchasers were selected from a ballot and sold lots at a 'pre-stated, below market price' (Troy 1978,11). Second, in the early 1990s, the Urban Land Authority (ULA) began selling smaller lots (300 m²) for not much more than half the price of larger lots (over 600 m²) to find that, if urban design and common facilities were better, smaller lots in a similar location were more attractive than larger ones (ULA 1993, 24).

Improving affordability remains an objective of VicUrban but the approach is different. Land prices are no longer discounted; no subsidies are provided against the market price. VicUrban's operating principle is to perform 'on a commercial basis' (Parliament of Victoria 2003:7) by setting an internal rate of return for projects, as other major metropolitan land developers do. During the 1990s all GBEs adopted competitive neutrality frameworks through the National Competition Policy, providing for non-commercial programs explicitly through a community service obligation, with budget expenditures meeting the costs (Cook 1999; Baird 2001).

Also, first-home purchasers have declined as a proportion of purchasers. Long-term declines in housing affordability and low-income householders' access to home ownership have become permanent features of the metropolitan housing market (Wood et al. 2005); it would make little difference if VicUrban provided first-home ownership by discounting the price of land.

In keeping with the ULA's practice, VicUrban mainly contributes to affordability by producing smaller, and therefore cheaper, lots than its competitors. The VicUrban average is 15 dwellings per hectare in fringe developments compared to other developers' average of 10 dwellings per hectare. Also VicUrban supports housing affordability through small-scale demonstration projects, such as the 2004 Affordable Home Design Competition, which invited architects to design a 120m² three-bedroom home with a six-star energy rating that could be constructed for a retail price of $A120,000 (VicUrban 2005,2). While it failed to implement a planned no-subsidy shared equity scheme for a for low-income purchasers (Broad and Lenders 2005; Millar 2006), VicUrban (2007) continues to explore partnerships with not-for-profit affordable housing associations to supply affordable rental housing for the disadvantaged and those on low incomes.

Provision of Services to New Suburban Areas

The second policy problem confronting VicUrban is the provision of services to accompany residential development, which has been a long-standing problem for fringe developments in Australian metropolitan cities (Neutze 1977; Neutze 1978). In the late 1960s social campaigns advocated improvements in suburban economic infrastructure, such as roads and sewerage, and social infrastructure, such as child care, community centres, health services and schools. There were two broad policy responses to the problem of suburban service development. By the early 1960s, developers were beginning to contribute to the cost of physical infrastructure services (Neutze 1995) and the federal Labor government (1972–75) developed a national urban policy and suite of programs. Significantly, such programs sought to redress physical and social infrastructure shortages and provide additional resources to areas experiencing 'locational disadvantage' (Sandercock 1983b; Whitlam 1985, Ch. 9).

The Commission of Inquiry into Land Tenures (1976) advanced a policy to tax capital increments as a consequence of land use changes. If successful, such revenues could have funded infrastructure. Given it failed, the possibility was raised that a land commission program provide infrastructure (Troy 1978, 183). By 1990 the Victorian Urban Land Authority (ULA 1993, 35) had established such a fund to provide for 'newly developing residential areas'.

Since then, two developments have focused public policy making on social infrastructure. First, by the mid-1980s, State governments responded to federal policy to reduce the total public sector borrowing requirement and cut intergovernmental transfers by relying more on developer contributions (Neutze 1997, 12). Second, the master planned community (MPC) became the preferred model for outer suburban development (Gleeson 2004; Gwyther 2004; Gwyther 2005). MPCs commonly feature a large area, a balanced mix of land uses, control by a master developer and master planning early in the development process (Minnery and Barjracharya 1999, 34). The origins of the MPC lie in new urbanism and assume that the built environment can create a 'sense of community' (Talen 1999, 1361). This model, suggesting orderly growth in new suburban developments and infrastructure paid for by developers (Minnery and Barjracharya 1999, 41), appealed to government, especially local government.

The MPC approach to land development contributed to changing the metropolitan land development industry. Because of their size, MPCs typically have long time-frames for planning, construction and sales. Consequently developers had to develop their organizational capacity to specify required professional services, manage them and run contract systems for delivery of works on site; the growth of MPCs increased the power of large developers to the detriment of smaller ones.

Environmental Impact of Low-Density Suburban Development

Reducing the environmental impact of low-density suburban development is the third policy problem that VicUrban and other State land commissions have identified and responded to through a range of initiatives. The Brundtland Report (WCED 1987) boosted debate about environmental planning objectives to lessen urban environmental impacts. 'Sustainable' became systematically used in policy statements about city planning and building. For example, the Victorian Department of Infrastructure (2002, 40) states that the 'government is committed to reducing resource use and waste generation, and to creating an environmentally sustainable path for future growth and development in metropolitan Melbourne and the surrounding region'.

Other responses by the urban land commissions to challenges presented by the environmental movement during the early 1990s included VicUrban's joining with the Broadmeadows City Council and a local newspaper to support greening the area through a substantial tree-planting program; actively promoting a 'smart block' program supporting solar efficiency in new housing design; and developing 'an energy efficient demonstration village' (ULA 1990; ULA 1991). By 1993 VicUrban was cooperating with the Australian Conservation Foundation to build a 'green home', designed to reduce consumption of water, energy and resources, from environmentally friendly materials (ULA 1993, 34). This focus on environmental performance of dwellings continued, leading to the completion in 2003 of the EcoHome by Metricon, a volume builder, on land developed by VicUrban – the focus of an action research project led by RMIT and Deakin universities in partnership with eight industry partners (Centre for Design 2005).

The commitment of VicUrban to environmental sustainability now extends to the energy and water efficiency of dwellings and provision of public transport, addressing building and material use to improve indoor environmental quality, selecting environmentally friendly building materials, reducing building waste, reducing impacts on the local ecosystem and maintaining biodiversity.

Chartering for Performance

The draft *Sustainability Charter* (VicUrban 2006) is most simply described as a system for guiding planning and assessing development outcomes for VicUrban projects against measurable criteria (see Chapter 8). As such it is an innovation in performance-based planning, an approach that sets 'standards that describe end-result and acceptable limits of practice' (Baker et al. 2004). VicUrban (2006, 5) states: 'The Charter has been designed to ensure that VicUrban's new urban communities and strategic development activities are underpinned by measurable principles of economic, environmental and social sustainability.'

As mentioned, the draft charter is structured around five headline corporate objectives: commercial success, community wellbeing, environment, urban design excellence and housing affordability. Priorities, objectives and performance measures have been specified for each. For example, commercial success is expressed through three priorities: financial appraisal, benefits optimization, and risk assessment and management. Objectives and performance measures have been set for each priority.

Performance assessment involves scoring against each performance measure up to a specified maximum score. Each headline corporate objective has a potential maximum score of 100 and the VicUrban scoring rule requires a minimum of 60 out of 100. There are two types of performance measures: 'mandatory' ones are scored and 'discretionary' ones are only scored if selected as part of the mix of features for a particular project.

At the outset judgments were made about the relative importance of priorities, objectives and performance measures evident in the maximum score setting for each performance measure and its classification as mandatory or discretionary and in the number of priorities, objectives and performance measures set for each of the five headline corporate objective areas (as presented in Table 15.1).

Table 15.1   Sustainability Charter priorities, objectives and performance measures

Headline Core Objectives	Number of Priorities	Number of Objectives	Number of Performance Measures	Mandatory Performance Measures (%)
Commercial Success	3	4	9	78
Community Wellbeing	5	11	20	0
Environment	8	29	38	29
Urban Design Excellence	9	9	39	15
Housing Affordability	4	6	10	10

An analysis of priorities, objectives and performance measures in the draft charter leads to other observations:

- The assessment of 'commercial success' is very precisely specified with little discretion over which performance measures are used.

- The assessment of 'community wellbeing' is specified using 20 performance measures but without mandatory measures, suggesting maximum flexibility in achieving the required score of 60 points.
- The assessment of 'environmental sustainability' has the second highest number of priorities (8), the highest number of objectives (29), the second highest number of performance measures (38) and the second highest number of mandatory performance measures.
- The assessment of 'urban design excellence' has the highest number of priorities, an objective to match each priority, the highest number of performance measures but a high degree of discretion over mandatory ones.
- The assessment of 'housing affordability' applies a small number of priorities (4), objectives (6) and performance measures (10) and only one performance measure is mandatory in project assessments.

The charter has been used to assess each project in five distinct stages – project vision, project goal setting, project design, project delivery and final review – with the scoring process at each stage drawing in broad organizational involvement. Experts in each of the headline corporate objective areas contribute to assessments by VicUrban project teams. Continuous project quarterly reports, using the measure tables, are submitted to the project control group, executive board and board, enabling a cumulative picture of each project's improving or declining performance.

Contributing to Increased Sustainability

This section assesses how VicUrban is responding to each of the policy challenges: housing affordability, service provision and environmental impact of new suburban development.

Housing Affordability

The national policy framework, which State governments have endorsed, insists on competitive neutrality of GBEs, constraining VicUrban to avoid net competitive advantage over competing private-sector land developers. This limitation is reflected in the 'housing affordability' element of the draft charter; only the first priority, 'low to moderate income housing', addresses the problem of home-ownership affordability and housing stress. A number of external measures track access to homeownership. The most prominent, produced by the Commonwealth Bank of Australia and the Housing Industry Association, measures the affordability of the median-priced established dwelling purchased by first-home buyers. The housing stress indicator is used to measure the proportion of renter and owner households in the bottom 40 per cent of the income distribution with housing costs above 30 per cent of their disposable income.

The first VicUrban priority included three measures against which to judge performance. The first, mentioned above, involved a rejected proposal for shared equity housing and exploring the possibility of meeting housing affordability objectives through partnerships with non-profit rental housing associations. Progress on the other two non-mandatory measures – to realize at least one project under the control of an accredited not-for-profit housing provider and to demonstrate a 'viable model for housing delivery' – depends on the Victorian Government Office of Housing's developing new models of social housing provision and on Commonwealth government support for a viable financing model (Berry 2003).

Three further priorities make little contribution to improving home-ownership affordability and reducing housing stress. 'Well located housing' refers only to access to transport, employment, education, shops and services. 'Diversity of housing' focuses on ensuring that a proportion of housing is built to accommodate people with disabilities and to ensure diversity in the size of lots and housing. This performance measure contributes to affordability only to the extent that reducing land lot size relative to that of other land developers lowers the price of entry. 'Housing costs' focuses on delivering 'affordable housing designs that achieve 6 star energy rating and 4 to 5 star heating and cooling', potentially influencing affordability by reducing dwelling running costs and increasing the proportion of household income available for housing costs.

In summary, the only substantive commitment to improving housing affordability in the draft charter – to establish a shared equity program for households with the same median income of households in neighbouring suburbs – was not delivered. VicUrban is reviewing its affordability policies but the broader housing policy framework limits its scope to address affordability issues. Future progress in improving housing affordability depends on developments in State and federal government housing policy, partly dependent on policy related campaigns and discourse, such as the National Summit on Housing Affordability (2004).

Services to New Urban Areas

VicUrban's commitments to improving service provision to its developments are mainly contained in the community wellbeing section, which contains no mandatory performance measures, maximizing VicUrban's flexibility in selecting the objectives and performance measures used to meet the 60-point minimum score. Five priority areas are identified – 'responding to community needs', 'building community capacity', 'economic benefit', 'healthy and active' and 'lifelong learning' – reflecting MPC characteristics of guaranteeing the provision of infrastructure and creating a sense of community.

The draft charter specifies *processes* for planning infrastructure and services that ensure the provision of facilities and services by State and local government agencies and investment by private sector firms, indicated in performance measures that, for instance, involve analyses of demographic needs, preparing a community master plan, planning for mixed use to promote local economic development, and framing service agreements with educational and vocational trainers.

The draft charter also requires alignment of the master plan with a statutory development contributions plan (DSE 2003, 3, 7) requiring all land developers to contribute to infrastructure for future suburban communities. The objectives and performance measures that aim to create a 'sense of community' include commitments to integrate public art and place-making activities using '1% of project costs' and allocating funds for a community development officer to organize activities and form residents' groups as they enter a new estate.

In summary, this element of the charter provides a framework for some infrastructure and service provision by VicUrban, the rest by State and local government providers, and a means to oversee numerous planning processes for VicUrban's new estates.

Environmental Impact of Low-Density Suburban Development

The priorities, objectives and performance measures of the 'environment' and 'urban design excellence' sections of the draft charter highlight VicUrban's commitments to improving the environmental sustainability of suburban developments. As shown in Table 15.1, these are the most detailed of the five sections. This level of detail is not surprising. Attaining many core objectives is most easily assessed using detailed performance measures. Also the various firms in the land development and building industries – such as engineers, excavators, environmental scientists, surveyors, urban designers and master planners, deliverers of electricity and installers of gas, water and telecommunications – as well as the builders and ancillary trades constructing dwellings on estates created by developers, are familiar with responding to, and generating, detailed specifications (Charter Keck Cramer 2006). In this organizational environment, exact and extensive specification has become the norm for controlling quality and costs from design to completion.

The eight priorities of the 'environment' section are: energy, water, transport, indoor environmental quality, materials, waste, landscape and atmosphere. All contain highly specified performance measures that VicUrban, as the project initiator, must continuously communicate to on-site trades people through the contracting and supervisory processes.

The first priority aims to lower the energy and water use of households living in the dwellings. For example, the water/potable water conservation objective entails a mandatory performance measure requiring that total consumption of households is 'modeled ≤ 160 L per person per day' through water efficient appliances, rainwater harvesting, grey-water harvesting, dual supply pipe and so on. Such a specification will affect the work of the many professionals involved, including engineers, urban designers, architects and landscape designers, and delivery service providers, including utilities, excavators, landscapers and plumbers. Another even more specific but not mandatory energy performance measure specifies the wattage and type of globe to apply for different lighting purposes throughout the residence.

The second priority seeks to reduce broader environmental impacts of housing construction through new building design and on-site systems. It sets performance measures which involve select building materials – each dwelling achieving 100 points according to the VicUrban Eco Materials Selector in order to reduce the up-stream environmental impact of building materials use. Construction waste minimization through '80% of construction and demolition waste to be recycled or reused' achieves the same end. Such provisions require on-site trades to change their practices.

An indication of the new dynamic that these requirements can establish between land developer and house builder is evident in the VicUrban Aurora Project Manager's description of a briefing workshop for potential builders of Aurora housing (Jolic 2004):

> We had 200 people ... who wanted to be involved, who had heard about the project ... they see that this is the way the industry is headed ... Partnering with us allows them to use our resources, because we have attachments to the different agencies – to EcoRecycle, the Sustainable Energy Authority – to get their R&D up and running. They ... are happy to be a part of it.

This statement suggests the development of new capacity within residential building firms resulting from specifying more sustainable products and materials, and new on-site requirements.

The third environmental priority relates VicUrban developments spatially within metropolitan Melbourne through a transport priority specifying performance measures covering spaces for bicycle storage and accessible transport alternatives to a private car. The latter performance measure has a criterion that '80% of dwellings are located within two of the following: 800m of a railway station, and 400m of a tram stop, 400m of a bus stop, and 400m of a ferry terminal or other'. The drive for improved environmental performance weakens here because transport priority performance measures are not mandatory and do not have to be scored. Therefore VicUrban does not have to consider the integration of households with the public transport system. This is not a VicUrban failing but reflects a fundamental weakness in the broader metropolitan planning system that has consistently failed to provide adequate public transport investment in outer metropolitan suburbs for new developments for many decades (Frazzetto 1999; Mees 2000).

Finally, the 'commercial success' performance measure indicates that VicUrban is seeking to calculate how its developments contribute to the environmental performance of urban infrastructure networks. Under an objective of 'optimizing the benefits of the project' it includes the measure to:

> Identify the external benefits of all significant initiatives (externalities) where the benefits are enjoyed by others and the cost potentially cannot be recovered. These may be environmental, social, economic, for instance, reduced need for a new dam, reduction by volume of waste flowing into the sea, job creation, visitors to Victoria etc.

The draft charter extends the requirement for residential environmental performance beyond the five-star standard required of all Victorian house builders. Therefore dwellings on VicUrban estates will be built to a higher environmental standard and could become a new benchmark. They will be better located in the suburban landscape. However, at least as importantly, the processes being used by VicUrban contribute to expanding the capacity of the housing industry to build dwellings and neighbourhoods with higher environmental standards while at the same time reducing environmental externalities of housing construction. The remaining problem that will not be solved by a triple bottom line instrument like the draft charter is how new outer suburbs will connect to the broader metropolitan area through public transport providing households with a viable alternative to car transport.

Conclusion

The Victorian Government's land development agency, VicUrban, systematically uses 'sustainability' as a wraparound term to describe its operations. VicUrban's definition and approach to sustainability is most clearly expressed in five headline corporate objectives: commercial success, community wellbeing, environment, urban design excellence and housing affordability. This chapter assessed VicUrban's pursuit of sustainability against three key issues that characterize outer suburban development since the 1960s.

The first, the issue of housing and land affordability, led to the establishment of State-owned land development agencies in the early 1970s. VicUrban is a direct descendant of this initiative. Second, inadequate infrastructure and services for expansive suburban developments led the State government to pressure VicUrban and private sector developers to provide more and more on-site infrastructure and to larger MPCs. Third, since the 1990s, environmental issues have become more prominent in requirements made of developers and house builders. VicUrban has gone further than other developers in greening its outer suburban estates.

Since 2004 VicUrban has adopted a triple bottom line method to plan and assess its outer suburban estate developments. The draft *Sustainability Charter* (VicUrban 2006) has been the instrument developed to achieve this: setting out priority areas, objectives and performance measures under headline corporate objectives applied to assess projects at five distinct stages from initial planning to completion. VicUrban uses such assessments internally at a number of levels, including the board.

The draft charter addresses three long-term urban development issues. However, with respect to housing affordability, VicUrban has done little to increase the supply of affordable housing for low-income households (see Chapter 16), largely supplying housing to moderate-income households. Alterations here rely on changes in State and federal government housing policy frameworks, which set the parameters for VicUrban operations. Developer contributions required by the State have increasingly provided community service provisions for new urban developments. The Victorian development contributions plan, which VicUrban and other developers work within, frames these levies and the provision of infrastructure. The draft charter contains detailed provisions for increasing the environmental sustainability of new areas, which represent a significant extension of those required by the new five-star provisions.

Finally, the processes being used by VicUrban to build estates using these new standards is setting a new benchmark for MPCs and may indicate that VicUrban has engendered a paradigm shift in the environmental performance of mass suburban housing.

References

Baird, K. (2001), 'What is a Community Service Obligation (CSO)? An Analysis of the Issues Involved in Identifying and Accounting for CSOs within Public Sector Organisations', *Australian Journal of Public Administration* 60:4.

Baker, D., Snipe, N. and Gleeson, B. (2004), 'Performance Based Planning: Perspectives from the United States, Australia and New Zealand' [paper] Planning Institute of Australia Queensland Division State Conference, Brisbane, 16 July 2004, School of Environmental Planning, Griffith University [website], <http://www.griffith.edu.au/school/evp/>, accessed 17 November 2006.

Berry, M. (2003), 'Why It Is Important to Boost the Supply of Affordable Housing in Australia – And How Can We Do It', *Urban Policy and Research* 21:4, 413–35.

Broad, C. and Lenders, J. (2005), 'Bracks Delivers Affordable Housing for "One in Ten"' [Media release from the Minister for Housing and Minister for Major Projects, 15 September, Melbourne] Department of Premier and Cabinet [website], <http://www.dpc.vic.gov.au/4A256811001D78BF?Open>, accessed 18 November 2006.

Centre for Design (2005), Sustainable Buildings: EcoHome (Melbourne: RMIT University), Centre for Design (RMIT) [website], <http://www.cfd.rmit.edu.au/programs/sustainable_buildings/ecohome>, accessed 9 May 2006.

Charter Keck Cramer (2006), *Residential Land Development Industry in Victoria – Assessment of Economic Benefits* (Melbourne: Urban Development Institute of Australia).

Commission of Inquiry Into Land Tenures (1976), *Final Report* (Canberra: Australian Government Publishing Service).

Cook, A. (1999), 'Community Service Obligations and Their Implications', *International Journal of Social Economics* 26:1/2/3, 211–21.

Department of Infrastructure (2002), *Melbourne 2030: Planning for Sustainable Growth* (Melbourne: Victorian Government).

DSE (2003), *A New Development Contributions System for Victoria* (Melbourne: Department of Sustainability and Environment), DSE [website], <http://www.dse.vic.gov.au/dse/index.htm>, accessed 1 November 2006.

Frazzetto, M. (1999), 'Public Transport Decline in Melbourne', *Urban Policy and Research* 17:2, 131–44.

Gleeson, B. (2004), 'Deprogramming Planning: Collaboration and Inclusion in New Urban Development', *Urban Policy and Research* 22:3, 315–22.

Gwyther, G. (2004), Paradise Planned: Community Formation and the Master Planned Estate, [PhD thesis] Submitted to University of Western Sydney [website], <http://library.uws.edu.au/adt-NUWS/public/adt-NUWS20051214.111331/index.html>, accessed 8 November 2006.

Gwyther, G. (2005), 'Paradise Planned: Community Formation and the Master Planned Estate', *Urban Policy and Research* 23:1, 57–72.

Jolic, A. (2004), *Transcripts of Evidence: Inquiry into Sustainable Urban Design for New Communities in Outer Suburban Areas* (Melbourne: Parliament of Victoria), Parliament of Victoria [website], <http://www.parliament.vic.gov.au/osisdc/inquiries/sustainableurbandesign/transcripts.html>, accessed 5 November 2006.

Mees, P. (2000), *A Very Public Solution: Transport in the Dispersed City* (Melbourne: Melbourne University Press).

Millar, R. (2006), 'Once-Mighty VicUrban Falls On Hard Times, Minister Criticises "Lack of Focus"', *The Age* 24 June.

Minnery, J. and Barjracharya, B. (1999), 'Visions, Planning Processes and Outcomes: Master Planned Communities in South East Queensland', *Australian Planner* 36:1, 33–41.

National Summit on Housing Affordability (2004), *Improving Housing Affordability: A Call for Action,* Canberra, Housing Summit [website], <http://www.housingsummit.org.au>, accessed 15 November 2006.

Neutze, M. (1977), *Urban Development in Australia* (Sydney: George Allen and Unwin).

Neutze, M. (1978), *Australian Urban Policy* (Sydney: George Allen and Unwin).

Neutze, M. (1995), 'Funding Urban Infrastructure Through Private Developers', *Urban Policy and Research* 13:1, 20–28.

Neutze, M. (1997), *Funding Urban Services: Options for Physical Infrastructure* (Sydney: Allen and Unwin).

Parliament of Victoria (2003), *Victorian Urban Development Authority Act 2003* [Act No. 59/2003], Australian Legal Information Institute [website], <http://www.austlii.edu.au/>, accessed 19 November 2006.

Sandercock, L. (1975), *Cities for Sale: Property, Politics and Urban Planning in Australia* (Melbourne: Melbourne University Press).

Sandercock, L. (1983a), 'Reforming Land Policy', in Sandercock and Berry (eds).

Sandercock, L. (1983b), 'Urban Policy: From Whitlam to Fraser', in Sandercock and Berry (eds).

Sandercock, L. and Berry, M. (eds) (1983), *Urban Political Economy: the Australian Case* (Sydney: George Allen and Unwin).

Talen, E. (1999), 'Sense of Community and Neighbourhood Form: An Assessment of the Social Doctrine of New Urbanism', *Urban Studies* 36:8, 1361–79.

Troy, P. (1978), *At a Fair Price: The Land Commission Program 1972–1977* (Sydney: Hale and Iremonger).

ULA (1990), *Annual Report* (Melbourne: Urban Land Authority).

ULA (1991), *Annual Report* (Melbourne: Urban Land Authority).

ULA (1993), *Annual Report* (Melbourne: Urban Land Authority).

VicUrban (2005), *2005 VicUrban Annual Report* (Melbourne: VicUrban), VicUrban [website], <http://www.vicurban.com/vic/publications.php>, accessed 3 November 2006.

VicUrban (2006), *Sustainability Charter Making Our Communities Better (Draft)* [February] (Melbourne: VicUrban).

VicUrban (2007), *Housing Affordability*, VicUrban [website], <http://www.vicurban.vic.gov.au/cs/Satellite?c=VPage&cid=1147912432935&pagename=VicUrban%2FLayout>, accessed 2 February 2007.

Whitlam, G. (1985), *The Whitlam Government 1972–75* (Melbourne:Viking).

Wood, G., Berry, M., Dalton, T., Pettit, C., Allan, I., Leong, K. and Stokes, A. (2005), *Affordable Housing for Low Income Victorians: A Summary of a Report on Research on Recent Trends and Issues in Affordable Housing Carried Out For* the *Victorian Department of Premier and Cabinet* (Melbourne: AHURI–RMIT University).

WCED (1987), *Our Common Future* [Brundtland Report, World Commission on Environment and Development] (Oxford: Oxford University Press).

Chapter 16

Who Can Afford Sustainable Housing?

Bill Randolph, Margaret Kam and Peter Graham

Introduction

Designing and constructing housing according to 'sustainability' principles has potential to provide a higher quality of life at a lower cost to both environment and householder. However, recent studies show that compliance with minimum environmental performance standards for new housing in Australia increases initial design and building costs. The argument of financial benefits from lower running costs persists due to lack of post-occupancy performance data while studies indicate life–cost benefits accrue mainly to second and third homeowners. Therefore, will sustainable housing be a luxury good? Can we afford not to ensure that all housing is 'sustainable'? This chapter argues that the provision of sustainable housing is a social equity issue and that current sustainable housing policy initiatives need to be reconsidered from this perspective.

Affordable Housing and Sustainable Development

There is a long-standing and substantial debate on housing affordability in Australian housing policy literature (National Housing Strategy 1991; Yates 2006). During the last century, much debate and policy development has been directed at understanding drivers and consequences of affordability problems for low-income and marginalized households. A parallel history of policy development on the question of solving housing affordability problems predates the establishment of the Commonwealth State Housing Agreement (1945), which represented a final political recognition that the provision of affordable housing of a socially acceptable quality to low-income Australians is a national priority and the mark of a socially progressive society (Hayward 1996). Social concern about the failure of the market to deliver affordable and appropriate housing for the poor and disadvantaged can be traced back at least to Engels's (1846) analysis of the housing conditions of the working class in mid-nineteenth century Manchester and Chadwick's (1842) equally ground-breaking treatise on poor housing and sanitary issues in England. Books and reports from social reformers later that century made provision of decent and affordable housing to the poor a key to social progress and fulfilment. In the twentieth century, the rise of public and philanthropic housing in Australia was a defining trend in the social progress of the poor (Merrett 1979).

In contrast, there is little serious engagement with environmental sustainability in the current literature on housing policy. In the light of the history of debates on affordable housing, this is a significant omission demonstrating how limited current housing policy has become in recognizing the importance of housing in wider social, economic and environmental debates. In fact, the origin of most policy delivering affordable housing in the later half of the twentieth century can be found in the public health and sanitary crises of the late nineteenth and early twentieth century –the great fear of the urban middle class – representing the great environmental crisis of that time. Quality housing with basic amenities to replace slums was not just for the poor but to prevent epidemics that threatened all social classes. There was a degree of enlightened self-interest in implementing the reforms: decent affordable housing was a public 'good' with spin-offs for the 'whole of society'.

Concern over affordability is not dead, of course. Housing affordability still hits the headlines following a prolonged period where house price inflation has pushed even the average home beyond the means of many low-income households, especially in Australia's largest cities (Berry and Hall 2001). However, recent debate on housing assistance policy has stressed strong social and economic sustainability implications of poor affordability outcomes (Bridge et al. 2004), without integrating the environmental component of the triple bottom line (although, see Blair et al. 2003).

From a completely different perspective, policy and regulations to reduce the environmental impacts of housing and improve ecological sustainability have rapidly increased in recent decades. For example, the Building Code of Australia was amended to include mandatory energy efficiency rating and performance standards for new housing, and there are the building sustainability index (BASIX) in New South Wales and Victoria's First Rate. Industry bodies are re-educating and certifying their members in green building: such as the Housing Industry Association GreenSmart program and the Australian Green Building Council's Green Star Accreditation. Most of these kinds of rating schemes and programs are reviewed in Reardon (2005) Section 1.10. Housing projects must comply with environmental performance regulation through local government developmental and environmental control plans as well.

The emergence of the 'green building' movement provides substantial building research on achieving much better environmental outcomes. With its roots in the oil crises of the 1970s, the international sustainable development agenda (WCED 1987) and mounting environmental concerns over greenhouse warming and global resource limits, the imperative for environmental design has become a major contemporary architectural paradigm. As with affordable housing, arguments for environmentally appropriate housing use the public-good position: reducing the environmental impact of housing provides long-term benefits to all.

The current environmental imperative in housing is predominantly physical, seeing green building as solved by applying well-grounded principles of environmentally appropriate design guidelines, technology and developing appropriate building materials. Behavioural aspects of environmentally sustainable building design have only recently come on to the agenda (Troy and Randolph 2006). Adherents of broader urban sustainability movements, such as the New Urbanists, do view environmental sustainability as a prerequisite for social and economic sustainability (Congress of New Urbanism 2000), but there has been little engagement by the green-building movement with mainstream housing policy debates on affordability. New Urbanists are largely silent on how social equity and housing affordability interrelates with better urban design, as if these issues might resolve themselves if we get the environmental settings right. With the exception of Blair et al. (2003), there has been virtually no attempt to relate needs for affordable housing to needs for environmentally appropriate buildings. Discourses on affordable housing and environmentally sustainable housing have moved in essentially parallel yet separate paths.

Addressing why this might be is beyond the scope if this paper. It suffices to say that the failure of environmental sustainability debates and affordable housing debates to engage at some level partly results from the narrow focus of adherents in an effort to get both positions heard and accepted. Yet critical and fundamentally important questions remain concerning the likelihood that environmental performance and affordability – both central to a socially and environmentally equitable housing system – might be complementary aspects of the overall sustainability of our housing system.

Three clusters of such questions are identified in this chapter. The first concerns how much more environmentally sustainable housing costs than 'traditional' housing. What is the basic 'cost–benefit' outcome of constructing housing to improved environmental standards? Would this reduce affordability, especially for those on low incomes? The second concerns who actually benefits from the development of environmentally improved housing. Stimulated by recent regulatory reforms, new environmentally improved housing is not often cheaper, and virtually no new affordable public housing is being built to higher environmental standards. Therefore low-income households are unlikely to be immediate beneficiaries. The third concerns the long-term question of how long it will take for low-income households to benefit from environmental gains in new housing. When will housing currently being built to higher environmental standards 'trickle down' to low-income households? This raises the acute question, with social equality implications, of whether the poor have been effectively excluded from recent environmental gains in housing construction. Put bluntly, is housing built to high environmental standards only for the middle class?

Here we segue neatly back to the issue of affordable housing. The great post-war slum clearance programs and mass suburban development undertaken by the various State housing commissions meant adequate homes of a contemporary standard became available to low-income households. Public housing provided contemporary levels of amenity to hundreds of thousands of Australians in the decades after 1945, thereby raising the standard of housing of those for whom it was built and helping solve the inner city environmental health crisis.

Today, the new standard of environmentally sustainable housing represents a contemporary equivalent of amenity improvements stimulated by public health and sanitary concerns of the early twentieth century. However, the cessation of growth in public housing stock means that most poor households do not have the option of benefiting from living in environmentally sustainable homes. Given the market is the predominant allocation mechanism for housing, low-income Australians are increasingly relegated to low-quality housing stock and, by implication, the least environmentally sustainable housing. The collapse of political backing for a mass affordable housing sector delivered through new-build programs has effectively excluded low-income Australians from access to environmentally sustainable housing.

The housing market is diverse, comprising many different segments, based on location, housing type and quality. The market is divided into renters and owner-occupiers. The home ownership rate in Australia is almost 70 per cent as a proportion of all households (Productivity Commission 2004). 'Affordability' of homes at any particular in time depends on house prices and household income levels, mediated by contributory and interrelated factors such as cost and availability of finance, taxation regimes, changing household demographics, the supply of new housing, the level of housing investor activity in the market, and so on. Despite the property slump of the early 1990s, house prices have been on a structurally driven upward trend in relation to household incomes for several decades. Affordability declined rapidly after 2000 due to various factors, prominently a surge in investor activity (Randolph 2006; Seelig et al. 2006). With the rise in the price of housing over the last few years, home ownership has gradually moved out of reach of an increasing number of young people and low-income households (Productivity Commission 2004). Examinations of how environmentally sustainable housing can more widely penetrate housing markets should be driven by considerations of short and long-term affordability, particularly for low-income households. An understanding of the costs and benefits of more environmentally sustainable housing is needed to understand the effects on housing affordability.

Costs and Benefits of Environmentally Sustainable Housing

While there is some emerging cost and benefit information on better environmentally performing homes in the Australian housing industry, there is still a lack of reliable and comparable benchmarking information on the 'actual' costs and benefits based on project cost experiences and performance evaluation.

Often cost information is proprietary or neither documented in design and building processes nor compared with baseline costing of a comparable standard conventional home. Furthermore, post-occupancy monitoring and evaluation for more sustainable houses is lacking and reporting such data is crucial to demonstrate achievement of the initially projected costs and benefits. Although anecdotal, evidence indicates that new housing is becoming more expensive as it becomes more environmentally friendly. Increasing the demand for this type of housing is contingent on the ability of new-home buyers to absorb these costs.

Costs

In a study of houses built in Queensland under the Housing Industry Association GreenSmart initiative, Luxmore (2005) found that initial capital costs for energy and water provisions varied, $A5,000–$A10,000. (Note that all Australian dollar figures in this chapter are based on net present value at the time of first publication.) Capital costs are potentially higher depending on levels and methods of fulfilling the standard. Annual cost savings for energy and water were estimated at $A500–$A600 (excluding annual costs). Payback periods can vary from seven years for some energy measures, such as solar hot-water systems, to 12 years for passive solar design (insulation, glazing, higher ceilings, shading). In another study of New South Wales (NSW) housing construction, Jamieson (2004) found that houses built to meet the BASIX cost an extra 6.3 per cent, on average, over conventional houses. Other evidence (ABCB 2002, CSIRO 2002; DHW 2002; Johnston 2002; Landcom 2003; Roberts 2001, SOLARCH 2000) indicates additional first costs of 1–8 per cent for more sustainable housing. For commercial and institutional buildings, 2–8 per cent increases have been found (Kats 2003; Steven Winter Associates 2004).

A cost–benefit study of BASIX (DIPNR 2004) prepared for the government to understand the impacts of implementing BASIX across NSW concluded that, to fully implement and comply with the BASIX energy target of 25 per cent and water target of 40 per cent, additional up-front costs are required for new homes as well as alterations and additions. The cost or financial implications of BASIX for a 'typical detached house' was projected at $A10,000 relative to current standard practice. However, additional up-front housing costs were expected to be offset by immediate and long-term benefits, including combined energy and water savings, estimated at $A300–$600 per annum for an average family household using electricity, with even greater savings for larger families in big houses. However, most of the estimated costs are relatively stable regardless of house size. Some recent housing case studies of project homes has found that actual cost estimates to meet the BASIX have coincided with projections. Project home builder, Masterton, offers an $A8,000 BASIX package. Cost estimates to meet BASIX for 'Shearwater', a Warriewood housing development by CPG Developments, are $A10,000 or $A50/m^2 additional to conventional housing.

An analysis (Allen Consulting Group 2002) of the costs and financial benefits of introducing a four or five-star energy rating regulatory standard for all new housing and major renovations of existing houses in the State of Victoria found that it would add to the capital cost of houses, affecting equity and access to home ownership. Of course, additional purchase costs can be met by increased borrowing given greater operational savings over time, but low-income households may not be able to afford this or banks may not lend them more.

First-home buyers generally purchase cheaper homes than changeover buyers. For example, in 2000–01 (Productivity Commission 2004), purchase prices ranged from a national average of $A120,000 for low-income first-home buyers to $A200,000 for home buyers at the upper end of the income distribution. Clearly a $A10,000 increase in capital costs would have a significantly greater impact on low-income first-home buyers.

The emerging number of demonstration projects show that early adopters are willing and able to pay a premium for green housing. Therefore, progress to sustainable housing depends on the ability of the critical mass of home buyers to afford its implementation. Equity is reduced if low-income buyers have to bear additional capital costs. Surveys (Centre for Design 2004) have found that home buyers would pay a premium for more sustainable housing, although there is a lack of supporting sales data. Preliminary market research (Centre for Design 2004; Yudelson 2004) indicates consumer demand for more sustainable housing, particularly for energy efficiency, but cheaper items are preferred and more commonly adopted.

Benefits

Financial benefits for home buyers include direct cost savings from reduced energy, water and waste, and lower operating and maintenance costs in the context of the life cycle of a home. For the average house in Australia, cost savings in energy efficiency measures from passive solar design principles have been estimated at $A400 per annum (AGO 2001). Higher valuation premiums, increased rental, higher occupancy and lower turnover have also been cited as benefits for homeowners and investors. Other value benefits include a streamlined approvals process and improved health, comfort and wellbeing through better environmental quality (Wilson et al. 1998). Better amenity, lifestyle and quality, flexibility and adaptability accrue for owners and renters. Theoretically, then, it is possible for more sustainable housing to be both financially feasible and socially beneficial.

Project homes are commonly seen as more affordable housing and account for around 80 per cent of all new homes built in 2003 (Hawley 2003). As the largest single house type constructed in NSW, volume project homes have a significant role in reducing environmental impacts (ISF 2003). The large-scale integration of sustainable building in the project homes industry can potentially increase its affordability and provide an opportunity for builders to differentiate their product in the marketplace by adding quality with least cost. Indications are that the project homes industry is moving in this direction. The introduction of BASIX has seen the development of better practice models for more environmentally sustainable project homes. Major project homebuilders, such as Masterton and Eden Brae, have developed BASIX-compliant display homes in GreenSmart villages.

The mandatory disclosure of a home's sustainability rating at the point of sale for new and existing homes can encourage some continuity of benefits between first-home owners who have borne the initial capital cost and second or third-home owners who benefit from operational costs. New-home owners can recoup financial benefits through resale, while the value for money, such as cost savings and health benefits offered by a more sustainable house, is also made more explicit to potential purchasers. Research indicates that better environmentally performing homes can attract a resale premium. An evaluation (Wilkenfeld 2001) of Canberra's house energy rating scheme (ACTHERS) has demonstrated that a better-rated house commands a higher sale price even when adjusted for land values and house area, might rent for more and offer better price stability.

Who Gets to Live in Environmentally Sustainable Housing?

New housing is not cheap housing. Randolph and Holloway (2004) estimate that Sydney households on median incomes, in 2003, could only afford a median priced home in two of Sydney's local government areas (Wyong and Campbelltown). The most recent (2001) data available on the prices of newly built homes in Sydney indicated only 4 per cent of new dwellings completed that year were priced under $A150,000 (Planning NSW 2002). A household earning about $A50,000 per annum (then roughly the Sydney median household income) might expect to generate that as a mortgage. Contemporary Sydney suburban housing built to BASIX standards is even less affordable. Park Central, in Campbelltown, at the south-west edge of Sydney, is being developed to the highest contemporary environmental standards (Landcom 2003). In early 2006, the starting price of one-bedroom apartments was around $A280,000, with three-bedroom houses around $A450,000, and $A450,000–$A623,000 for a four-bedroom home. Households earning $A50,000 per annum would have struggled to afford even the smallest in one of the more affordable areas in Sydney.

However, it is not all bad news for those on low incomes. New metropolitan plans for Sydney, Melbourne and south-east Queensland envisage a much higher density future for all these Australian cities. Flats or attached dwellings will account for up to 70 per cent of new housing in Sydney, 60 per cent in Melbourne, and 50 per cent in south-east Queensland. This might benefit those on lower incomes for at least two reasons. First, flats are cheaper than houses. With more flats being built over the next thirty years, some low-income households (many being single households or households with only one wage earner) might be able to afford homes in new higher density developments built to contemporary environmental standards. Second, the current trend for investors to own over half of new higher density housing means that many thousands will be rented. Until recently, rent levels have generally risen at a modest rate. This implies that new flats built to more environmentally exacting standards are likely to accommodate many low-income households for whom renting is the only option, although most of them are transient students and Generation X households. Moreover, while they may benefit from living in housing built to higher environmental standards, their life style and behaviour does not necessarily mean that positive environmental outcomes are achieved (Troy and Randolph 2006).

The Elusive Trickle Down

The standard position in traditional theories of land economics is that housing produced at the margins for high-income households will eventually 'trickle down' to low-income households. By the time the housing reaches them (or they reach it), the standards of amenity are significantly below those at the margin of new production (hence the lower relative price). This theory reasonably approximates the way the poor get housing in a pure market economy. The question then arises: if the poor are excluded from the new wave of housing built to higher environmental standards, how long will it take for this stock to trickle down to them? This question is almost impossible to answer. It depends on how fast the relative value of new housing (or the neighbourhood it is in) declines to a point where low-income households are able to afford to buy, or where numbers of investors begin to move into the area, thereby providing cheaper rental opportunities. Judging from contemporary metropolitan housing markets, this might take 30–40 years.

Again, it is not all bad news. Recent research on western Sydney (Randolph and Holloway 2004) showed that, in 2001, 17 per cent of the housing in the most recently built suburbs was rental. It is possible that similar proportions of new suburban stock are still being bought as investments. Given that rents are not excessive – typical house rents in the Park Central (Campbelltown) development mentioned above were $A260– $A360 per week in early 2006 – some households on modest (not the lowest) incomes might be able to live in environmentally improved homes in new suburbs.

While this may contribute to better environmental outcomes for some low-income households, it will be many years before most of the latest-built housing filters down to the relative price range that the bulk of low-income households can afford to buy or rent. Taking Sydney as an example again, in 2001 there were 500,800 household incomes below the 33rd percentile in the poorest third of the population (Randolph and Holloway 2004). At this time, the Sydney housing market was being supplied with an average of around 28,500 additional dwellings per year (Cardew et al. 2000). In other words, the marginal addition to the net stock of dwellings was about 2 per cent per annum, of which about a fifth was replacement of stock lost to demolition and conversion to other uses. With just 4 per cent at notionally affordable prices, approximately 1,100 new affordably priced homes were available to low-income Sydneysiders that year. If such figures still prevail and even all 1,100 were sold or rented to low-income households, it would take almost 450 years to provide all of them with homes built to current environmental standards!

Conclusion

The cost implications of mandatory standards, such as BASIX, applied to residential building, do not benefit recipients of low-cost housing. Given the significant environmental, social and economic costs to society of not implementing sustainable housing, sustainability requirements cannot be seen as tradable to increase housing affordability. An appropriate policy mix would need to target this imbalance and increase availability of more sustainable housing in the short and long terms by, for example, subsidizing the retrofitting of existing private and public housing stock to increase environmental performance (see Chapter 17). This would shorten the 'trickle down' time for more sustainable buildings to become available to low-income earners.

Financing mechanisms, such as the provision of low-interest green-home loans promote the construction of more sustainable housing and the retrofitting of existing housing to improve environmental performance, effectively targeting additional up-front costs and increasing affordability for home buyers. Such schemes presume that reduced household expenditure on energy can increase the borrower's ability to repay the loan and reduce the financial risk to the lender. It has also been proposed (Vale and Vale 2002; Beyer 2002) that sustainable building criteria be integrated as a prerequisite for financial incentives offered by the government, for example to first-home owners. With the release of the *Sustainable Cities Report* (Crouch 2005), an additional $A3,000 assistance package has been proposed for first-home buyers, a fraction of what existing energy efficiency regulations already cost.

Compliance costs are reducing housing affordability by increasing the capital costs of new housing. However, it is important that a home buyer understands that long-term housing affordability is directly linked to the life-cycle cost implications of the home that they purchase. More environmentally sustainable 'affordable' housing requires a holistic approach that views low life-cycle cost as defining affordability. The affordability of different types of housing also needs to be considered in terms of the external (such as infrastructure) costs.

Federal, State and local governments have a leadership role in providing social or low-income affordable housing, reporting project experiences and making available associated cost and benefit information. Policies need to stimulate demand for more affordable environmentally sustainable housing in the short and long terms. The failure of successive governments to provide sufficient incentives for developing new affordable housing stock over the last twenty years continues to limit the access of low-income households to new housing built to higher environmental standards. The trickling down of new housing to low-income households will take many years to significantly improve environmental outcomes for this group. The imminent (2008) renegotiation of the State and federal housing compact, the Commonwealth State Housing Agreement, offers a major opportunity to incorporate environmental sustainability principles into new affordable housing. The dominant argument for affordability based on capital cost alone (as opposed to life-cycle costs) is inadequate in the context of sustainability in housing. A more environmentally sustainable house will increasingly be a more affordable house. Future affordability would be assisted by better cost and benefit information that reflect market realities and render the true long-term costs of occupying housing more transparent.

This chapter has sought to raise awareness of the need for debates on housing affordability and environmental performance to coalesce in Australian housing policy discourse. Unless these two issues are tackled concurrently in policy development we risk having to compromise both qualities, which would undermine the triple bottom line equity aspirations of genuine sustainable housing.

There can be little doubt that greater environmental performance regulation is increasing the capital cost of new house construction while housing markets in Australia's capital cities are pricing out low-income earners. Early research into the financial benefits of improved environmental performance shows that there are long-term benefits in reduced operating costs and potential resale values. However, no one knows yet whether the financial benefits at point of sale will overcome the first-cost penalties. The private sector is unlikely to bear this risk. Therefore, housing policy must address these issues.

All Australians must have access to the environmental and operational-cost benefits of more sustainable building. Affordable sustainable housing should be a right, not a privilege.

References

Allen Consulting Group (2002), *Cost-Benefit Analysis of New Housing Energy Performance Regulations: Impact of Proposed Regulations* [Report for the Sustainable Energy Authority and Building Commission], Sustainable Energy Authority of Victoria [website], <http://www.seav.vic.gov.au/ftp/buildings/5starhousing/acgr.pdf>, accessed September 2004.

ABCB (2002), *Assessment of Costs of Regulated Energy Savings Measures* (Canberra: Australian Building Codes Board and Page Kirkland Group).

AGO (2001), *Cool Communities*, Australian Greenhouse Office [website], <http://www.greenhouse.gov.au/coolcommunities>, accessed 9 December 2006.

Berry, M. and Hall, J. (2001), *Policy Options for Stimulating Private Sector Investments in Affordable Housing Across Australia* (Melbourne: Affordable Housing National Research Consortium and Australian Housing and Urban Research Institute).

Beyer, D. (2002), *Sustainable Building and Construction: Initiatives and Regulatory Options Towards a Sustainable Planning, Building, Design and Construction Sector in Western Australia* [Background Paper for State Sustainability Strategy] (Perth: Sustainability Policy Unit of the Department of Premier and Cabinet).

Blair, J., Prasad, D., Judd, B., Soebarto, V., Hyde, R., Zehner, B. and Kumar, A. (2003), *Affordability and Sustainability Outcomes of 'Greenfield' Suburban Development and Master Planned Communities – A Triple Bottom Line Assessment* [Final Report] (Sydney: University of New South Wales–University of Western Sydney Research Centre of the Australian Housing and Urban Research Institute).

Bridge, C., Cockburn-Campbell, J., Flatau, P., Whelan, S., Wood, G. and Yates, J. (2004), *Housing Assistance and Non-Shelter Outcomes* [Final Report] (Melbourne: Australian Housing and Urban Research Institute).

Cardew, R., Parnell, A. and Randolph, B. (2000), *Sydney Housing Affordability Review* (Sydney: Joint Housing Industry Group and Landcom).

Centre for Design (2004), *'Environmentally Conscious Home Buyers' Who Are They And What Do They Want?* (Melbourne: Centre for Design RMIT).

Chadwick, E. (1842), *Report on an Enquiry into the Sanitary Condition of the Labouring Population of Great Britain and on the Means of its Improvements* [1982 Reprint] (London: Clowes and Sons).

Congress of New Urbanism (2000), *Charter of the New Urbanism* [M. Leccese and K. McCormick (eds)] (New York: McGraw Hill).

Crouch, E. (2005), 'Sustainability Making for Unaffordability.' *Online Opinion* [journal website], <http://www.onlineopinion.com.au/print.asp?article=196>, accessed 28 March 2006.

CSIRO (2002), *Energy Efficiency Measures for Houses: A National Approach – Feasibility* (Canberra: CSIRO Building Construction and Engineering Division for the Australian Greenhouse Office).

DHW (2002), *Proposed Energy Efficiency Measures: Amendments to the Building Code of Australia: Volume 2, Housing Provisions* [Comments to Australian Building Codes Board] (Perth: Department of Housing and Works, Office of Planning Policy).

DIPNR (2004), *Summary of Cost Benefit Study for BASIX,* Department of Infrastructure, Planning and Natural Resources, at BASIX [website], <http://www.basix.nsw.gov.au/information/common/pdf/summaryofcba.pdf>, accessed 10 May 2005.

Engels, F. (1846), *The Condition of the Working Class in England* (Harmondsworth: Penguin Books).

Hawley, J. (2003), 'Be It Ever So Humungous', *Sydney Morning Herald Good Weekend* 23 August, 24–8.

Hayward, D. (1996), 'The Reluctant Landlords? A History of Public Housing in Australia', *Urban Policy and Research* 14:1, 5–35.

ISF (2003), *Sustainable-Affordable Housing: Submission to Inquiry into First Home Ownership*, Institute for Sustainable Futures [website], <http//www.isf.uts.edu.au/ whatwedo/SustainableAffordable.pdf>, accessed 2 August 2004.

Jamieson, S. (2004), 'Sustainable Housing Construction in New South Wales', [Honours thesis] Submitted to Faculty of the Built Environment, University of New South Wales (Sydney).

Johnston, D. (2002), *Actual Costs – Is Building Green Too Expensive? Building Green in a Black and White World* (Washington: Builderbooks).

Kats, G. (2003), *The Costs and Financial Benefits of Green Buildings: A Report to California's Sustainable Building Task Force*, <http://www.ebcne.org/pdfs/CostsFinBeneGreenBld.pdf>, accessed 7 March 2004.

Landcom (2003), *Energy Smart Solutions from Landcom: The Edmondson Park Model* (Parramatta: Landcom).

Luxmoore, D. (2005), 'Evaluation of Three GreenSmart Houses: a Comparison with Current Mainstream Housing and Sustainable Housing', [Masters thesis] Submitted to Faculty of Engineering, Queensland University of Technology (Brisbane).

Merrett, S. (1979), *State Housing in Britain* (London: Routledge and Keegan Paul).

National Housing Strategy (1991), *The Affordability of Australian Housing,* National Housing Strategy Issues Paper 2 (Canberra: Australian Government Printing Service).

Planning NSW (2002), *Land and Housing Monitor, January–June 2001* (Sydney: NSW Department of Housing).

Productivity Commission (2004), *First Home Ownership* [Report 28] Melbourne, Productivity Commission [website], <http://www.pc.gov.au/inquiry/housing/finalreport/index.html>, accessed 10 February 2006.

Randolph, B. (2006), 'Trends in the Lower Income Residential Investment Market', [Paper] Australian Financial Review Housing Congress, Sydney, 31 March.

Randolph, B. and Holloway, D. (2004), *The Need for Moderating Income Housing in the Sydney Region*, [prepared for Landcom] (Sydney: Faculty of the Built Environment, University of New South Wales).

Reardon, C. (ed.) (2005), *Your Home Technical Manual* [3rd Edition] (Canberra: Commonwealth of Australia, Department of the Environment and Heritage, Australian Greenhouse Office).

Roberts, J. (2001), *The State of Green Building*, Cahners Residential Group, Housing Zone [website], <www.housingzone.com/green/index.asp>, accessed 9 July 2006.

Seelig, T., Burke, T. and Morris, A. (2006), *Motivations of Private Investors in the Rental Market* [Position paper] (Melbourne: Australian Housing and Urban Research Institute).

SOLARCH (2000), *Project Homes: House Energy Rating, New South Wales Industry Impact Study* [Report for the Sustainable Energy Development Authority] (Sydney: National Solar Architecture Research Unit, University of New South Wales).

Steven Winter Associates (2004), *GSA LEED Cost Study Final Report*, Flex Your Power [website], <http://www.fypower.org/pdf/gsaleed.pdf>, accessed 6 February 2007.

Troy, P. and Randolph, B. (2006), *Water Consumption and the Built Environment: A Social and Behavioural Analysis* [Research Paper 5] (Sydney: City Futures Research Centre, Faculty of the Built Environment, University of New South Wales).

Vale, B. and Vale, R. (2002), 'Sustainable Development Begins At Home', *Online Opinion* [journal website], <http://www.onlineopinion.com.au>, accessed 10 February 2004.

WCED (1987), *Our Common Future* [Brundtland Report, World Commission on Environment and Development] (Oxford: Oxford University Press).

Wilkenfeld, G. (2001), *Mandatory Energy Performance Disclosure Requirements for Dwellings: Impacts in the Australian Capital Territory and Potential Impacts in Other Jurisdictions* [Report to the Australian Greenhouse Office, Planning and Land Management Group, ACT Department of Urban Services, Canberra].

Wilson, A. Uncapher, J., McManigal, L., Lovins, L., Cureton, M. and Browning, W. (1998), *Green Development: Integrating Ecology and Real Estate* [Rocky Mountain Institute] (New York: John Wiley & Sons).

Yates, J. (2006), *Housing Affordability and Financial Stress* [Collaborative Research Venture 3: Background Paper 3] (Melbourne: Australian Urban and Housing Research Institute).

Yudelson, J. (2004), *The Insider's Guide to Marketing Green Buildings* (Portland: Green Building Marketing).

Chapter 17

Retrofitting the Australian Suburbs for Sustainability

Tony Dalton, Ralph Horne, Wim Hafkamp and Margaret Lee

Considerable effort has gone into regulating for improved environmental performance of the approximately 150,000 new residential dwellings built each year in Australia, mainly in urban areas. However, there has been relatively little attention to strategies to systematically improve the environmental performance of the existing 7.5 million residential dwellings. Energy and water use and the environmental impacts associated with the production, use and disposal of materials used to build homes are key sustainability concerns. Given that environmental sustainability is high on government agendas – enshrined in policy at national, State and local levels – it follows that such issues should be addressed and appropriate measures incorporated into housing improvements.

Various resources are available to assist in 'greening' the home and include on-line advice offered by the non-profit environmental organization, Australian Conservation Foundation (2007), and the government *Your Home* manual (Reardon 2005). However, most renovators neither utilize these nor incorporate environmental sustainability as a key consideration in renovating. Initiatives for existing stock lag even further behind those for new-build which, in Australia, are behind the rest of the western world in energy performance (Horne et al. 2005).

This chapter argues that there is considerable potential to influence the continuous and ubiquitous process of housing renovation to make a greater contribution to improving the environmental performance of existing housing stock. It outlines potential gains to be made through a more strategic approach to housing renovation and proposes a framework for considering the key actor groups and stakeholders with interests in housing renovation.

Trends and Potential

Despite projected improvements in residential energy efficiency, energy use in Australian dwellings is rising and expected to rise at 1.7 per cent per year (Akmal and Riwoe 2005) for reasons discussed below. Residential water consumption increased for the four years prior to 2001, although water restrictions have contributed to a net reduction in domestic water use in the period 2001–2004 (ABS 2005a). Other, less well-documented, impacts associated with housing renovations and new furnishings and finishes include biodiversity losses – see Chapter 18 – and the health impacts of poor indoor environment quality.

Energy is perhaps the most well-documented problem and is linked to the main global problem facing humanity – climate change. Most residential energy is used in heating and cooling spaces (44 per cent), with a further 28 per cent for water heating (EMET Consultants 2004, 6). For water use, ABS (2001, 89) reported the main areas of consumption as outdoor use (44 per cent) and bathroom/toilet use (35 per cent). Hence, efforts to reduce energy and water use through the renovation of residential housing should focus on this ubiquitous process.

However, aggregate consumption figures conceal the variability of housing stock. Factors such as type, age, condition, size, material composition, climate and appliance use affect the environmental performance of existing housing. Most Australian dwellings are detached and over 20 years old. This indicates that most current housing was built before building codes required energy efficiency and water conservation. Nevertheless, the Australian Bureau of Statistics (ABS 1999, 19) reports that 80 per cent are in good condition and have no major structural problems.

Meanwhile new houses contribute to rising per capita resource use by adding larger sized new dwellings despite diminishing household size (ABS 2002). Since each person occupies more space the environmental impact of material use, heating and cooling is rising accordingly. Moreover, different configurations of housing types (such as weatherboard, brick veneer and solid brick) and climates (such as cool-climate Tasmania and sub-tropical southern Queensland) provide varying performance, with varying potential for retrofitting to improve performance.

Householder Behaviour

Lifestyle choices also add to current trends in the decline of residential environmental performance. To emphasize the human factor, as we use more appliances with operational power and/or water needs our resource consumption tends to rise.

However, there is evidence that householders are becoming more energy and water efficient. The proportions of households with reduced-flow showerheads and dual-flush toilets increased from 22 to 44 per cent and from 39 to 74 per cent respectively, 1994–2004 (ABS 2004). Behavioural changes in and around the dwelling include shorter showers, full loads for clothes and dish washers, recycling and reuse of water, turning off and repairing taps, using less water in baths and basins, and using buckets to wash cars (ABS 2004). Nevertheless this positive trend in water practices does not seem to have translated into reversing the aforementioned trends in rising per capita consumption – a phenomenon begging further research. Moreover, this behaviour trend is tempered by mixed results on energy use.

While modest gains in insulation use, energy saving, lighting and solar-energy use are apparent, electricity remains the main energy source for cooking and hot-water systems. According to the ABS (2005b), there has been a rapid, significant increase in the number of households with air-conditioners, from 33 up to 60 per cent (1994–2005) and household willingness to support green power schemes fell from

26 down to 23 per cent (2002–2005). Is this a telling indication of householders' lack of commitment tackle global warming? Or, are there other factors to do, say, with retailing green power that explains this negative trend? Either way, the result reduced household environmental sustainability.

Retrofitting Activities and Stakeholders

The size of the housing renovations and retrofit industry varies according to definition. The Housing Industry Association (HIA), the ABS and BIS Shrapnel all publish renovations data, producing estimates for 2004–2005 of $A3 b (HIA 2005, $A6 b (ABS 2005c) and $A24 b (BIS 2006) respectively. The HIA collect data from builder insurance records, while ABS collects building approvals information, and BIS conducts a major survey with a wider definition of housing improvement. The HIA suggests that extensions provide the bulk of renovations activity by value, while the BIS results suggest that the total retrofitting industry is of a similar order of value to the new-build industry. This relative share of construction activity has risen rapidly over the past two decades, and forecasts suggest this trend will continue (Construction Forecasting Council 2005; Cuming 2006).

Retrofitting Australian housing is a large and diverse set of practical and cultural practices, involving households and housing industry firms and contractors, subject to State and local government building and planning regulations. However, continuous retrofitting is not leading to substantial gains in the environmental performance of existing housing stock. This is a problem given that the need for increased energy and water conservation is becoming increasingly urgent. We argue that this lack of focus is not a technical problem. There is an extensive body of building science research used to develop products and specifications for use in dwelling structures to reduce environmental impacts of dwellings. This science provides sound guidelines about how households can reduce their energy and water use. Instead the poor environmental performance of Australian housing has to be understood as an institutional and cultural problem. Figure 17.1 presents a conceptual framework to analyse this problem in institutional and cultural terms. This framework consists of three key interconnected elements:

- Households, both owner-occupiers and tenants.
- Industry, comprising many firms and unincorporated contractors supplying goods and services and undertaking on-site work.
- Government agencies that regulate the built environment.

Households

As with research in other countries, for instance the UK and the US (Ball 2003; Barlow and Ozaki 2003; Hassell et al. 2003), studies of innovation in the Australian housing industry, such as Greig (1992) and Dowling (2005), have not incorporated households. They have focused on new dwellings, leaving households aside or in the background as a consumer or demand factor. Since householders are central and

Figure 17.1   Residential housing renovation institutional practices

have significant views about how their dwellings meet their needs and preferences about how they might change their dwellings in the future, it is essential that they, and their perceptions and experiences, are included in analyses of environmental sustainability and home improvements.

Multiple motivations guide householders in ways to modify and use dwellings. It is not sufficient to assume that motivations are limited to economic self-maximizing objectives, as evident in the Productivity Commission (2005) analysis of potential for domestic energy saving. The household is a complex set of relations, and utility-maximizing calculations fail to capture all motivations and outcomes. As Wheelock and Oughton (1996) argue, the household is a 'network of relations' including economic alongside social and technological relations. Baum and Hassan (1999) confirm the multi-causal nature of household decisions about renovation, relating household decisions about whether to move or not to decisions about renovating. These views are important for understanding how households engage with energy and water efficiency initiatives.

Economic research by Lenzen et al. (2004) suggests that household income is the strongest predictor of household energy consumption in Sydney. A Canadian study confirms the importance of disaggregating motivations for three apparently distinct household energy efficiency behaviours – 'investment for efficiency', 'management of energy use' and 'curtailment of energy use' – which, however, 'do not constitute a single environmental behaviour construct' with broader social networks as an important explanatory variable (Scott et al. 2000, 75–6). Berglund (2006) confirms the importance of distinguishing between motives by arguing that moral motives can guide preparedness to sort waste for recycling in ways which are not rational in utility-maximizing terms.

Industry

A diversity of actors participate in the renovations industry: financial agents such as investment and mortgage lenders and insurers; real estate agents; fabricators of structural building components and fittings for rooms such as kitchens; knowledge providers such as architects, industry associations and housing/design media; on-site doers, such as plasterers, plumbers and builders; and building materials and appliances manufacturers and suppliers.

Firm size is critically important. On-site doers are mostly small firms and frequently subcontract. They are involved in all aspects of maintenance, repair, alterations and additions. They focus on current market conditions, short-term planning horizons and maintaining small-scale businesses. This provides a flexible overall approach to dividing and managing the risks associated with small capitalization and reserves. However, despite this diversity, there is little innovation. Larger firms are mainly building materials manufacturers, domestic-appliance manufacturers or financial intermediaries, traditional hierarchical organizations that are not focused on innovation.

With renovations, there is a significant overlap between the on-site doers and households, and this involves two important features. First, those working in the renovations industry are also members of households and often help relatives and friends; the carpenter is also a brother-in-law and takes charge of a renovation or repair job within the extended family, doing work for 'mates rates' and organizing subcontractors.

In UK research, Davidson and Leather (2000) show that the level of skill available to households is a significant determinant of 'do-it-yourself' (DIY) retrofit jobs. A Sensis (Cussen 2005) analysis of on-line information searching indicates that 'Australians love their home … Australians enjoy home renovation, especially if they can do it themselves'. Davidson and Leather (2000:749) estimate that, in 1991, 'the proportion of DIY and unpaid work by value rose to 45 per cent of overall work value' on UK houses. Unfortunately, at the time of writing, there were no equivalent Australian data.

Government

In 1994, the Australian Building Codes Board (2007) developed a 'nationally uniform approach to technical building requirements' to enable 'the building industry to adopt new and innovative construction technology and practices'. However, such standards, mainly responsible for recent higher energy efficiency standards, only apply to new housing. Meanwhile the national government has generally ignored seeking to green the extensive growth in housing renovation.

Reflecting a wider lack of engagement with major energy-related environmental issues, Australia has neither ratified the Kyoto Protocol nor followed up a joint initiative with the US Government to improve energy efficiency (Lowe 2005). The $A1.8 b committed to a national climate-change strategy is spread over a number of areas, such as low-emission technologies, energy efficiency strategies and local-area advisory and educational programs (Australian Greenhouse Office 2005). There has been no sustained focus on built environment energy conservation. An analysis (Armstrong 2004) of the overarching policy review, *Australia's Energy Future* (Energy Task Force 2004), confirmed the absence of a coherent policy analysis within national government.

The Productivity Commission (2005) presents a picture of residential energy as a minor issue, identifying a plethora of complex economic barriers, including imperfect information, information asymmetries, and split incentives (which are discussed further below). The overriding emphasis is on short-term dollar costs and benefits, with little recognition of social factors and motivations, product durability, comfort, safety, or environment. Consumers appear as rational, fully informed individuals, with no relevant social networks nor concern about the health of the environment. Where savings are mentioned, they are presented as insignificant figures, with no awareness of potential transformative effects.

This approach to human behaviour runs counter to research indicating that we do not act rationally by investing in energy efficiency measures that produce substantial financial savings – a phenomenon termed the 'energy-efficiency gap' (Huntington 1994). Literatures that explore this gap are technological and engineering-based (see Sanstad and Howarth 1994), economics-based, or social science-based – involving innovation diffusion and organization theory (see Lutzenhiser 1994).

Nevertheless certain government agencies, especially at the State and local levels, have supported and promoted measures to improve the environmental performance of existing residential housing. Notable examples include:

• State housing authorities renewing their public housing stock through maintenance, upgrade and urban renewal programs, including measures aimed at improving the water and energy efficiency of dwellings.
• The New South Wales (NSW) Government's extending BASIX – the Building Sustainability Index – to housing renovations by requiring design for less potable water and energy use by households (NSW Department of Planning 2006).
• The ACT House Energy Rating Scheme involving mandatory disclosure of the energy efficiency rating of all dwellings when sold.
• The ACT Energy Wise program offering energy efficiency audits for pre-1996 homes (for a small fee) and recommending measures, including minor structural and behavioural changes.

Anecdotal evidence (Home Energy Advice Team 2006; Office of Sustainability 2006) suggests that a significant number of participants have changed their behaviours and are seeking to use less energy and water.

The future role of government in encouraging greater energy efficiency through regulation and developing programs in the residential sector will be significant. However, two important features of these processes need to be borne in mind. First, as Gann et al. (1998, 186) argue, it is important to recognize that, to be successful, regulation requires innovation; new regulation should encourage participants in the house building industry to change their behaviour. They suggest that it is useful to distinguish between four types of innovations in the house building industry: *product, process, configurational* and *systemic* innovation. By examining processes of regulation and innovation, they conclude that it is possible to 'envisage a new regulatory process in which the order caused by standards can create a stable and supportive environment for focused change' (Gann et al. 1998, 293). Their analysis suggests that new regulation must be based on a very detailed and sophisticated understanding of the industry.

Second, it is important to recognize that new regulation is often highly contested. Already there has been opposition from the house building sector to the increasing energy efficiency requirements of new housing through regulation. In early 2006 housing industry bodies, in particular the HIA and the Master Builders Association, ran a campaign against the inclusion of the energy performance measures in the Building Code of Australia and mobilized support from some federal ministers, who committed the national government to an 'appropriate ex-post evaluation' (Dunckley 2006; Tyndall 2005).

Barriers to Retrofitting for Environmental Sustainability

The energy efficiency gap must be taken seriously as a barrier to retrofitting for environmental sustainability. Associated controversies centre on whether or not the gap is evidence of imperfect markets or market failures, and whether or not government intervention is appropriate or justifiable. Issues arising include some specific to tenants and landlords, others specific to owner-occupiers, and the more generally applicable problems of perceived and real costs and benefits, and finally risk.

Tenants and landlords have different interests in housing improvement, known as the 'split incentive'. The tenant may wish to make improvements but sees no way of recovering the investment if the lease ends before the end of the investment's payback time. Meanwhile, landlords are mainly interested in capital costs, not recurrent costs associated with energy and water use. In Australia, landlord–tenant legislation provides no basis for reconciling distinct interests. As a result, tenants are more likely to buy cheap appliances, such as expensive-to-run electric heaters. The main reason 34 per cent of respondents gave the ABS (2005c, 7) for living in dwellings without insulation was that they were 'not the home owner/not responsible for insulation'.

Owner-occupiers face other obstacles, such as what economists call 'imperfect information' – limited information on and ability to evaluate options. Similarly, 'information asymmetry' refers to instances where suppliers do not divulge information. Even if households have information on energy-efficient options, and discuss them with contractors or suppliers, they may discover costs or perceive risks. Supply chains can be impenetrable to new environmental products due to market protection or inertia. Resource efficient options may not be produced at sufficient scales to make them price competitive. Contractors may not have sufficient expertise and experience with the resource efficient option, causing them to quote higher prices for installation. In innovation diffusion theory, these difficulties are associated with the take-off or early-adoption phase of a product.

Notwithstanding cost, risk and information factors, householders may not attach much weight to a financial benefit which is small compared to their consumption budget. The private gross benefit of not taking into account the costs of an energy saving option may be of little consequence to many household budgets, while the social gross benefit may be significant. Indeed the Australian Productivity Commission (2005) uses this argument when it notes the small fraction of household budgets spent on energy. Lee and Yik (2004) point to household motivation as a significant factor. Egmond et al. (forthcoming) use the term 'predisposing factors', including attitude, awareness and self-efficacy.

Mills et al. (2006) include other costs and benefits in their typology such as indoor environment (comfort, health, safety), noise, amenity/convenience, water, waste and the indirect benefits from downsizing equipment. Clinch and Healy (2003) present a model which estimates the value of increased thermal comfort as equal to or higher than energy savings. Risk for early adopters also can be significant in the initial stages of innovation diffusion. Another risk is uncertainty about actual energy savings obtained compared to conventional options either because the technology does not perform according to expectation – Koomey and Sanstad (1994) discuss inadequate parameter specification – or because the specific building characteristics and/or the household context in which it is applied affect those savings. In sum, the way householders understand the situation and assess costs and benefits in dwellings, which are both investments and produce a complex bundle of services, is crucially important but poorly understood.

Conclusion

The considerable potential for retrofitting the Australian suburbs for environmental sustainability remains unrealized, mainly due to:

* The inherent diversity in householders' interests.
* The ways in which householders consider improvements to their homes.
* Market failures.
* Poorly developed innovation and adoption processes in the retrofit industries.

As mentioned, this latter point relates to the complex structure integrating small on-site firms and contractors, and large materials, finance and appliance firms. The economic actions of households are embedded in broader social relations that are shaped by multiple and interacting motivations and relate to a larger institutional environment. This is overlooked in economic analyses and technologically based appraisals of the potential for environmental sustainability outcomes. Understanding the complexity of household relations is key to realizing this potential, requiring sophisticated approaches. Simple 'technical' fixes alone cannot be expected to work.

Le Heron (forthcoming) sums up the required approach by arguing that it is essential to go beyond thinking about sustainability as a desirable end-state and then simply encouraging everyone to try harder. Instead, it is important to think institutionally and for analyses to include investment processes, production and consumption issues, private and public sector organizations, households, and holistic thinking that relates sustainability to ecological, economic and cultural dimensions. In summary, we argue for an approach that recognizes residential renovation as an Australian institution that needs reshaping in order to embed environmental sustainability in the housing sector.

References

ABS (1999), *Australian Housing Survey: Housing Characteristics, Costs and Conditions* [Cat. No. 4182.0] (Canberra: Australian Bureau of Statistics).

ABS (2001), *Water Account Australia* [Cat. No. 4610] (Canberra: Australian Bureau of Statistics).

ABS (2002), *Australian Social Trends 2002* [Cat. No. 4102.0] (Canberra: Australian Bureau of Statistics).

ABS (2004), *Environmental Issues: People's Views and Practices* [Cat. No. 4602.0] (Canberra: Australian Bureau of Statistics).

ABS (2005a), 'Household Water Use and Effects of the Drought', *Australian Economic Indicators* [Cat. No. 1350.0] (Canberra: Australian Bureau of Statistics).

ABS (2005b), *Environmental Issues: People's Views and Practices* [Cat. No. 4602.0] (Canberra: Australian Bureau of Statistics).

ABS (2005c), Australian Social Trends 2005 [Cat. No. 4102.0] (Canberra: Australian Bureau of Statistics).

Akmal, M. and Riwoe, D. (2005), *Australian Energy: National and State Projections to 2029–30* [ABARE eReport 05.9, October, prepared for the Australian Government Department of Industry, Tourism and Resources, Canberra].

Armstrong, G. (2004), 'Securing Australia's Energy Future, the Federal Government White Paper, 18 June 2004', *National Economic Review* 56, 55–9.

Australian Building Codes Board (2007) History of the Building Code of Australia, [website], <http://www.abcb.gov.au/>, accessed 26 February 2007.

Australian Conservation Foundation (2007), ACF [website], <www.acfonline.org.au>, accessed 15 February 2007.

Australian Greenhouse Office (2005), *Tracking to the Kyoto Target 2005: Australia's Greenhouse Emissions Trends 1990 to 2008–2012 and 2020* (Canberra: Australian Greenhouse Office, Canberra).

Ball, M. (2003), 'Markets and the Structure of the Housebuilding Industry: An International Perspective', *Urban Studies* 40:5–6, 897–916.

Barlow, J. and Ozaki, R. (2003), 'Achieving "Customer Focus" in Private Housebuilding: Current Practice and Lessons from Other Industries', *Housing Studies* 18:1, 87–101.

Baum, S. and Hassan, R. (1999), 'Home Owners, Home Renovation and Residential Mobililty', *Journal of Sociology* 35:1, 23–41.

Berglund, C. (2006), 'The Assessment of Households' Recycling Costs: The Role of Personal Motives', *Ecological Economics* 56:4, 560–69.

BIS (2006), *The Home Improvements Market in Australia 2006* (Melbourne/Sydney: BIS Shrapnel).

Clinch, J. and Healy, J. (2003), 'Valuing Improvements in Comfort From Domestic Energy-Efficiency Retrofits Using a Trade-off Simulation Model', *Energy Economics* 25:5, 565–83.

Construction Forecasting Council (2005), *Renovations to Rescue Residential Construction from Negative Outlook: New Construction Forecasts,* Construction Forecasting Council [website], <http://www.cfc.acif>, 6 December 2006.

Cuming, A. (2006), 'Banks Milking Home Renovations Boom', *The Age*, 9 January, 67.

Cussen, J. (2005), 'Home Sweet Home' [media release] 16 March, Sensis [website], <http://sensis.com.au>, accessed 15 February 2007.

Davidson, M. and Leather, P. (2000), 'Choice or Necessity? A Review of the Role of DIY in Tackling Housing Repair and Maintenance', *Construction Management and Economics* 18, 747–56.

Dowling, R. (2005), 'Residential Building in Australia, 1993–2003', *Urban Policy and Research* 23:4, 447–64.

Dunckley, M. (2006), 'Drive to Stall New Code Blocked', *Australian Financial Review* 6 March, 57.

Egmond, C., Jonkers, R. and Kok, G. (forthcoming), 'Target Group Segmentation Makes Sense: If One Sheep Leaps Over the Ditch, All the Rest Will Follow', *Energy Policy*.

EMET Consultants (2004), *Energy Efficiency Improvement in the Residential Sector* (Melbourne: Sustainable Energy Authority of Victoria).

Energy Task Force (2004), *Australia's Energy Future* (Canberra: Department of the Prime Minister and Cabinet).

Gann, D., Wang, Y. and Hawkins, R. (1998), 'Do Regulations Encourage Innovation? The Case of Energy Efficiency in Housing', *Building Research and Information* 26:4, 280–96.

Greig, A. (1992), *Structure, Organisation and Skill Formation in the Australian Housing Industry,* National Housing Strategy Background Paper 13 (Canberra: Australian Government Publishing Service).

Hassell, R., Wong, A., Houser, A., Knopman, D. and Bernstein, M. (2003), *Building Better Homes: Government Strategies for Promoting Innovation in Housing,* (Santa Monica: RAND).

HIA (2005), *Renovations Monitor, December Quarter* (Canberra: Housing Industry Association).

Home Energy Advice Team (2006), *Home Energy Audits* (Canberra: Home Energy Advice Team).

Horne, R., Hayles, C., Hes, D., Jensen, C., Opray, L., Ron, W. and Kendra, W. (2005), *International Comparison of Building Energy Performance Standards.* Prepared for Australian Greenhouse Office and Department of Environment and Heritage (Melbourne).

Huntington, H. (1994), 'Been Top Down So Long it Looks Like Bottom Up to Me', *Energy Policy* 22:10, 833–9.

Koomey, J. and Sanstad, A. (1994), 'Technical Evidence for Assessing the Performance of Markets Affecting Energy Efficiency', *Energy Policy* 22:10, 826–32.

Le Heron, R. (forthcoming), 'Towards Governing Spaces Sustainably – Reflections in the Context of Auckland, New Zealand', *Geoforum*.

Lee, W. and Yik, F. (2004), 'Regulatory and Voluntary Approaches for Enhancing Building Energy Efficiency', *Progress in Energy and Combustion Science* 30:5, 477–99.

Lenzen, M., Dey, C. and Foran, B. (2004), 'Energy Requirements of Sydney Households', *Ecological Economics* 49:3, 375–99.

Lowe, I. (2005), 'Greenhouse, a Scientific, Political, Moral Issue', *Arena Journal* 24, 161–79.

Lutzenhiser, L. (1994), 'Innovation and Organizational Networks Barriers to Energy Efficiency in the US Housing Industry', *Energy Policy* 22:10, 867–76.

Mills, E., Kromer, S., Weiss, G. and Mathew, P. (2006), 'From Volatility to Value: Analysing and Managing Financial and Performance Risk in Energy Savings Projects', *Energy Policy* 34:2, 188–99.

NSW Department of Planning (2006), *BASIX* (Sydney: Sustainability Unit, NSW Department of Planning).

Office of Sustainability (2006), *Home Energy Advisory Team and ACT Energy Wise Program* (Canberra: Office of Sustainability, Chief Minister's Department).

Productivity Commission (2005), *The Private Cost Effectiveness of Improving Energy Efficiency* (Melbourne: Productivity Commission).

Reardon, C. (ed.) (2005), *Your Home Technical Manual*, 3rd Edition (Canberra: Commonwealth of Australia, Department of the Environment and Heritage, Australian Greenhouse Office). Online version: <http://www.yourhome.gov.au>, accessed 15 January 2007.

Sanstad, A. and Howarth, R. (1994), '"Normal" Markets, Market Imperfections and Energy Efficiency', *Energy Policy* 22:10, 811–18.

Scott, D., Parker, P. and Rowlands, I. (2000), 'Determinants of Energy Efficiency Behaviours in the Home: A Case Study of Waterloo Region', *Environments* 28:3, 73–96.

Tyndall, F. (2005), 'Industry Has BASIX Problems', *Australian Financial Review* 22 June, 58.

Wheelock, J. and Oughton, E., (1996), 'The Household as a Focus for Research', *Journal of Economic Issues* 30:1, 143–59.

Chapter 18

Nurturing Nature in the City

Sarah Bekessy and Ascelin Gordon

If one accepts the simple proposition that nature is the arena of life and that a modicum of knowledge of her processes is indispensable for survival and rather more for existence, health and delight, it is amazing how many apparently difficult problems present ready resolution. (McHarg 1969, 7)

Introduction

Engaging with 'nature' in places they live and work, many people around the world gain benefits, including aesthetic and cultural inspiration, recreation, and purer air and water. Often local plants and animals are the only exposure that city people have to natural environments so urban habitat represents an important educational opportunity. Preserving 'nature' requires managing biodiversity, the variety of life, at both the gene and species levels. It also requires managing the ecosystems of which species form a part, as well as the ecological and evolutionary processes that maintain them.

Worldwide, nurturing nature in our cities has become increasingly challenging over the last one hundred years, as cities have dramatically increased in size (Global Urban Observatory and Statistics Unit 1999). Urban growth has resulted in profound impacts on natural areas, including: loss of natural habitats and fragmentation of the landscape; introduction of pests and weeds; modification and pollution of natural waterways; increased roads and traffic; problems of sewage and waste disposal; and disturbance from intensive recreation and tourism.

In Australia, urban areas are generally located in regions of regular rainfall and fertile soil, most often with high biodiversity (Yencken and Wilkinson 2000). Therefore the biodiversity value of remnant areas is often highly significant. For example, in Australia, over 40 per cent of nationally listed threatened ecological communities (Newton et al. 2001) and more than 50 per cent of threatened species (Yencken and Wilkinson 2000) occur in urban fringe areas. For these reasons, urbanization is considered one of the greatest current threats to biodiversity and there is an urgent need to improve conservation planning in cities.

Despite the introduction of planning legislation and frameworks to preserve biodiversity, many cities around the world are facing a looming extinction crisis; short-term economic gains consistently win over biodiversity concerns on a localized case-by-case basis. As an example, the following statistics highlight recent trends in biodiversity loss in some of the major cities of Australia:

- In Sutherland Shire, Sydney, a recent Science Unit (2006) risk assessment showed that bushland and mammal species have declined steadily over the past 40 years (losing 3000 ha and 12 mammal species) and identified urban expansion, particularly new release areas, as the main culprit.
- During 1994–2003, an estimated 23 per cent (121,900 ha) of the remnant vegetation on Perth's Swan Coastal Plain was cleared (Perth Biodiversity Project 2003, 5).
- In Melbourne, 50 per cent of the extremely limited area of native grassland remaining in 1985 was lost to development and weed invasion over the subsequent two decades (Williams et al. 2005).

This chapter outlines key issues for biodiversity management in urban areas and outlines the paradigm shift required to respond to the substantial challenge of nurturing nature in the city. Our recommendations focus on the protection of high value habitat in greenfield developments, rather than recreating habitat on brownfield sites.

Unique Challenges

Protecting extensive tracts of wild land, free of development, is critical for the conservation of biodiversity. However, such areas are insufficient. Many species and ecosystems exist primarily on either private land or areas subject to human disturbance. Additionally, the protection of biodiversity should aim to conserve species across a broad range of climatic regions and to conserve all races, variants and subspecies (Williams et al. 2001). Therefore, it is critical to find ways to inhabit and use lands in peri-urban and urban environments in a manner compatible with biodiversity conservation.

Governments at all levels in many parts of the world emphasize urban planning, and have commitments to ensure that developments are socially and ecologically sustainable. However, often there is little scientific input into the biodiversity aspects of the urban planning process and consideration of biodiversity values is, at best, ad hoc. Despite the introduction of key planning legislation and frameworks that aim to preserve biodiversity, many regions are facing a looming extinction crisis in the suburbs.

Planning for biodiversity conservation in urban areas poses several key challenges, including: strategic, long-term management at the appropriate scale; economic and social trade-offs; coping with the 'extinction debt'; the need to manage biodiversity on private land; lack of acknowledgement of scientific complexity; and supporting the paradigm shifts required to protect biodiversity.

Strategic, Long-Term and Appropriate Scale Management

Preserving biodiversity requires a long-term strategic view. Ad hoc conservation efforts will ultimately fail to protect remnant patches of vegetation from outright loss and gradual degradation due to incremental pressures of urbanization (Pressey et al.

1993). In most urban areas, biodiversity is considered too late in the development process, at the project or development assessment phase, when decisions about spatial arrangement have already been made (Fallding 2004). Threatened species legislation is typically triggered when specific sites are being assessed for development, not when strategic plans are formulated (Fallding 2004). Furthermore, vegetation management policies are typically produced and reviewed in a policy cycle that is too slow to adapt to the rapid changes occurring in peri-urban environments. Ideally, management should be able to respond to findings from monitoring and advances in scientific understanding.

Often the planning process fails to link strategic planning, impact assessment and ongoing management (Fallding 2004). For example, Victoria's net-gain policy (DSE 2002, 16) requires decisions to be made regarding the location of vegetation offsets, but is less effective at identifying ongoing management of the areas selected. Many areas in the urban fringes are essentially unmanaged, having been taken out of agricultural production to await decisions regarding zoning, development proposals and applications. This poses risks to biodiversity, as land can degrade through weed invasions and lack of appropriate fire and grazing regimes.

The scale of biodiversity management in peri-urban regions is another significant challenge, as both site-focused and ecosystem-scale management are required (Briggs 2001; Fallding 2004). Biodiversity encompasses biota at the gene, species, population, community and landscape levels. Interactions between these levels of biota create complex systems that vary in composition, structure and function and are in a constant state of flux. Therefore, the conservation of biodiversity must follow a dynamic, multi-scaled approach that allows for continuous change and complex interactions between species at numerous scales. Hence, the conservation of biodiversity requires a coordinated response from a national scale through to on-ground managers. Broad conservation objectives are set at national and State scales, interpreted at regional and local scales, and implemented at the on-ground or backyard levels. These scales relate to strategic and development assessment phases of planning, but often, simultaneous consideration of both issues at both scales is required when making decisions (Fallding 2004). Also, ecological data scales are not easily comparable with town planning scales, making that data difficult to incorporate into development plans (Brunkhorst 2000).

Economic and Social Trade-Offs

Protection of habitat for biodiversity in urban fringe areas involves trade-offs between a complex range of land uses, including housing development, agricultural production, recreation and conservation. The intensity of the pressures placed on natural areas is often much higher than other regions. The case for development is driven by the potential for large economic gains, so biodiversity concerns tend to lose on a local case-by-base basis. For example, studies of the results of the principal legislation designed to protect threatened species in Australia – the Environment Protection and Biodiversity Conservation Act 1999 – demonstrate an alarming rate of failure in attempts to protect biodiversity in site-based decisions. Only two of the

1504 decisions assessed through the Act have resulted in refusals to grant approvals (DEH, 2005). The problem of cumulative impacts stems from the difficulty of demonstrating that, even though a single land use change might have a low overall impact on biodiversity, an accumulation of individual changes over time might well constitute a major regional impact (Theobald et al. 1997).

A key problem with existing legislation and policy involves the principles of the ecologically sustainable development paradigm, which hinges on the idea of achieving a questionable 'balance' between economic growth and ecological sustainability. The assumption that a compromise can be reached seems contradicted by on-ground facts, almost inevitably leading to incremental loss in ecological values. Similar failings exist in many market-based approaches – 'biodiversity banking schemes' and trading in 'habitat hectares' (Parkes et al. 2003) – proposed as mechanisms for managing vegetation loss in urban areas. All these approaches are highly problematic considering the 'extinction debt' already existent in most urban areas.

Coping with Extinction Debt

Many ecosystems existing in peri-urban areas have been substantially cleared and modified. For instance, estimates (Commonwealth of Australia 2001) suggest that only 8 and 11 per cent of the pre-settlement native vegetation remains in Victoria's volcanic plains and south-east coastal plains bioregions respectively. Actions in the past incur 'extinction debts', future loss of species as a consequence of land management practices. For example, in areas surrounding Adelaide, the capital of South Australia, the extinction debt estimate (Possingham 2000) is 40 terrestrial bird species. Thus, even if no further habitat is cleared, 40 species are predicted to become extinct in years to come as a result of historical vegetation clearance and land management. Hence, it is unlikely that many urban vegetation remnants and threatened species will have long-term viability without substantial revegetation and restoration. Such debts might be partly avoided by short-term research and management and long-term large-scale habitat reconstruction (Possingham 2000).

Clearly, restoration and reconstruction are necessary in many urban and peri-urban areas, but implementing such change is not always simple. Unlike a building that can be retrofitted for sustainability, destroyed habitat may well be impossible to reconstruct. Revegetation and restoration can increase tree cover, improve aesthetics and human livability, and create habitat for some species. However, to date, no ecosystem with all component species and habitat functioning has been recreated. Assessments (Hynes et al. 2004) of revegetation success indicate that we are not very good at creating habitat for biodiversity. Hobby farmers, with good intentions but lacking environmental knowledge, manage many urban and peri-urban properties – resulting in inappropriate revegetation, planting non-indigenous species, and ecologically insensitive landscape design.

In many urban areas, significant funding is available for restoration and revegetation, often required through habitat trading or offset policies (Parkes et al. 2003). Yet decisions regarding location and type of planting tend to be ad hoc, which questions the biodiversity value of current approaches (McCarthy et al.

2004). Much current reforestation is motivated by net gain in vegetation, carbon sequestration, reducing salinity, or soil erosion, without thorough exploration of potential biodiversity benefits. However, carefully planned restoration efforts could meet both objectives.

Managing Biodiversity on Private Land

Historically, conservation planning has been largely ad hoc and opportunistic, based on a reserve system privileging areas of low production value and 'charismatic' sites (Pressey et al. 1993). The result is an unrepresentative reserve network unlikely to adequately conserve biodiversity. The success of future biodiversity conservation efforts in peri-urban areas is likely to depend heavily on off-reserve habitat management to ensure the persistence of threatened species (Cabeza and Moilanen 2003), implying systematic landscape planning that explicitly incorporates biodiversity values across all tenures, including private land.

Regulation aims to reduce the rate of native vegetation clearance on private land, but has little influence on managing remaining vegetation. Biodiversity conservation strategies that encourage private landholders to conserve biodiversity on their land need to be implemented. In rural areas, voluntary agreements – such as Land for Wildlife, a Victorian Government program currently supporting nearly 6,000 land holders to manage habitat for wildlife on their private property – aim to conserve biodiversity on private land, and land purchase mechanisms aim to improve biodiversity within public reserve systems. These schemes can be effective where rural landholders understand the economic benefits of conserving biodiversity for the health of ecosystem services and where low-cost land is added to an adjacent reserve for ease of management. However, such schemes are not easily transferable to urban settings, where land prices are much higher, land parcels much smaller, and land-use variation is greater.

Successful models have been created to finance the preservation of natural values on private land in urban areas, including:

- The Brisbane City Council (Queensland) bushland preservation levy, which uses a proportion of rates to buy environmentally significant bushland.
- The City of Boulder (Colorado) open space preservation scheme has operated for over sixty years, using a small sales tax increase to buy property on the periphery of the city to prevent urban sprawl. Some properties had environmental values while the city leases others for farming.
- Funding ecosystem services through water or biodiversity trusts (Binning et al. 2001).

Scientific Complexity

The complexity and uncertainties of biodiversity management are rarely acknowledged in planning systems. Bennett (1998) suggests that successful urban biodiversity management must take into account key conservation planning principles:

- protect key sites of biodiversity;
- maintain the viability of populations and increase the diversity of species within remnants;
- ensure movement of migratory species; and
- reduce susceptibility of species to disease and threats such as weed invasion and predation from pest animals.

However, none of these objectives are simple to achieve from a scientific perspective, even ignoring political and social obstacles. For example, protecting key sites of biodiversity requires knowing the composition and location of biodiversity and quantifying levels of threat. Very little is known about most of the world's biodiversity. An estimated 87 per cent of species on earth have not even been described yet (Heywood 1995). Lack of knowledge makes assessing management impacts on most species impractical or impossible (Burgman and Lindenmayer 1998). Acting without detailed knowledge of ecosystem composition and processes presents a major challenge for conservation planning.

Maintaining the viability of species also requires consideration of many factors, including landscape elements, such as fragmentation of habitat and size and shape of remnants and types of land uses as well as the requirements and characteristics of individual species, such as mode of dispersal, rate of replacement and response to urban impacts. Currently, no methods are available to predict the viability of more than a few species. Tools need to be developed to enable planners to assess and prioritize potential planning strategies to maximize the long-term probability of species' persistence (Margules and Pressey 2000). Although simple conceptually, incorporating species viability in evaluations of conservation planning options remains a significant challenge to conservation planners.

Paradigm Shifts Required to Protect Biodiversity

While there are many examples of innovative responses to the challenge of preserving peri-urban biodiversity, most cities in the world are far from achieving best practice. Considering the rate at which urban centres are growing, cities are at risk of rapidly losing biodiversity values and the associated ecosystem goods and services, such as purification of air and water.

Australia's pattern of human settlement has been characterized by particularly high rates of urbanization, low-density cities, and concentrations of population within fifty kilometres of the coast (Newton et al. 2001). Without adequate planning, future development has the potential to impinge further on remaining habitat and substantially reduce the biodiversity value of urban and peri-urban areas (Lowe et al. 2003). Establishing legislation to protect biodiversity values in urban areas is a significant step towards ensuring the ecological sustainability of these regions. However, it is important that ecological knowledge is incorporated into decision-making processes (Wilson and Lowe 2003). Currently, the design of natural areas in many urban and peri-urban landscapes is not assessed in terms of the comprehensiveness or adequacy of the protection of biodiversity. There is an opportunity to improve the planning process through a sound, scientific understanding of landscape patterns, species requirements and environmental pressures.

Conservation planning requires a long-term view, rather than simply reactions to threats as they arise. Areas of remnant bushland and open space close to cities and major roads are most likely to be lost. Therefore it is essential that conservation planners work in concert with town planners and those responsible for developing major infrastructure. Using this approach, plans for freeways, highways or subdivisions can avoid significant native vegetation. Just as importantly, areas of high biodiversity significance can be targeted for purchase by conservation management agencies early in the planning process before inflationary pressures from development impacts on land prices, which has often prohibited State and local governments from purchasing for preservation. Furthermore, it is important to incorporate ecological knowledge into conservation planning and decision-making processes. Currently, the design of natural areas in many urban and peri-urban landscapes is not assessed for comprehensive or adequate protection of biodiversity. There is a need to improve the planning process by integrating sound, scientific understanding of landscape patterns, species requirements and environmental pressures.

Effective biodiversity conservation will require changes to current approaches to land use, pollution control, resource consumption, waste and recycling, valuation of natural resources and the role of the community and individuals in protecting the environment. Good government policy is fundamental to implementing the changes needed. However, history has shown that biodiversity conservation policies are not commonly matched by effective implementation with good biodiversity outcomes. Urban ecologically sustainable development will be impossible unless more financial and human resources are directed to support improved understanding and management.

Despite the scientific complexity of assessing the conditions required for persistence of urban biodiversity, it is possible to provide some recommendations to dramatically improve current practices. The following narrative, 'Biodiversia', describes simple changes to greenfield developments to accommodate biodiversity considerations. These changes are immediately achievable within the constraints of current practices. More radical and substantial changes could be made over a longer time scale, requiring fundamental changes to current development paradigms. Table 18.1 provides a summary of the main actions described, as well as broad estimates of the comparative value to biodiversity and the ease of implementation in new and existing suburbs.

Biodiversia

What would a suburb look and feel like if designed with the preservation of biodiversity as a top priority? Whilst the resources required to nurture nature in the city can be more onerous at the planning stage, suburbs developed with the preservation of biodiversity as a top priority may well be appealing places to live. Consider the following scenario.

Table 18.1   Actions to prioritize biodiversity in suburban development design

Action	Effect on Biodiversity	Ease of Implementing in Existing Suburbs	Ease of Implementing in New Suburbs
Clustered Housing – 50% Open Space	High	Low	High
Green Corridors Linking Conservation Areas	High	Low	High
Controlling Pets	High	High	High
Managing Weeds	High	Medium	Medium
Native Gardens	Medium	High	High
Roads and Impervious Surfaces, Swales to Stop Runoff	Low	Low	High
Reduced Lighting at Night	Medium	Medium	High
Fencing Remnants	High	High	High

The scene: a large city (over one million inhabitants) in the developed world, a new suburb built on a greenfield area on the city fringe, a housing estate designed with the preservation of biodiversity as a top priority, a house in the centre of the estate...

It's 5pm, a hint of the day's heat still lingers. You leave your house, heading towards the community centre for the monthly meeting of the local land stewardship program. On the agenda is a presentation about optimal monitoring strategies for detecting invasive weed species and coordinating volunteers for weed control work. While only about 30 per cent of the residents have participated in the stewardship program, much has been accomplished in the two years it has been running. This has included biodiversity education programs at local schools, the implementation of strategies for dealing with feral animals, monitoring populations of rare birds and a captive breeding and release program to help recover the depleted population of a local ground-dwelling mammal. All this was possible due to the budget obtained from a fraction of all house sales in the estate.

You pass through woodlands, following one of the many walking and cycling tracks within the estate. Over half of the total estate area is open space, with well over half the open space reserved for conservation. Some conservation areas have walking and cycling tracks through them. Sensitive areas are fenced off from the public.

When the estate was planned, conservation areas were selected using systematic conservation planning principles (Margules and Pressey 2000). Areas were selected large enough for flora and fauna to persist and representative of the regional biodiversity, taking into account their local, regional, national and international significance (McHarg 1969). The spatial context of each conservation area was also considered: how it contributed to the overall connectivity in the landscape and complemented existing conservation reserves in and around the city.

The houses were grouped into clusters of about seven, each house with views onto areas with natural values, vital to inspire residents' connections with them. During construction, clearing of vegetation was minimized, and unavoidable clearing offset by revegetation. While the overall density of housing was not significantly lower than in other areas in the city, the 'clumped' (Arendt 1996) layout was very different. Although free standing, the houses were built close together with small gardens around them, reducing the amount of private outdoor space around houses, but most residents agreeing that the access to open space and views more than made up for this.

Passing though the woodland, you approach the next cluster and notice a caged area behind the first house owned by one of the few residents with a cat. To ensure protection of the local fauna, cat and dog owners are required to have an enclosed run if they want to let their pet outside the house. Residents with dogs keep them on a leash while walking. The community centre provides other rewarding options for people who enjoy interacting with animals: caring for injured wildlife at home and helping with breeding programs for threatened species.

Walking past this cluster of houses you see how creative some residents have been in designing gardens using only native and indigenous plant species. You spot gardens designed to attract native birds and others to attract local butterflies (informed by the community centre's information on plant–animal associations). Reaching the end of the cluster you see one resident even has several garden ponds with vegetation designed to attract frogs. Several houses have small areas set aside for non-native gardens consisting of herbs, vegetables, fruit trees and other traditional garden plants. All non-indigenous species were carefully selected so they would not become environmental weeds.

The path rejoins one of the few roads through the estate. You see the community centre ahead, and notice a striking design contrast between the gently curving olive-coloured road and swales spaced on either side with carefully chosen indigenous plants. The swales absorb road runoff and filter out petroleum-based residue in water. The light-coloured material used in road construction absorbed much less heat than conventional bitumen and produced much smaller microclimatic effects, especially in summer. Apart from the few roads in the estate, impervious material use was minimized. The walking tracks were made out of water-pervious materials, their slight sponginess also making walking much more pleasant. All houses feature water tanks. All this significantly reduces the negative impacts of peak flows on local waterways in other residential estates (Arnold and Gibbons 1996, 243).

In the distance you see where the road joins the old arterial leading into the city. There are structures on the road sides designed to act as noise barriers and fences to keep wildlife off the road. A recently constructed wildlife bridge with small trees and shrubs is visible, reminding you of several new underground wildlife tunnels.

Just before you reach the estate centre, a car drives slowly past, obeying the reduced evening speed limit designed to reduce road kill. Car use in the estate is discouraged. Since the light-rail extension was completed it is much easier to use a combination of public transport and cycling, some residents selling the family car and renting one of the electric neighbourhood cars (see Chapter 7). The light-rail extension has a raised section to avoid destroying a rare vegetation community. Remembering back to your previous residence near busy major roads, you can't decide which is more pleasant, the lack of traffic noise or the absence of air pollution...

It's dusk as you leave the stewardship meeting. Starting the walk home you notice how little light pollution there is. The houses were carefully designed to emit minimal light, especially important for some bird species during migration (Savard et al. 2000). As you pass a fenced conservation area, you notice the dimmed street lamps – a compromise between human convenience and biodiversity preservation.

As you near home your mind wanders. An estate designed to prioritize the preservation of biodiversity was also the most pleasant place you have ever lived in, not only because of the natural values retained in the area, but also the sense of community nurtured by the spatial arrangement of houses. Without this sense of community, it would have been impossible to undertake all the activities so vital in preserving the biodiversity of the area.

References

Arendt, R. (1996), *Conservation Design for Subdivisions: A Practical Guide to Creating Open Space Networks* (Washington: Island Press).

Arnold, C. and Gibbons, C. (1996), 'Impervious Surface Coverage: The Emergence of a Key Environmental Indicator', *Journal of the American Planning Association* 62:2, 243–58.

Bennett, A. (1998), *Linkages in the Landscape: The Role of Corridors and Connectivity in Wildlife Conservation* (Gland: IUCN).

Binning, C., Cork S., Parry R. and Shelton D. (2001), *Natural Assets: An Inventory of Ecosystem Goods and Services in the Goulburn Broken Catchment* (Canberra: CSIRO Sustainable Ecosystems).

Briggs, B. (2001), 'Linking Ecological Scales and Institutional Frameworks for Landscape Rehabilitation', *Ecological Management and Restoration* 2, 28–35.

Brunkhorst, D. (2000), *Bioregional Planning: Resource Management Beyond the New Millennium* (Amsterdam: Harwood Academic Publishers).

Burgman, M. and Lindenmayer, D. (1998), *Conservation Biology for the Australian Environment* (Chipping Norton: Surrey Beatty and Sons).

Cabeza, M. and Moilanen, A. (2003), 'Site-selection Algorithms and Habitat Loss', *Conservation Biology* 17:5, 1402–13.

Commonwealth of Australia (2001), *Australian Native Vegetation Assessment* (Barton: National Land and Water Resources Audit for Land and Water Australia), Australian Natural Resources Atlas [website], vegetation biodiversity [webpages], <http://audit.ea.gov.au/ANRA/vegetation/docs/Native_vegetation/nat_veg_vic. cfm>, accessed 1 February 2007.

DEH (2005), *Referrals, Assessments and Approvals Statistics* Department of Environment and Heritage [website], <http://www.deh.gov.au/epbc/statistics/ march-2005.html>, accessed 12 November 2005.

DSE (2002), *Victoria's Native Vegetation Management – A Framework for Action* Department of Sustainability and Environment [website], <www.dse.vic.gov.au/ dse/nrenlwm/nsfframework.pdf>, accessed 6 October 2004.

Fallding, M. (2004), 'Planning for Biodiversity', *Australian Planner* 41, 45–50.

Global Urban Observatory and Statistics Unit (1999), *Human Settlements: Conditions and Trends* United Nations Human Settlements Program [website], <http://www.unhabitat.org/habrdd/CONTENTS.html>, accessed 2 October 2003.

Heywood, V. (1995), *Global Biodiversity Assessment* (Cambridge: Cambridge University Press).

Hynes, L., McDonnell, M. and Williams, N. (2004), 'Measuring the Success of Urban Riparian Revegetation Projects Using Remnant Vegetation as a Reference Community', *Ecological Management and Restoration* 5, 205–9.

Lowe, K., Fitzsimons, J., Gleeson, T. and Straker, A. (2003). 'Biodiversity Conservation and Natural Resource Management Planning: Mechanisms for Improved Integration at the Regional Level' [Unpublished paper].

Margules, C. and Pressey, R. (2000), 'Systematic Conservation Planning', *Nature* 405, 243–53.

McCarthy, M., Parris, K., van der Ree, R., McDonnell, M., Burgman, M., Williams, N., McLean, N., Harper, M., Meyer, R., Hahs, A. and Coates, T. (2004), 'The Habitat Hectares Approach to Vegetation Assessment: An Evaluation and Suggestions for Improvement', *Ecological Management and Restoration* 5:1, 24–7.

McHarg, I. (1969), *Design With Nature* (New York: The Natural History Press).

Newton, P., Baum, S., Bhatia, K., Brown, S., Cameron, A., Foran, B., Grant, T., Mak, S., Memmott, P., Mitchell, V., Neate, K., Pears, A., Smith, N., Stimson, R., Tucker, S. and Yencken, D. (2001), *Human Settlements, Australia State of the Environment Report 2001* [Theme report] (Canberra: CSIRO Publishing for Department of the Environment and Heritage), available at the CSIRO Publishing [website], <http://www.publish.csiro.au/pid/3002.htm>.

Parkes, D., Newell, G. and Cheal, D. (2003), 'Assessing the Quality of Native Vegetation: the 'Habitat Hectares' Approach', *Ecological Management and Restoration* 4 February Supplement, 29–38.

Perth Biodiversity Project (2003), *Councils Caring for Their Natural Communities* [booklet] (Perth: Western Australian Local Government Association, National Heritage Trust and Department for Planning and Infrastructure).

Pressey, R., Humphries, C., Margules, C., Vane-Wright, R. and Williams P. (1993), 'Beyond Opportunism: Key Principles for Systematic Reserve Selection', *Trends in Ecology and Evolution* 8, 124–8.

Possingham, H. (2000), 'The Extinction Debt: the Future of Birds in the Mount Lofty Ranges', *Environment South Australia* 8:10.

Savard, J-P., Clergeau, P. and Mennechez, G. (2000), 'Biodiversity Concepts and Urban Ecosystems', *Landscape and Urban Planning* 48:3–4, 131–42.

Science Unit (2006), Sutherland Shire Council's assessment of environmental risks in Sutherland Shire and costs and benefits of risk management [personal communication] 3 May.

Theobald, D., Miller, J. and Hobbs, T. (1997), 'Estimating the Cumulative Effects of Development on Wildlife Habitat', *Landscape and Urban Planning* 39, 25–36.

Williams, J., Read, C., Norton, T., Dovers, S., Burgman, M., Proctor W. and Anderson H. (2001), *Australia State of the Environment Report 2001: Biodiversity* [Theme

Report] (Canberra: CSIRO Publishing for Department of Environment, Sport and Territories).

Williams, N., McDonnell, M. and Seager, E. (2005), 'Factors Influencing the Loss of Indigenous Grasslands in an Urbanising Landscape: A Case Study from Melbourne, Australia', *Landscape and Urban Planning* 71, 35–49.

Wilson, J. and Lowe, K. (2003), 'Planning for the Restoration of Native Biodiversity Within the Goulburn Broken Catchment, Victoria, Using Spatial Modelling', *Ecological Management and Restoration* 4:3, 212–9.

Yencken, D. and Wilkinson D. (2000), *Resetting the Compass: Australia's Journey Towards Sustainability* (Melbourne: CSIRO Publishing).

Chapter 19

How Smart is 'Smart'? – Smart Homes and Sustainability

Mike Berry, Mark Gibson, Anitra Nelson and Ingrid Richardson

Introduction

This chapter on the smart (new information and technology enabled) home acts as a warning on 'transforming' the suburbs. It presents a critical perspective on the concept of the smart home from four distinct angles: a history of smart suburban homes; policy making; innovation; and reviewing non-determinist ways of interpreting human–technology relations.

The smart home has featured mainly in marketing (Smart Wired 2007), but governments are supporting automated sustainability-related developments, such as water and energy metering, broadband infrastructure (to encourage smart cities and smart communities) and 'high tech' home demonstration projects. What drives innovation in technology-intensive areas such as information and communication technology (ICT) for domestic settings? How do human technology relations really emerge to transform economic and social relations? This chapter raises deep issues and offers no simple answers. It demonstrates how complex steering sustainability is, especially if policy makers do not question traditional or international directions and simply respond to market forces.

What is 'smart'?

During the 1990s Australian policy makers commandeered the term 'smart' to describe strategies for urban (and rural) developments. While in Western Australia 'smart' referred to sustainability, especially environmentally sustainable initiatives, in Queensland 'smart' has referred mainly to expanding use of new ICTs in business, households and neighbourhood communities. In other States, such as Victoria, 'smart' is a confusing descriptor because it is regularly used both ways.

To compound the confusion – or partially explain it – certain new ICTs either directly or indirectly enable more sustainable practices. For instance, energy and water meters offer households detailed information on current consumption comparative to past use and local consumers, as well as signalling overuse, offering options for households to reduce the rate of delivery or even stop it if a certain level of usage is breached. Also, public transport users can access timetables and up-to-the-minute information on delays and expected departures and arrivals via the

Internet, smart screens located at transport nodes, and mobile phones. Home-based e-work (ICT-enabled work from home) is touted as more sustainable because of savings on transport and greenhouse gas emissions responsible for global warming (Goodman et al. 2004). Here ICT advances align with sustainable practices. Could the sustainability performance of smart households offer a basic solution to currently unsustainable domestic practices?

The Emergence of the 'Smart Home'

'Environment' is a key word in the concept of the smart home, but it is not usually the natural environment that is called to mind. It captures the idea, rather, of controlled ambience – subject to technological modulation, but in which the technologies recede, blending seamlessly with walls, ceilings and doors, furniture, decorative features and outdoor spaces. For example, the first issue of *Australian Smart Home Ideas* (2005, 36) carries an advertisement for a sound system which has been made invisible: 'There are 42 speakers in this room. Can you find them?' Lighting is another common area of attention. A feature in that journal (Haycock 2005, 19) outlines the benefits of the smart home, asking us to imagine a future freed of the 'barrage of switches on every wall': 'Instead, via the control system you can access a series of "scenes" such as "dining" or "watching TV" – the lights are set in certain configurations perfect for every moment of your day'. The 'environment' of the smart home is the total domestic surroundings, minutely managed, yet discreetly concealed.

The smart home has a long history in more general imaginings of technological domestic spaces attuned to the desires of their inhabitants. While it still conjures up futuristic science fiction images, it has a closer material connection with the development, since the 1950s, of a consumer economy focused on the suburban home. Concealed surround sound, lights controlled through 'occupant sensors' and Internet refrigerators are seen as sophisticated extensions of television, multiple power points and domestic electrical appliances. They give new life to the idea of the 'dream house' established with the growth of new suburban developments in the post-war period (Spigel 2001). The housing boom over the last fifteen years has seen a new round of image-making around this idea, from television home and garden makeover programs to exhibitions and trade journals. *Australian Smart Home Ideas* takes its place, in this context, beside *Vogue Living*, *Better Homes and Gardens* and a host of domestic lifestyle magazines.

The specific designation 'smart home' dates from the mid-1980s, when first used officially by the American Association of Home Builders (Harper 2003,1). It captured some of the meaning of the older term 'wired homes', used by hobbyists from the early 1960s, while riding on the proliferating use of 'smart' as a popular way of branding new products exploiting the potential of information and computer technologies – 'smart card', 'smart phone' and 'smart bomb'.

The key feature distinguishing the smart home from the merely comfortable or well appointed home was a new element of interactivity, not just between user and technology, but also between technologies. The smart home does not simply offer an array of devices; it offers devices programmed to respond continually to changes in surroundings and to others around them. This interaction produces the 'environment'.

Three technological developments have been particularly important in the current topicality of the smart home. The first has been breakthroughs in the miniaturization of integrated circuits at a cost such that digital electronic components can be built into ordinary consumer items. A process that started with larger white goods such as dishwashers and washing machines has now extended to toasters, coffee making machines, lights and fans. While 'ubiquitous computing' has been slower to emerge than was hoped by Mark Weiser (1993) when he coined the term in the early 1990s, it has become a realistic possibility.

The second and related development has been the potential for communication between previously distinct technologies, allowing them to be thought of as belonging to a network or system. A central focus here has been the mobile phone, which has evolved from its use in telephony to Internet connections, location-based games, image transmission and remote control functions such as the control of air-conditioners and other domestic appliances. Wireless and cabling systems have also opened up communicative possibilities for a range of other items.

The third development has been the emergence of platforms capable of integrating diverse technologies in a single digital hub. The home 'media centre', integrating television, DVD and MP3 players, stereo sound systems, digital cameras and computers, are probably the best-known development in this direction, but can be seen as only the first stage of more ambitious projects of digital integration. The technology solutions company Majitek (2006) offers products promising 'interoperability between systems' and integrated control over a 'distributed network of devices' 'a Universal Component Model that can encapsulate any software components – these are completely interoperable and ensure backward and forward compatibility with legacy systems and new technologies that you may be required to deal with'. The technology has the capacity to integrate entertainment, communication, data traffic/storage, monitoring, metering of utilities, security and tracking.

But the key questions for the future of the smart home are likely to be as much economic as technological. It is still difficult to know what business models will drive the uptake of the technologies. After some efforts at working with property developers, the telecommunications innovator, Majitek, focused on the sale of digital platforms for business applications. As Richard Harper (2003: 2) argues, there is little business incentive to increase the productivity of domestic labour, and design for the home has continued to focus on stand-alone devices sold independently. However, there are opportunities to change models of service. Some of the main interest in smart homes – such as the 'Orange at Home' project sponsored by the UK mobile network operator, Orange (2006) – has been from telecommunication companies and other service providers.

This provides reason, perhaps, to look again at the possible alignment between the technologized 'environment' of the smart home and the 'environment' as the term might be used in thinking about sustainable housing. As an important body of European theory has begun to outline, the shift towards services models has the potential to deliver significant environmental benefits. Services can often substitute for products, bringing a decrease in the 'materials component' required for the fulfilment of needs (Goedkoop et al. 1999, 18). Simple examples are the provision of packaging as a service, allowing recycling, or the substitution of video on demand for material items such as DVDs or videotapes. Services are also developed around a systems perspective, bringing greater attention to environmental questions.

The smart home is not so much a clearly defined phenomenon as a fluid and unstable field of possibilities. While the concept references technological innovations, it is as dependent on economic, social and political factors for its continuing interest and relevance. It subtly activates concerns intersecting with sustainability, but in ways that could be steered in various directions. As an object or potential object of policy, it should be considered in this broad context.

Creating ICT-Related Policies

The smart home might be seen as just the smallest concept in a suite of Russian doll-style ideas that stretch through smart business precincts (such as the Docklands in Melbourne), smart communities (promoted by Telstra 2006), smart cities, smart States and smart nations. The Australian Department of Communications, Information Technology and the Arts and State bodies such as MultiMedia Victoria herald a brave new future of the networked nation: ICT-enabled work, play and social practices. Liberal and Labor governments, from federal down to local levels, have mainly sought and received advice from technical, business and commercial experts in the development of their ICT policies. Such 'responsive' policies to provide infrastructure for the 'network society' epitomize a weak position, relying on market and industry decisions and delivery. The opportunities and risks of smart high tech developments either coinciding or conflicting with sustainability principles is a sadly ignored feature of current policy. This also highlights the holism of a sustainability perspective and the inadequacy of current state structures, which departmentalize policy such that sustainability is just one aspect of government or one department's responsibility.

When we look at ICT policy we discover that public debates have centred on traditional political divides such as the optimum role of the once-public telecommunications monopoly, Telstra, and ways to privatize it. A parallel focus has been developing a competitive yet adequate and efficient telecommunications sector able to address challenges such as economic inefficiencies resulting from a national population spread in relatively low densities over vast areas of land. In fact, there has been much more thought, funding and action for implementing hard infrastructure (such as broadband) than in soft, social, programs which explore, analyse and encourage ICT use in small and medium-sized enterprises, neighbourhood communities and homes. Yet only at this level can the sustainability impacts of ICT developments be reliably audited and monitored. Property developers of new estates, who have the greatest capacity to integrate new ICT capacities to individual households and neighbourhoods in cost-effective ways, have been difficult to convince about the profitability of integrating broadband and related services into typical home packages.

As just one node in the connected community, the connected home has further potential to integrate sustainability features. At an international level there have been pressures to increase community participation in environmental governance and programs that aim to encourage and support more sustainable grassroots practices. Indeed new ICTs enable more and different forms of communication and information sharing as well as a variety of tools for non-synchronous discussion and decision making over vast geographical distances (PlaceMatters 2007). For instance, GIS tools that present visual displays of complex information are being developed to support new and inclusive forms of community-based information storage and sharing as well as decision making. However, the inclusion of all stakeholders and interests runs the risk of continuing the status quo in terms of balancing conflicting interests and the rule of the market in terms of opportunities and directions. The 'triple bottom line' version of sustainability exemplifies this danger as the urgent priority of achieving environmentally sustainable solutions is diluted by trade-offs with 'social sustainability' and 'economic sustainability'. Simply providing more information and more interactive means of communication does not necessarily lead to more social engagement or conflict resolution, although it may facilitate these outcomes when other necessary preconditions are met.

How can policy makers constructively address the challenges of regulating and/ or supporting new ICT developments in such a way as to maximize their social and environmental benefits? How can policy makers best develop a proactive position when uncertainties and risks are high because we are dealing with speculative future scenarios? Questions surrounding the appropriate role of government in managing technological applications not only drive to the heart of democratic values and processes but also raise issues that have occupied the minds of social scientists for centuries.

The compounding of 'smart' meaning technologically savvy with 'smart' meaning more environmentally sustainable has parallels with interpretations of the historical role of technology, especially within capitalism, and social analyses of techno-futures which emphasize clean, automated and efficient living. In the classic and most popular perspective, capitalism magically delivers technological solutions to all human problems, so environmental sustainability becomes just one more challenge that inevitably and ultimately will be addressed and 'solved'.

Concrete models of a high tech, sustainable future of smart homes and lifestyles are hard to find: government sponsored models of innovative sustainable housing – such as Innovation House in Coomera, Queensland – fail sustainability tests by simple measures such as ecological footprint assessments. While the Innovation House (2007) website promotes it as 'smarter, greener, easier', 'a formula for future living', combining 'sustainable living' with 'smart design', if everyone in the world lived in Innovation House, we would need many more planets with equivalent resources of our earth just to sustain the current world population (Strengers 2006). It is clear, then, that a strong government role in steering sustainable outcomes from technological opportunities and advances would not only be preferable but might well be necessary.

The sustainability literature is split by those arguing that capitalist technology can and/or will provide answers and those who argue that the mass production and consumption implicit to capitalist developments is responsible for environmental damage and risks. The latter argue that small, appropriate and alternative technologies and approaches that strongly regulate or undermine capitalist practices are necessary to avoid crises associated with environmental sustainability. Therefore there are suspicions from this quarter that new ICTs are not adequate to address issues that mainly involve altering daily practices in highly conscious and conscientious ways. These socio-technological questions will be fundamental to research for evidence-based policy making in this area, and also suggests that we need to think of alternative ways of understanding and implementing sustainable practices and technologies at the everyday 'disruptive' level.

Disruptive Innovation

Visions of the smart home are essentially technology driven; new technological possibilities are reified as inevitable future norms. Business plans are written on the confident basis of a rapid consumer response. That confidence is reinforced by reassuring references to past success-stories – the almost universal spread of conventional television in the West and, before that, the refrigerator and washing machine as well as the more recent video recorder and mobile phone. Once unleashed, new ICTs such as digital television and Internet shopping redefine the aspired-to home. However, sceptics point out that, while some households are pioneers, rushing ahead of the crowd, early take-up at best prefigures or predicts the subsequent rolling waves of conversion. What tends to be politely, if uncomfortably, forgotten are the failures, the bombs, the modern-day Edsels – little or no mention here of Internet fridges and (arguably) digital television.

However, there is a strong economic dynamic underlying the 'technology as destiny' story. Proponents of evolutionary economics (Berry 2003) argue that competitive processes in advanced economies like Australia place 'innovation' at the centre of the economic engine. Innovation drives productivity improvements that create competitive advantage for successful innovators, the close followers realizing profits that can be ploughed back into further innovation. New technologies are the object and outcome of innovation. Once launched on a new technological trajectory, development continues in the same direction, at least for a while. Economic development is, in this sense, 'path dependent' (Arthur 1988; 1996). It is what gives the first mover and close followers a distinct though not permanent advantage. Getting to market first with a technically sophisticated new product allows an innovator to establish a strong position and set the contours of subsequent competition.

Competitors are locked into the new technological paradigm. Lock-in occurs for three main reasons:

- High-tech innovations generally require very large and risky up-front investments. Once a new technology appears that is demonstrably superior to existing ones, it is usually less risky to jump on board rather than risk

investing in another new technology.
- Many high tech products depend on compatibility with an appropriate network. Hence, the more products depend on a particular network system, the more likely that further applications will be developed for that system.
- Customers must invest significant time and money in skilling-up to use many high tech products. This investment is 'sunk', lost, if customers subsequently shift to other products requiring further skills.

The combined lock-in impact of high up-front firm investment, network effects and 'customer groove-in' is nowhere more apparent than in ICT.

For example, once Microsoft established the Windows operating system as the industry standard, software developers focused on producing new products to work on this platform. As the volume and diversity of Windows-specific software grew, more computer users turned to Windows-based computers, expanding the market for applications and encouraging software developers to produce further applications on this platform and so on. An earlier, oft-quoted case of lock-in, getting in first and establishing the standard was the humble keyboard. The QWERTY configuration is not the functionally or ergonomically most efficient option yet continues to rule more than a hundred years after its introduction. Similarly VHS triumphed over the better BETA in the world of the video cassette recorder.

Path dependence, however, sometimes leads to a dead end or a cliff. Indeed, there is increasing evidence that many complex human–technology systems fail. In his aptly titled book, *Why Most Things Fail*, economist Paul Omerod (2005) offers a range of biological and social examples from species extinction to the bankruptcy of the typical firm to demonstrate this seemingly ubiquitous fate. From a different perspective but with a similar message, Christensen (1997) distinguishes between innovations (and their underlying technologies) that are 'sustaining' and those that are 'disruptive'.

Sustaining innovations deliver ever greater functionality to technology-savvy consumers willing to pay a premium to be at or near the leading edge – like snapping up the next generation mobile phone, new model car or integrated home entertainment system. Market leaders generally drive sustaining innovations, seeking to defend and extend their dominant market shares. Disruptive innovations, on the other hand, are modest attempts to meet the modest needs of low-end users who don't want or can't afford most of the functions provided by current products or, even more importantly, to cater for non-users for whom current products don't meet their needs at all. As such, disruptive innovation is of little interest to market leaders who are focused on capturing the sophisticated, cashed-up high-end users and attempting to up-sell others to the new cutting-edge products. Small entrants pioneered low-cost, no-frills airlines, while the established airlines continued to compete for the high-value business customers. Minicomputers were not successfully introduced by the main-frame giant, IBM, but by firms like Digital Equipment, Data General and Wang. The latter, in turn, missed out on the move to personal computers, which were ushered in by Apple, Tandy, Commodore and IBM on the comeback trail. Portable computers saw a different set of innovators – Toshiba, Sharp and Zenith – disrupt and extend the market. Similarly hand-held devices are disruptive innovations introduced by start-ups or established firms from other sectors coming in under the radar of the current market leaders.

These examples suggest the sting in the tail – the disruptive side of disruptive innovation. Often, the modest start-up bottom-feeders, chasing what appear to be crumbs from the table by satisfying the needs of low-end and non-users, start moving progressively up-market and out-competing market leaders in mainstream markets. They do this because they are able to improve functionality of their products from a lower cost base. Eventually their products catch up to and satisfy the main needs of the core of users who switch away from the more sophisticated and expensive products that offer extra functions that they do not want. Increasingly, the previously dominant firms are confined to the minority of users at the technological leading edge. In this way, the producers of mainframe computers lost out to the producers of minicomputers who, in turn, were overtaken by the producers of personal computers, who were subsequently blind-sided by the laptops and, later, the hand-helds. At each stage, the 'new kid on the block' overtook the dominant player, locked into improving its current market winner. A parallel process occurred in the development of computer components like disc drives (Christensen 1997, Ch. 2). More recently, some of the small low-cost airlines have taken on the major markets of the big carriers by seeking to attract business-class passengers, introducing frequent-flyer schemes and club lounges, etc. Christensen and Raynor (2003, 48) give dozens of similar examples, like desktop photocopiers, digital cameras and Amazon.

This familiar, repeated pattern of business success and failure in the face of disruptive innovation has a number of causes argued in detail by Christensen (1997) and Christensen and Raynor (2003). Two causes, however, stand out. First, market leaders understandably seek to better serve existing mainstream customers. But the functionality built into technologically advanced products, as a result of sustaining innovations, runs further and further ahead of the actual needs of these 'average' consumers, appealing only to a declining proportion of cutting-edge customers willing to pay a premium for the rapidly improving result.

Second, this opens up opportunities for low-end disruptors to move up-market, by developing and improving low-cost, low-functionality products currently serving low-end users, to meet the needs of mainstream consumers increasingly left behind by the market leaders. Disruption works because it is the disruptors who now meet the actual, as opposed to assumed, needs of the bulk of consumers, existing and potential, and do so at a price the latter are willing to pay. In the words of Christensen and Raynor (2003), it is the disruptive innovator who delivers products or services that 'do the jobs they want done' for an acceptable price. Sustaining innovations, on the other hand, eventually push prices beyond the reach of most consumers by bundling too many functions that do jobs that most consumers don't want done, and charging for them in a 'take all' manner.

The key implication of successful disruption is that firms, policy makers and policy-based researchers need to better understand what jobs consumers want done. In the context of smart homes: how smart? The fact, noted above, that Majitek has chosen to move the focus of its integrated digital platforms from home to office gives cause for caution. What ICT innovations in the home matter and to whom (and why)? What potential exists for new products to meet the particular needs of different groups (and different members within the household) at different levels of functionality? In particular, how do the possible ICT-driven sustainability options scan with different groups, including those who currently exhibit no appetite for available fare like smart metering, distributed electricity systems, movie downloads and Internet banking? The ICT-driven shift from products to services, noted above as a technological possibility, will only occur to the extent that households perceive that this helps them to get done the jobs they actually want done and new or existing providers find ways of delivering those services at an acceptable price. In this latter context, who is best placed to offer an attractive product? According to Christensen, often the answer will be a recent start-up (an Apple or Microsoft bursting out of a garage) or a firm from a different industry. Government policy can also influence the extent to which innovations, both sustaining and disruptive, unfold and bite, through both incentive structures (taxes, subsidies, community education) and regulation (energy ratings, standards, and so on).

From the viewpoint of innovation as an economic process, then, technology is not destiny but a deeply uncertain, dynamic, unpredictable, problematic and surprising journey. Producers who lock into the 'wrong' technological trajectory face a grim Hobbesian world in which life is indeed 'solitary, poore, nasty, brutish, and short' (Hobbes 1982, 186).

The Human–Technology Relation

Several themes and interpretive concepts have been discussed here, including the emergence of the 'smart home' amidst the growth of suburbia and an increased focus on the home as stylized environment, issues of sustainable policy at the grassroots and government levels, and the processes of 'disruptive' and 'sustaining' technological innovation. Each might be seen as interpreting or representing a set of complex relations between humans, environments and technologies. In steering sustainability, understanding these relations is of some importance, and can be usefully understood by combining the actor–network approach with the materialist philosophy of Donna Haraway and Don Ihde (Ihde 1990; 1993). This combination allows a way of critically and concurrently interpreting systems and institutions (networks), the minutiae of everyday practices, and the materiality of environments and built spaces.

As discussed above, articles and advertising in smart-home magazines highlight the need and ability to control the domestic environment, the necessities of automation and remote micromanagement of domestic space though smart lighting, integrated media, and intelligent control systems. An Eaton Electric (2005) advertisement describes monitors as a 'solution' to both the human–home relation and the management of people within the home: 'If the iron has been left on, Home Heartbeat will tell you. If the front door is ajar, it will let you know. It will even alert you when the kids come home from school'.

Much of this discourse is in keeping with commonly understood definitions of technology and its uses. As Simpson (1995: 24) points out: 'Technology can be viewed as that constellation of knowledge, processes, skills and products whose aim is to control and transform... [T]hat set of practices whose purpose is, through ever more radical interventions into nature (physical, biological and human), to systematically place the future at our disposal.' Yet, in the context of sustainability, the very notion of 'control' is problematic. In particular, if we are to understand both the complexities and 'everydayness' of sustainable practices in the home, then we must reconsider in non-hierarchical ways the 'relationality' between humans, their tools and technologies, and the environment. That is, as Latour (1994), Haraway, Ihde (1990; 1993) and others have argued, tools and technologies have their own mode of 'being-with', emergent trajectories that are not always intentional (such as the silicon chip or telephone), the world is itself an 'agent' that in its materiality has determining effects, and humans are nodes in a network of relations that recognizes all of these things – people, objects, technologies, matter – as socio-technical 'actors'. In this way, the notion of disruptive innovation can be seen to emerge out of a socio-technical network of relations between humans, tools and the material world. Serres and Latour (1995: 107) stressed: 'Relations spawn objects, beings and acts, not vice versa'.

Ihde (1993) suggests that all human–technology relations (which is really just another way of saying 'ways of being human') have particular consequences for how we exist in and know the world; our tools fundamentally affect our sensory access to the world, the extent to which our body extends into and adapts to that world, and what we can say we know about the world. That is, each specific human–technology relation has its own set of cultural, technical, experiential, sensorial and interfacial loci and histories.

In actor–network terms, technologies, environments and humans together constitute complex socio-technical systems. Moreover, each human–technology–environment relation can be considered as having specific 'world-making' effects. In terms of recent developments in 'smart' technologies, then, on the one hand we can critically examine exactly what is meant by ascribing a fairly vacuous notion of 'smartness' to home monitoring, media systems and the domestic environment, how it follows the centuries-old vectors of humanism and the understanding of technologies as means of control over nature.

On the other hand, we can think about how smartness can be interpreted in different ways, to see technologies, environments and domestic/built spaces as having their own complex kind of agency, partially determining how we live and move about in them – their own functionality and ways of arranging spaces and bodies (Sofoulis 2001; 2002), in particular, how the ubiquitous computing and connectivity technologies wired into the smart home are themselves inclined towards particular 'affordances' and 'readings' of the environment (as quantitative, data-based, remote-controllable, and open to surveillance).

The phenomenon of remote control and its deep embedment in our perception and experience of the smart home is an interesting case study. Put simply, we can interpret our use of the remote control device as a negotiated and adaptive extension of the hand. Designed to 'fit' the adult hand in consonance with the handy familiarity of other numbered keypads in everyday use, most remote devices are organized in such a way that the environment is rendered a spatial extension of our perceptual or physical reach – controllable, orderly and immediate. Yet, conversely implicit in this relation is the way remote control devices of all kinds organize both domestic space and our bodily movements through and within that space, constraining and enabling our relation to the immediate and distant environment.

The use of remote-control devices and systems, and the 'smartness' seemingly intrinsic to some of them, can also be usefully interpreted by Ihde's (1990) categorization of several broad types of human–technology relations: embodiment relations (semi-transparent relations such as wearing eyeglasses, where we experience the world through technology); hermeneutic relations (semi-opaque relations which require us to 'read' a device such as a thermometer or gauge); and alterity relations (technology as 'other', such as computers or artificial intelligence). Each relation speaks a certain attitude towards the world. Interestingly, remote controls and smart technologies cross these relation types: they are embodied particularly when also wearable or miniaturized, hermeneutic in their monitoring capacity, and alterative in terms of being (at least potentially) intelligent. In later work Ihde (1993) captures the automated and hidden aspect of technologies in the smart home by bringing critical attention to ambient and background technologies, those that are either taken for granted or go unnoticed as an aspect of our environment. This typology of relations can also be a useful way of interpreting the development of both sustaining and disruptive innovations, and the way in which sustainable practices emerge from and configure socio-technical networks and human–technology relations.

The understanding that technologies are both culturally embedded (social) and materially specific (technical) is also captured by Heidegger's (1977) notion of 'equipmental environments' – the idea that all human–technology relations fit within a milieu of cultural habits and broader contexts of tool use. The success of home monitoring and security systems, for example, is situated within broader cultural narratives and technologies of protection. Thus technologies do not exist in isolation but belong within a larger set of cultural beliefs and practices. Historically the term 'smart', when coupled with technology, connotes information, data-based and communication technologies over more mundane domestic devices. The prototypes for smart houses and the technologies that are integrated into the working of the smart home pay almost no attention to domestic work: they predominantly feature home entertainment systems, safety and security, communication (screens in every room and perpetual Internet connection), environment (heating and cooling), and centralized control and monitoring of all these.

In an early case study of the gender-technology relation in the context of the smart home (Berg 1994) a designer claims to have considered the issue of housework by inserting automatic light switches; upon entering a room with a basket full of wet clothes, for example, the houseworker would not have to put them down to turn on the light. Similarly, in Eaton Electric (2005, 47) we are told that the Home Heartbeat™ system – the 'world's first personal, wireless awareness system' – will 'monitor the inner workings of the house' and enable the user to check if you've left the hair straightener on or if the washing machine is overflowing. These very cursory concessions to household work show the widespread hierarchism of 'high' technologies, such as media centres and connectivity, over 'low' domestic technologies, such as cleaning. The Internet fridge becomes high-tech once it has the capacity to communicate and inform as a mediatic and/or informatic assemblage.

This hierarchy reflects social relations and inequalities already existing between public paid work and domestic labour, and a particular interpretation of 'smartness', prioritizing control and surveillance, not relationality.

Conclusion

There are histories and contemporary contexts of ICT use and innovation that need to be understood in order that effective sustainability policies be initiated and maintained in the domestic home. We have offered a critical history of the concept of 'smart', and considered how the smart home has emerged out of a complex field of technological capacity and innovation, along with socio-economic and political factors that intersect with environmental impact concerns. This chapter indicates that policy makers need to diversify their approach to sustainability and consider a range of stakeholders while proactively supporting a milieu of creative possibilities and scenarios at both the institutional and 'everyday' level; to move past the traditional provider/consumer dichotomy that typifies perceptions of resource use; understand and support the way technological innovation often emerges at the grassroots or 'garage' level to disrupt that dichotomy; and rethink ICTs as agents or intermediaries within social contexts and environments rather than simply as 'objects' of consumption.

References

Angerer, M-L., Peters K. and Sofoulis, Z. (eds) (2002), *Future Bodies: Zur Visualisierung von Körpern in Science und Fiction* (Wein/New York: Springer-Verlag).

Arthur, B. (1988), 'Competing technologies, increasing returns and lock-in by historical events', *Economic Journal* 99, 113–16.

Arthur, B. (1996), 'Increasing returns and the new world of business', *Harvard Business Review* 74:4, 100–09.

Australian Smart Home Ideas (2005), 1, 36 [advertisement].

Berg, A-J. (1994), 'A Gendered Socio-Technical Construction: The Smart House', in Cockburn and Dilic (eds).

Berry, M. (2003), *Innovation by Design: The Economic Drivers of Dynamic Regions* [lab report 01] (Melbourne: lab.3000).

Christensen, C. (1997), *The Innovator's Dilemma: When New Technologies Cause Great Firms to Fail* (Boston: Harvard Business School Press).

Christensen, C. and Raynor, M. (2003), *The Innovator's Solution: Creating and Sustaining Successful Growth* (Boston: Harvard Business School Press).

Cockburn C. and Dilic, R. (eds) (1994), *Bringing Technology Home: Gender and Technology in a Changing Europe* (Philadelphia: Open University Press).

Eaton Electric (2005), 'Peace of Mind in a Heartbeat', *Connected Home Solutions* [advertisement] November/December, 46–7.

Goedkoop, M., Van Halen, C., Te Riele, H. and Rommens, P. (1999), *Product Service Systems, Ecological and Economic Basics* (Amersfoort: PRéConsultants).

Goodman, J., Alakeson, V. and Jorgesen B. (2004), *Encouraging Green Telework* (London: Forum for the Future).

Harper, R. (ed.) (2003), *Inside the Smart Home* (London: Springer-Verlag).

Haycock, K. (2005), 'Get Smart – Just What Is An Intelligent Home?', *Australian Smart Home Ideas* 1, 17–22.

Hobbes, T. (1982), *Leviathan* (Harmondsworth: Penguin).

Heidegger, M. (1977), *The Question Concerning Technology and Other Essays* (New York: Garland Publishing).

Ihde, D. (1990), *Technology and the Lifeworld: From Garden to Earth* (Bloomington: Indiana University Press).

Ihde, D. (1993), *Postphenomenology: Essays in the Postmodern Context* (Evanston: Northwestern University Press).

Innovation House (2007), Innovation House 2 [website], <http://www.ih2.com.au/>, accessed 13 January 2007.

Latour, B. (1994), 'Pragmatogonies: A Mythical Account of How Humans and Nonhumans Swap Properties', *American Behavioural Scientist* 37:6, 791–808.

Majitek (2006), *Intermajik* [flyer], [website], <http:www.majitek.com>, accessed 13 June 2006.

Munt, S. (ed), (2001), *Technospaces: Inside the New Media* (New York: Continuum).

Omerod, P. (2005), *Why Most Things Fail: Evolution, Extinction and Economics* (London: Faber and Faber).

Orange (2006), 'Orange at Home', Digital World Research Centre [website], <http://www.dwrc.surrey.ac.uk/Research/OrangeSmartHouse/tabid/84/Default.aspx>, accessed 20 July 2006.

PlaceMatters (2007), PlaceMatters [website], <http:www.PlaceMatters.com>, accessed 7 February 2007.

Serres, M. and Latour, B. (1995), *Conversations on Science, Culture, and Time* (Michigan: Michigan University Press).

Simpson, L. (1995), *Technology, Time and the Conversations of Modernity* (New York: Routledge).

Smart Wired (2007), [website], At Home with Automation and Reading Room (Smart Homes) [webpage], <www.smartwiredhouse.com.au>, accessed 5 February 2007.

Sofoulis, Z. (2001), 'Smart spaces @ The Final Frontier,' in Munt (ed.).

Sofoulis, Z. (2002), 'Post- Non- and Para- Human: Toward a Theory of Sociotechnical Personhood,' in Angerer et al.

Spigel, L. (2001), *Welcome to the Dreamhouse* (Durham: Duke University Press).

Strengers, Y. (2006), 'Research on Information Communication Technologies, Households and Environmental Sustainability: The Case of Innovation House 2, [Unpublished paper, 3 August draft].

Telstra (2006), Telstra Smart Community [website], <http://www.telstrasmartcommunity.com/>, accessed 7 February 2007.

Weiser, M. (1993), 'Hot Topics: Ubiquitous Computing', *IEEE Computer* October, 71–2.

Chapter 20

Sustainable Futures

Anitra Nelson

Introduction

The task of creating sustainable futures has never been as critical or as challenging as it is today, with global warming and other ecological damage resulting from human activities now threatening the future of the species itself. This threat is neither distant nor contained. Many experts prescribe immediate, urgent, global and local action, arguing that, already, it may be too late.

Sustainability in urban settings has greater significance as the year 2007 marks the shift in urban–rural composition of the world. Over half of the world's population now resides in cities in contrast to our past history when a (decreasing) majority lived and worked in rural areas (Worldwatch Institute 2006). Concurrently, as globalization of production and trade has strengthened interconnecting networks between national capitals and urban centres of commerce and finance, cities are centres of power.

However, analyses and decision making for strategic action on urban sustainability challenge current national and international economic, political and social structures. Our strikingly capitalist institutions and practices have all developed to support more and more production for human consumption. Most political forces have supported the market and focused on social issues of distribution. Yet economic growth has occurred without sufficient understanding or care for ecological systems, which are stretched to provide materials and ecosystem services to support the overwhelmingly artificial environments and diversity of lifestyles in contemporary cities.

Human–nature dualisms reverberate in urban–rural dualisms. Thus a sustainability challenge is to address the fact that the city's hinterland extends like an elongated body away from its urban head all the while providing the heart and pulse of urban society. This challenge parallels the sense, heightened by city life, that humans have conquered or can manage and insulate themselves from nature, rather than constantly being in tension with the natural environment, which is a part of ourselves, not apart from us.

The authors of this collection have sought to contribute to the analytical, practical and creative thinking necessary to plan for and establish sustainable living in urban areas. They have discussed aspects of sustainability that can be guided or regulated by governments, implemented by business and industrial practices, and applied in mundane living by citizens. Despite common objectives and many shared values, the contributors represent a diverse set of views.

In this final chapter of *Steering Sustainability in an Urbanizing World* we discuss some general aspects of sustainability in the context of the development of this manuscript. We reveal an underlying tension between some authors with respect to visions of sustainability, specifically with respect to urban and rural settlement. While opening a thorny and perhaps overly theoretical debate, this chapter also seeks to close with a very practical signpost to the future by exploring elements and lessons from a thirty year old environmental living zone (ELZ) aptly located on the very edge of the urban–rural 'divide'. Experiences of the activists and residents in the Bend of Islands ELZ exemplify the potential and limits of concerted action for environmentally friendly and socially sustainable living, offering a fallible yet optimistic real world model from which the principles of working with people and with nature endure as mainsprings not only of dualism but also of *dynamism*.

Sustainability

At a preparatory meeting for the dialogue between the contributors and sustainability experts from the Victorian Department of Sustainability and Environment – see Chapter 1 – a policy maker suggested that this work should elaborate on one bold idea or strategy. Another call for unity was sounded the next day in the contributors' workshop when one author suggested a need to agree on a definition of sustainability.

In the event we chose a heterogenous collection with approaches that do not so much collide as work at distinct levels or elaborate on aspects of sustainability. As a result readers can appreciate that there are numerous ways to perceive, approach and apply sustainability, indicating distinct definitions in context. Indeed I often suggest to students that pursuing and achieving sustainability is similar to seeking and discovering 'love' – sustainability is a state, not a thing. Visions and strategies are useful but not foolproof; working 'on your feet' is critical and there is always more to learn. The point that policy makers and researchers alike must appreciate is that sustainability is a seriously and subtly complex state that cannot be easily planned and managed. Further, it is a shared responsibility and result. The *State of the World 2007: an Urban Planet* (Worldwatch Institute 2006) reports that grassroots forces, community groups and local government, have outpaced the achievements of national governments in many places – see Chapters 11–14, Part III, this collection.

In fact, the question is not so much how to define sustainability as to decide what is it that we want to sustain. Similarly in directing and assessing policy making, it is not just a matter of questioning or recommending policies and processes to achieve those policies but also of analysing who makes and changes a policy and who implements or enacts policy. Sustainability discourse is riven by differences about what is to be sustained, intermingled with dialogue fabricating such distinctions in terms of method. The triple bottom line approach, with its apparently even-handed and well-balanced treatment of the economic and social as well as environmental spheres, epitomizes confusion. This approach submerges and marginalizes bold questions, such as: Can capitalism ever achieve environmental sustainability? Meanwhile the dynamics of capitalist economies work profoundly – even irredeemably (Kovel 2002; Nelson 2001b) – against environmental values and social justice.

From the outset, the contributors to this collection were selected and guided to stress *environmental* sustainability and to consider the necessary integration between a citizen's daily practice and community or neighbourhood systems, the 'local', as well as state controls, regulations and support. In such a framework, policy making and implementation rely on community awareness and education, neighbourhood systems and processes, and regionally managed services (including research) to support comprehensive grassroots measures for household sustainability. As such, policies tend to evolve from dialogues and experiments, which might be initiated at the grassroots or from the top, but will be enacted in necessary unison between, say, the generators and consumers of energy and so on.

Therefore, given their original brief, the contributors have emphasized holistic approaches, such as the ecopolis and permaculture (Part I), synergies required between individual practices and local and regional systems (Part II), community and neighbourhood action (Part III), as well as the physical space of the household (Part IV). Overseeing and monitoring the necessary synergies between such levels, recreating processes of household service provision, more appropriate planning and design of built environments and social techniques of living practical sustainable lifestyles are likely to be the foci of future policy discourse, experimentation and action.

Urban or Rural Settlement?

In the workshop involving most of the contributors to this work a serious tension developed between certain authors, on rural and urban aspects of sustainability. While acknowledging that the city is embedded in a bioregion, Newman's position – asserted in Chapter 2 – claims that, by nature, human beings are urban (*homo urbanus*). While lauding urban ecovillages he criticizes the back-to-the-land movement and hobby farmers whose practices, he claims, are less sustainable than those of urban dwellers. Instead, he writes that 'we need to ensure that the countryside is more rural and the city more urban'.

Newman's arguments counter many perspectives, such as permaculture – see Chapter 4 – and David Suzuki (1997, 181), who suggests that:

> In the urban environment that is today's most common human habitat, science and technology perpetuate the illusion of dominance and shape the way we see the world. Cities manifest a way of thinking that reflects mechanical or technological models based on standardization, simplicity, linearity, predictability, efficiency, and production.

Similarly, *Small is Possible* (McRobie 1981), extends arguments developed by Schumacher (1997), who stressed in *Small is Beautiful* (1999, 50) that cities were 'a pathological growth'. Such directions suggest decentralization and indicate ways in which sustainability might be achieved by cities becoming more rural. However, this whole debate begs the question of what is rural and what is urban: surely there are examples of sustainability in both contexts? Nevertheless, as pointed out by Pears in Chapter 6, sustainability cannot be reduced simply to a matter of density.

This is not the only serious area of tension between advocates of sustainability. Further divisions centre on, for example, the extent of confidence in state institutions, and whether direct regulation or indirect encouraging measures, such as economic incentives, are likely to be most successful. Indeed others, as mentioned, have no confidence that capitalism can be made environmentally sustainable at all, arguing that a new system of production and distribution is critical to creating environmental and social sustainability. The latter perspective indicates that triple bottom line and other approaches that privilege rather than challenge economics are likely to result in more of the same, sustaining capitalism rather than nature (including the human species).

Often the subtexts of such theoretical discussion are based in well-grounded experiences and practical applications. They are not simply dogma. Dissention is not always a problem. However, in the context of collective action, conflict is often damaging, leading to disconcerting actions or paralysis, which is scary in this case of establishing sustainable practices at five minutes to midnight. For the same reason, however, deliberation is crucial; we cannot afford to follow unsound directions or strategies now.

The controversy on the relative sustainability of urban and rural settlement might appear purely theoretical in the face of a seemingly unstoppable trend to urbanization, our now overwhelmingly urban world. However, the urban–rural settlement question is pertinent in regions, including most of Australia, where it might be argued that space for such a choice still exists. Indeed, if there is any doubt on the matter, it represents a key issue to consider in strategic policy making for a sustainable future. Decisions regarding provision of infrastructure, regional planning, sustainable regional development, and so on all depend on what kind of settlements are deemed most sustainable.

Community and Neighbourhood

As the chapters on water (Chapter 9) and waste (Chapter 10) indicate, managing the environment is no longer seen as the responsibility of governments or industry with short-term powers and perspectives. It is increasingly acknowledged that the responsibilities for living in sustainable ways must be broadly shared, sustainability must be generally valued and understood, and sustainable futures will exhibit sophisticated interactions – collaborations and complementarity between individual practices and collective systems. Thus, whole-of-government approaches, multi-stakeholder forums and whole-of-community processes are emerging to address sustainability issues in integrated, global–local, ways.

In Chapter 3 of this work, Downton elaborated on urban fractals, practical demonstration models of ecopolis approaches. In Chapter 12, Mike Hill and Lorna Pitt presented the example of Westwyck, and Bekkesy and Gordon (Chapter 18) outlined a utopian scenario for protecting biodiversity. The examples that they describe are relatively recent and focused on dreams and trials with sustainable community living. However, experimentation with sustainable living in ecovillages has been a global phenomenon and philosophies of environmentally friendly societies have long histories. Thus this chapter on sustainable futures explores some key elements of steering sustainability by drawing on personal experiences in the Bend of Islands ELZ.

The residents of the Bend of Islands ELZ – located on the rural fringes of suburban Melbourne, the capital of Victoria – have over thirty years of experience learning about and actively conserving their natural environment as well as engaging with local government and developers to protect the box-ironbark woodlands within which they live. Whilst not established with the specific aim of being a model of sustainable living – residents of the ELZ follow minimal impact environmental practices to maintain the bushland within which they live for its natural ecological values – the ELZ presents sufficient characteristics and objectives of living in sustainable ways to make its experiences relevant to a discussion of strategies for achieving sustainable futures.

Rural Histories, Urban Futures

David Holmgren (2002, 235), co-originator of the permaculture concept, with Bill Mollison, agrees with Downton (Chapter 3) that 'we will only succeed in dealing with the environmental crisis when we do so in cities', with the following qualification:

> I believe the inspiration, examples and wisdom for the solutions come not from the centre but from the margins, where people live at the edge between culture and nature, between modernity and the past. The idea that the hinterland provides a wellspring of human biological vigour, values and renewal for civilisation is an old one, but I believe the ways in which this is happening are diversifying and intensifying as we approach the end of the fossil-fuel era.

The Bend of Islands ELZ is a fine example of Holmgren's point. (Note: all references for the following data on the Bend of Islands ELZ appear in BICA 2007; Nelson 2001a; Nelson 2001c; RBCC 2007.)

Incorporating many of the features of the imaginary 'Biodiversia' (Chapter 18), residents in the ELZ have pioneered grey-water systems involving transpiration beds for growing kitchen gardens, they live without fences between properties, they have established design, siting, construction material and technical guides and regulations for environmentally friendly housing, and have developed two models for collectively managing the environmental aspects of a neighbourhood precinct. ELZ residents have long practised the kinds of water-saving techniques discussed by Hurley and Mercer in Chapter 9 and exemplify the kind of community action analysed by Whelan in Chapter 11.

Stewardship and Praxis

Inspired by the activities of the residents of the Round the Bend Conservation Co-operative, which started five years earlier (1971), the Bend of Islands Conservation

Association (BICA) initiated and maintains the ELZ as a living reality (1976–). This voluntary association and the residential cooperative are model organizations appropriate for structuring community-based sustainability. They perform learning, managing and monitoring functions, representing the community and neighbourhood interests in negotiations with relevant government bodies and developers.

BICA covers 400 ha of box-ironbark woodlands, incorporating over 130 land titles and the cooperative (136 ha), which represents 32 shares (titles to households). Box-ironbark forest is Victoria's most endangered type of native bushland – around one-seventh of what existed in the early 19th century when white settlers colonized the State remains intact – and only a few per cent is protected in parks. The ELZ provides a significant ecological link in a corridor of bush between a State park and a national park, it is a designated site of zoological significance and most is classified of biological significance. As such the vegetation offers habitat for 134 native species, including two endangered ones. BICA and the cooperative have developed special management strategies and working groups to care for this land and its ecological values in relatively intensive and ongoing ways.

In a wholly unconscious way ELZ residents created processes to develop and share knowledge and skills to care for the local bushland that demonstrate a 'learning by living' model advocated by the radical educationalist Ivan Illich (1973, 75), who argued that the task of modern civilizations was 'the creation of a new style of educational relationship between man and his environment'. The essence of Illich's model – and what makes it most appropriate for application in terms of community-based sustainability – is self-motivated learning in a democratic polity of self-management and popular participation. BICA and the cooperative have ensured that locally appropriate conservation principles, practices and policies are followed, through a flexible mix of discourse, field experience, expert advice, research, experiments and mentoring.

Wider Relations

The activities and operations of BICA and the cooperative focus on their locale and community. They have developed in distinct ways to reflect and express the needs of, and opportunities offered by, their specific ecological landscape and its human inhabitants. At the same time this neighbourhood and community is part of a wider and more complex suburban landscape and networks and faces developments comparable with the rest of Melbourne's green suburban fringes. Its identity and influence draw much from this public profile and negotiations with developers, infrastructure service providers and government agencies.

Indeed the history of the ELZ indicates its challenges. BICA had already been in operation some years and was recognized for its residential conservation strategies (ACF 1975) when the locals decided, at a public meeting held in October 1976, to formally become an ELZ with a unique classification and regulations. However, it took a full six years for the State Minister for Conservation to proclaim it. While the slow bureaucrat has become a community joke, the association and cooperative work hard to keep up with developments at all levels of government, making submissions to relevant inquiries, negotiating, advocating and working with government departments. Locals try to solve difficulties by talking them through face-to-face but observe and report instances of infringements of regulations to local government, frequently too distracted with other duties to monitor such developments. Testimony to the success of the ELZ, it appears on the website of the Nillumbik Shire Council (2007) and in such documents as the final report on its future, 2020, strategies (Nillumbik Shire Council n.d., 10).

BICA exists to inform and assist. The association facilitates real estate dealings in the area by providing local agents with an information pack on regulations and expectations of residents. When the Melbourne Water agency decided to sell off public land in the area several years ago, BICA met with representatives and proposed how to sell off the land in such a way as to best preserve its environmental values. Similarly BICA negotiates with the local electricity supplier over how and to what extent it prunes and cuts trees in the area. The association supports broader environmental organizations and its members regularly report back on developments to facilitate joint, supportive and complementary efforts. In these ways the association and cooperative illustrate how strong, reliable and responsible local organizations can help large governments avoid the pitfalls of 'one size fits all' policies and facilitate constructive two-way engagement to benefit the environment.

The Bend of Islands – like much of Australia, including significant sections of its urban populations – is bushfire-prone. Concepts of sustainability are especially contentious in this area where Grant's concept of 'folklore' (see Chapter 5) is peculiarly applicable. Every year as damaging bushfires rage out of control – in January 2003 a firestorm destroyed 474 homes on the suburban fringes of the national capital, Canberra, in just one day (Catalyst 2003) – experts, victims and know-alls argue how best to protect the built and natural environments from bushfire. Under the auspices of the Country Fire Authority, the Christmas Hills volunteer fire brigade offers a final demonstration of the achievements of its local ELZ residents. Besides printed information and sessions, householders are encouraged to belong to 'telephone trees', which network members of the community for fire-warnings and assistance. Members of the cooperative are required not only to plan but also to rehearse to other members their bushfire plans, which often show far more detailed preparedness and far more sophisticated knowledge than in other comparably affected communities. Fire management, specifically the appropriate fuel-reduction strategy, is a highly contentious issue. With the banner, 'Red Truck, Green Heart', the brigade has initiated various environmentally friendly approaches, including the incorporation of minimal-impact suppression tactics and a recovery action team to minimize environmental disturbance caused by fire and fire suppression activities.

While developed for conservation purposes, the Bend of Islands ELZ shows the potential for small communities to develop knowledge and skills to creatively nurture their neighbouring environment and processes to work with wider, regional, forces to improve sustainable outcomes.

Policy

What approaches to making and implementing policy are most likely to support sustainable practices by neighbourhood-centred citizens and communities? Many of the chapters in this collection indicate how the roles of policy makers in resource management, urban planning and infrastructure provision have changed over the last decade or so to accommodate new developments and understandings of sustainability challenges. Supporting sustainable futures would seem to require policy makers to share more responsibilities for the sustainable use of resources with users, especially citizens and industry.

A framework characterized by state control of resources and management of service provision along with state regulation and space for free market activities has given way to emerging structures within which government acts most successfully as a sustainability leader, with a dedicated interest in all resource use and service provision, facilitating sustainable practices, adopting flexible and experimental approaches requiring vigilant monitoring and constant engagement with stakeholders. Within this new model, policy making and implementation is necessarily more complex and subtle, requiring distinct skills in community engagement, discourse and leadership while maintaining powers to enforce limits increasingly deemed necessary to ensure the sustainable use of resources, energy and so on.

The challenges of urban sustainability imply radical, not just incremental, changes. For instance, whereas large industry and government consumers have received discounts for massive energy and resource use in the past, a sustainability rationale suggests that higher users ought to be charged disproportionately more than modest users. In other words there is a strong logic supporting policies that estimate reasonable rations of resources and services across the board and strongly deter or stop flagrant consumption. Life cycle assessment (see Chapter 5) would be a tool for policies taking this direction. The Community Ecosystem Trust model (M'Gonigle et al. 2001) recommends policies favouring tenders who promote and achieve best practices in sustainability above economically cheaper ones. Such models turn capitalism – competition using monetary measures of efficiency and competence – on its head.

Throughout human history people have dreamed of futures to achieve all kinds of ends, from preserving and extending their royal dominions, to abolishing poverty, saving cultures and creating democracies. Today we must dream a future for the survival of our species.

References

ACF (1975), *Residential Conservation* (Melbourne: Australian Conservation Foundation).
BICA (2007), Bend of Islands Conservation Association [website], <http://home.vicnet.net.au/%7Ebica/index.html>, accessed 3 February 2007.

Catalyst (2003), 'Canberra Firestorm', at Australian Broadcasting Commission [website], Catalyst [program webpage], <http://www.abc.net.au/catalyst/stories/s794270.htm>, 27 February 2003, accessed 17 February 2007.

Holmgren, D. (2002), *Permaculture: Principles and Pathways Beyond Sustainability* (Hepburn: Holmgren Design Services).

Illich, I. (1973), *Deschooling Society* (Harmondsworth: Penguin).

Kovel, J. (2002), *The Enemy of Nature: The End of Capitalism or the End of the World?* (London/New York/Nova Scotia: Zed Books/Room 4000/Fernwood Publishing).

McRobie, G. (1981), *Small Is Possible* (London: Abacus).

M'Gonigle, R., Egan, B. and Ambus, L. (2001), *Developing Sustainability Through the Community Ecosystem Trust: Report 1 When There's a Way There's a Will* (Victoria: University of Victoria Eco-Research Chair of Environmental Law and Policy).

Nelson, A. (2001a), 'Learning by Living: Conservation in Community: Two Models from the Bend of Islands, Victoria' [paper], The Future is Here Environmental Education Conference, RMIT University, Melbourne, 15–19 January 2001, Marine Education Society of Australasia [website], <http://www.mesa.edu.au/aaee_conf/Nelson-Anitra.PDF >, accessed 3 February 2007.

Nelson, A. (2001b), 'The Poverty of Money: Marxian Insights for Ecological Economists', *Ecological Economics* 36, 499–511.

Nelson, A. (2001c), 'Two Models of Residential Conservation: Communal Life in an Australian Box-Ironbark Forest', *International Journal of Heritage Studies* 7:3, 249–72.

Nillumbik Shire Council (n.d.), *Nillumbik 2020 – A Preferred Future (Final Report) Abridged Version* (Eltham: Nillumbik Shire Council).

Nillumbik Shire Council (2007), [website], <http://www.nillumbik.vic.gov.au/>, accessed 3 February 2007.

RBCC (2007), Round the Bend Conservation Cooperative [website], <http://kerryc.customer.netspace.net.au/>, accessed 3 February 2007.

Schumacher, E. (1997), 'No Future for Megopolis' in his *This I Believe and Other Essays* (Totnes: Resurgence/Green Books), 161–71.

Schumacher, E. (1999), *Small is Beautiful, Economics As If People Mattered: 25 Years Later...With Commentaries* (Point Roberts/Vancouver: Hartley and Marks Publishers).

Suzuki, D. with McConnell, A. (1997), *The Sacred Balance: Rediscovering Our Place in Nature* (St Leonards: Allen and Unwin).

Worldwatch Institute (2006), *State of the World 2007: An Urban Planet* (Washington: Worldwatch Institute).

Index